Around the World in 80 Years

RANULPH FIENNES

Around the World in 80 Years

A Life of Exploration

Edited by Barry Johnston

HODDER & STOUGHTON

First published in Great Britain in 2024 by Hodder & Stoughton
An Hachette UK company

1

This book has been compiled and edited from the following previously published works:
Living Dangerously, Macmillan, 1987 and *Mad, Bad and Dangerous to Know*,
Hodder & Stoughton, 2007. Chapter 4 from *To the Ends of the Earth*, Simon
and Schuster UK, 2014, copyright © Westward Ho Adventure Holidays Limited,
1985, 2014. Chapter 9 from *A Talent for Trouble*, Hodder & Stoughton, 1970.

With contributions as follows:
Page 21: copyright © Monty Don 2024; page 41: copyright © Dr Mike Stroud 2024;
page 63: copyright © Anton Bowring 2024; page 87: copyright © Oliver Shepard 2024;
page 107: copyright © Erling Kagge 2024; page 125: copyright © Levison Wood 2024;
page 143: copyright © Stephen Venables 2024; page 165: copyright © Ian Parnell 2024;
page 189: copyright © Børge Ousland 2024; page 211: copyright © Dr Mike Stroud 2024;
page 233: copyright © Kenton Cool 2024; page 255: copyright © Bear Grylls 2024.

A CIP catalogue record for this title is available from the British Library

Hardback ISBN 9781399729734
Trade Paperback ISBN 9781399729741
ebook ISBN 9781399729758

Typeset in Sabon MT by Hewer Text UK Ltd, Edinburgh
Printed and bound in Great Britain by Clays Ltd, Elcograf S.p.A.

Hodder & Stoughton policy is to use papers that are natural, renewable
and recyclable products and made from wood grown in sustainable
forests. The logging and manufacturing processes are expected to
conform to the environmental regulations of the country of origin.

Hodder & Stoughton Ltd
Carmelite House
50 Victoria Embankment
London EC4Y 0DZ

www.hodder.co.uk

Contents

Introduction

My first encounter with Sir Ranulph Twisleton-Wykeham-Fiennes was when I was a schoolboy at Eton College, although I didn't know it at the time. The Fourth of June is an annual holiday at Eton, when parents and families come down to the school and numerous events take place, ending with the Procession of Boats.

Hundreds of spectators gather on a field beside a narrow branch of the Thames as each of the school rowing eights glide slowly past the crowd, the crews dressed like eighteenth-century midshipmen. One by one, the boys have to stand up, holding their oars vertical, then take off their straw boaters to salute the crowd. Sometimes an oarsman loses his balance and falls in, which brings loud cheers from the crowd.

In 1966, something extraordinary happened. The first boat went by successfully, but as the second boat appeared, it suddenly tipped over and the whole crew fell into the water. When the third boat arrived, the same thing happened, to more cheers by the spectators, soon followed by another. There was now complete chaos and the crowd was in uproar.

There were reports that a frogman in a face mask and diving suit was seen in the river and even rumours that he was an Old Etonian serving in the Army, but he was never caught.

Nearly forty years later in 2004, now an audiobook producer, I went to Chester to record Ranulph Fiennes giving one of his brilliant lectures on behalf of the Royal Geographical Society. As we talked in his dressing room before the show, he revealed to me that *he* was the frogman, then a 23-year-old in the SAS, who had returned to Eton to have some fun. I told him it was the highlight of my time there.

Later I produced Ran reading his excellent autobiography *Mad, Bad & Dangerous to Know* and the radio programme *An Hour with Ranulph Fiennes* and abridged his book *Fear* for BBC Radio 4's *Book of the Week*.

All through his life, Ran has never been afraid to break the rules, take enormous risks, and test the limits of human endurance. As he turns eighty, this book is a celebration of his extraordinary expeditions and adventures and his travels around the globe. He has written several books about his life and many of the stories selected here are from his earlier volumes *A Talent for Trouble* (1970), *To the Ends of the Earth* (1983) and *Living Dangerously* (1987, 1994), as well as *Mad, Bad & Dangerous to Know* (2007, 2020), and are being published together for the first time.

Barry Johnston,
2024

Prologue

This was all my wife Ginny's idea. I had spent eight years serving in the armed forces in Germany and Oman, and after we were married in 1970, I needed to find a way to earn a living. Ginny had been working as a mountain guide for the National Trust in Scotland and I had already led a couple of expeditions to Norway and up the River Nile. So she suggested we combine our skills. We would organise an expedition every year during the summer months and I would earn money by writing a book about it and giving lectures during the winter.

Our first expedition together was in Canada, a river journey crossing British Columbia from the Yukon to the US border, and Ginny came too as the road party leader and radio operator. After we returned, she was cooking dinner in 1972, when she suddenly said, 'Why don't we go around the world?' Her idea was that a core group of an expedition team would travel over the entire surface of the world via both Poles without flying one yard of the way.

This became known as the Transglobe Expedition and it changed our lives forever. It took us seven years to plan the itinerary, find the sponsorship, secure all the equipment and recruit a team of fifty-two volunteers, and a further three years to traverse both ice caps and achieve the first surface circumpolar journey round the Earth.

Following this success, sponsorship became easier to obtain, but it relied on us getting good publicity in the newspapers or on television. That meant breaking more world records of a geographical or physical nature.

At that time, the holy grail of the international polar fraternity was to reach the North Pole with no outside support and no air contact. In 1986, Mike Stroud and I managed to get only 300 miles from the Pole, though we still broke the previous unsupported record, and I was installed in the *Guinness Book of Records* World Hall of Fame as the 'World's Greatest Living Explorer'.

After two further unsuccessful attempts to reach the North Pole, our next expedition was in the deserts of southern Arabia and the archaeological search for Ubar, the fabled Atlantis of the Sands. After many years and eight expeditions, Ginny and I finally uncovered the ruins of the ancient lost city in Oman in 1990.

Our main rivals at the North Pole were always the Norwegians, especially Erling Kagge and Børge Ousland. Now I learned that Kagge was planning a solo unsupported journey to the South Pole. So in 1993, Mike Stroud and I set off on our own journey, pulling 485-pound sledges and in 95 days we crossed 1,350 miles to be awarded the world record for the first totally unsupported crossing of the Antarctic landmass.

Two years later, I needed another expedition. By then, all the great polar challenges, north and south, had been achieved by groups of two or more. All that was left was for an individual to try them unaided and I heard that Børge Ousland was planning a solo crossing of the Antarctic continent. So I returned to Antarctica at the age of fifty-two, but only halfway to the South Pole I was halted in my tracks by the excruciating pain of a kidney stone and had to be airlifted back to base.

I lost that particular race, but no one had yet completed the final polar grail of reaching the North Pole solo and unsupported along the North American route. It was an expedition that I would pay dearly for. In early 2000, I set off with two sledges carrying all my equipment and enough food for a journey that would take about eighty-five days.

After about two weeks, the sledge containing all my food and communications gear broke through the ice and fell into the Arctic sea. I took off the mitt on my left hand to untangle a rope and pull the sledge back on to the ice. Within minutes, I had severe frostbite and the fingers on my left hand were ramrod stiff and ivory white. The pain was extreme and so I radioed for help. I was flown out by plane to the nearest hospital in Ottawa.

Back in England, I was told it would take at least five months for the undamaged stumps to heal enough so they could amputate the frostbitten ends. But after four months, I could stand it no longer, so I bought a fretsaw and cut off the dead, purple ends myself.

I spent the next three years writing books, including a biography of Captain Scott. After which I needed a break, so when Mike Stroud suggested that we run seven marathons on seven continents in seven days, I agreed immediately. Shortly afterwards, I was on board a plane at Bristol airport, when I had a massive heart attack. I was rushed by ambulance to Bristol's Royal Infirmary, where I underwent double heart bypass surgery.

I now had only sixteen weeks to recover and teach myself to run again before the start of our marathon challenge, which could not be postponed for sponsorship reasons. Somehow I managed to do it and in late 2003, Mike and I ran the seven marathons in seven days, starting in Antarctica and finishing in New York, and together we broke another world record.

When I got home to our farm in Exmoor, however, I discovered that Ginny was seriously ill. She had suffered from sudden stomach pains for years, but the doctors never found anything wrong. Now she was diagnosed with a virulent form of stomach cancer and only three months later, she died.

In the long weeks that followed, I tried to lift my head above the deep ache of Ginny's death, telling myself that she would want me to attack life again, but I was becoming morose, inactive and full of self-pity. So I contacted my friend Sibussio Vilane, the first black person to summit Everest, who had earlier invited me to climb Everest with him. But first of all, I had to learn how to climb, and over the next year I undertook weeks of training in the Alps and in Ecuador with the mountain tours company Jagged Globe.

Ginny had told me often that if she should die before me, I was to remarry as soon as possible. At a lecture in Chester for the Royal Geographical Society, I met Louise Millington, who was full of life and she made me feel happier again. A year after Ginny's death, Louise and I were married in March 2005.

We spent our honeymoon at Everest Base Camp in Tibet. With the help of Sibu and the Jagged Globe group, I made it all the way to the Death Camp at 27,560 feet, but after we began the steep climb to reach the summit, I became dizzy and was gasping for breath. I knew if I had another heart attack, I would be dead in minutes. So I had to turn back and descend to lower altitudes at once.

Someone suggested that a tougher challenge would be the North Face of the Eiger, which was at a much lower altitude than Everest. I also wanted to confront my irrational fear of heights. So I contacted the mountain guide Kenton Cool, who agreed to teach me how to climb on rock and ice in the Alps. After further climbing lessons in the UK, I was deemed ready to go in March 2007. It was an extremely tiring and often frightening experience. But on the fifth day of our climb, I conquered my fears and stood on the summit of the Eiger North Face at 14,000 feet.

I had resolved not to climb any more mountains, but no one had yet achieved the ultimate adventurers' crown of crossing both polar ice caps and summitting the 'Third Pole', which was Mount Everest. So in 2008 I joined a group led by Kenton Cool from the easier Nepali side, but once again, I found myself fearing that if I carried on, I would die.

I realised that I was pushing myself too hard. I was sixty-five. If I could take things at a slower pace, I felt my body would be able to adapt. A year later, I went back to Everest with the ever-patient Tundu as my Sherpa, and keeping to a slow pace all the way, I finally reached the summit. I now hold the world record for the Global Reach Challenge, as the first person to have crossed both polar ice caps and summitted Mount Everest.

But age has a way of catching up with you. I turned seventy in 2014 and I had noticed some aches and pains in my legs and lower back. I was advised to take more exercise and so I went into training for the Marathon des Sables in Morocco, often described as 'the toughest foot race in the world', a six-day, 250km ultramarathon across the Sahara Desert. I struggled in the intense heat and at times my running was reduced to a shuffle. I managed to finish the race as the oldest British runner, but I recognised that I was now of geriatric status.

I have often been asked if I felt guilty risking my life on these expeditions, especially since I married Louise and we had our daughter Elizabeth. But explorers very rarely die, so in reality it is much safer. You are far more likely to die if you are a miner or truck driver, both professions with far higher death rates than mine. Both Ginny and Louise married me in the full knowledge that this is how I make a living. I have never been paid for the expeditions, but without them, there would have been no books and no lectures.

People also wonder why I chose to do challenges that are so dangerous and life-threatening. But if they were not so dangerous, people would already have done them and there would be no world records left to be broken.

I have no regrets. I would like to have completed a solo unsupported walk to the North Pole and to summit all seven of the highest mountains on each continent. Mike Stroud and I also had to abandon the first ever winter crossing of Antarctica, after it became too dangerous for the team to continue. But that's another story.

Above all, I am happy that my expeditions have raised millions of pounds for UK charities. When we started, raising money was never an objective, and it was our patron Prince Charles, as he was then, who first asked us to raise money for the Multiple Sclerosis

Society. Since then we have raised millions for the British Heart Foundation, Marie Curie Cancer Care, and many other charities. Ultimately, it was my obsession with raising big funds for Marie Curie to pay their nurses and to train new ones that encouraged us to take on further challenges. As I write, the total has now reached almost £20 million, all as a result of the King's suggestion.

Ranulph Fiennes,
2024

Joseph Skibinski, Ran, Jack McConnell and Stanley Cribbett by the River Thames before departing for the Headless Valley Expedition in Canada, 1971.

1

Canada

*The first transnavigation of British Columbia
by river from the Yukon to Vancouver
1971*

*fter leaving Eton College in 1962, Ranulph Fiennes joined
the Royal Scots Greys, the regiment commanded by his late
father during the Second World War, and he spent five years as a
tank troop leader in Germany, with a brief secondment to the
SAS in Hereford. He then commanded a reconnaissance platoon
in the Sultan of Oman's Armed Forces for two years, fighting
Marxist rebels in Dhofar.*

*In 1970, aged twenty-seven, Ran decided it was time to leave
the armed services to begin a new career as an expedition leader
and author.*

For a while, I continued to train with 'R' Squadron, 22nd SAS
Regiment in Hereford as a trooper, but the long drives and low
pay sparked a call to the 21st SAS Regiment (Territorial) in
London, whose CO agreed to take me on straightaway as a
captain. I spent most weekends with my new unit, very grateful
for the bigger pay packet. Then in February, a letter arrived from
the Royal Scots Greys, on whose list of reserve officers I still
figured. They had an expedition for me to lead.

That year British Columbia was celebrating the centenary of its

joining the Canadian Confederation and wished to commemorate
the early pioneers, most of whom had been Scots who had explored
their impenetrable territory by river. The centenary committee in
Vancouver had suggested that a river journey by Scotsmen from
their northern border with the Yukon to the United States border
on the 49th parallel would be a feat to match those of their fore-
bears. If successful, it would also be the first recorded north–south
transnavigation of British Columbia. The route, along nine inter-
connecting water systems, ran deep through the Rocky Mountains
and included some of the roughest rivers in the world.

The Canadians approached the Ministry of Defence in London
and they passed the suggestion on to the Greys, who liked the
idea, especially since in June they were due to lose their identity
and their famous grey berets through regimental amalgamation.
The Headless Valley Expedition would be a fine last fling but, as
they had no regular officers available to lead it, my name came up.
I was told the regiment would provide 'two or three soldiers and
some supplies'.

My wife Ginny, whom I had married a few months earlier,
agreed to join us as the road party leader and radio operator, and
when two of my old *langlauf* team from Germany volunteered, I
accepted both at once. One was an ex-butcher's apprentice from
Edinburgh called Joseph Skibinski (we used to call him an Oatmeal
Pole); the other, Jack McConnell, was a skilled radio operator.
My last acquisition was a tank mechanic called Stanley Cribbett,
who according to Skibinski, though short in size, could repair
anything from a clock to a sputnik. The *Observer* sent their top
photographer, Bryn Campbell, and the BBC *World About Us*
supplied a two-man film team, and a Yorkshire policeman with
lifeboat experience, Ben Usher, was recruited to steer for them.

An RAF Hercules flew us to Edmonton, from where we drove
our sponsored Land Rover and a four-ton lorry lent by the
Canadian Army north-west to Fort Nelson. Here the plan was for
the three boats to undertake a 400-mile trial journey before
committing ourselves to the main expedition and attendant

publicity. This seemed sensible, since our UK training had only been on the Thames and none of us had wild water boating know-how.

The trial goal was to reach the little known Virginia Falls, twice the height of Niagara, and 110 miles up the South Nahanni River. American river-runner and author Colonel Snyder, not given to understatement, described the South Nahanni as 'the fastest river in North America and the most dangerous in five continents'. To reach the Nahanni itself involved a further 290 miles of river travel. It would be a fair test.

We Royal Scots Greys wore our grey berets with their silver eagle badges as we left Fort Nelson. This was out of respect for our famous regiment, which four days previously had ceased to exist after 300 years as Scotland's own cavalry regiment. During the Second World War my father had seen the last of the grey horses in the 1940s; I wore the last grey beret in the 1970s.

The three boats slid away, edging into the current as we gathered speed. A Mountie, two Sekani people from the First Nations, and a group of press from Vancouver waved us off. Ginny stood alone on the bank, small and forlorn in her dusty jeans, soon a fading blur in the willows.

The river was 300 yards wide, both banks were thickly wooded and the world passed by quite silently but for the rush of water, the soft plunk of paddles and the sudden boil of converging eddies. An hour from Fort Nelson things changed with a vengeance.

'The current's racing along,' Bryn mused, 'as though there's a waterfall ahead.'

'There's no rapid on this river,' I assured him.

From up ahead I heard a sound as of breakers lashing a shingle beach; the same dull double boom and the rushing hiss of undertow. The channel ahead curved right but the local current sucked us left. The other boats were out of sight.

Along the left-hand bank fallen trees rose and fell in the water. Torn down by the force of the floods upon the elbow of the river's curve, their gnarled roots clung to the bank and their trapped trunks threshed to the pulse of the rushing water. If a boat was sucked into this chaos of tangled roots, the tubing would be torn and punctured. We stabbed deep with our paddles, straining to move into mid-river.

Before Stan could reach the outboard, a branch lashed across and cut his face. A splintered root dug into the hull behind Bryn and ripped it open. The port air tube wrinkled and subsided and the boat shuddered as we struck a grounded log. We bounced off. If the boat had been of wood, we would probably have foundered and been sucked beneath the mass of heaving vegetation.

For a moment we were free, spun away from the bank by an eddy. This was merely a brief respite, for the shock of our narrow escape was soon eclipsed by the horror of the scene ahead. Now we could see the source of the earlier wind-borne roar, an island in mid-river on which, it seemed, every log borne downriver by recent floods was impaled. The whole force of the current, channelled by the acute bend, ran full tilt against the upstream apex of the island, and every piece of flotsam, from floating stumps of juniper to eighty-foot logs, was ensnared where the current split in two against the island.

We could not go left because that channel was a moving mass of tangled debris. So we swung right, sweating over the paddles.

Stanley wrestled with our outboard, swung its drive-shaft down until it locked vertically and tugged hard on the ignition cord. Again and again he pulled and twice the engine spluttered hopefully. Bryn stopped paddling to look over his shoulder, distracted by the shocking sound of log crashing on to the log.

The water about us was disturbed now by back eddies surging around the jam. We were sucked inexorably backwards to where the river rushed under the sieve of logs. I thought to myself: 2,000 miles to go and here we are drowning on the first day. Then we smashed into the logs, sharp branches whipped at us and the boat up-ended. Someone screamed and a heavy object rammed my chest. I felt a branch rip down my back and the shock of cold water.

4

For a moment the boat was held by a branch and I scrabbled up from the floor to the mid-tubing. The branch broke and our bows disappeared, sucked inch by inch under the churning debris. Water poured over the bagged gear and the lashed fuel drums.

A branch flailed at Bryn and tore him away. He disappeared underwater, his hands clawing the air as he went.

The boat was about to go under. We must get on to the logs while there was a chance or we would all drown. I shouted to warn Stan and tried to scramble on to the nearest log above us. But it was too large and too slimy to grip. Then the boat shuddered and I fell back among the fuel drums. Stan shouted with excitement. He had started the engine. All this time he had single-mindedly tugged at the cord, not noticing the disappearance of Bryn. Now he engaged gear and the forty-horsepower engine roared in reverse cavitation.

There was hope. We both jumped up and down on the half-submerged craft to vibrate the trapped bows loose. A lashing line snapped, a ten-gallon drum broke loose and the bows shot free. Stanley grabbed the tiller and, with painful slowness, we edged away from the log jam.

Then I saw Bryn, or rather his mop of black hair. An underwater surge had spewed him up further down the log jam and his smart denim 'ranger' jacket was caught up on a branch. As we watched, his head sank a few inches. The full force of the undertow was dragging at him from the waist down.

We donned life-jackets and Stanley nosed the boat as near as possible to the downstream end of the log. I jumped on to it and edged along its bucking length towards Bryn. Sometimes the tree spun through half a turn. Reaching Bryn, I held his jacket scruff firmly and, with our combined strength, he came clear of the water. He was white, cold and shaken, but managed a rueful grin. His frail stature and normally immaculate garb belied a tough and resilient spirit.

The other crews both managed to keep clear of the great jam. We learned our lesson about the danger of snags and thereafter warmed our engine for a while each morning and started it at the first sign of any likely threat.

The BBC crew wished to camp an hour before dusk each evening to sort out their tent and bedding gear in the light. My own policy was not to waste good river-time, so I stopped only when I could no longer spot floating snags. They were annoyed by this.

Each evening Ben Usher erected two two-man tents for himself, Richard and Paul, and cooked a meal from special rations. We put up a single four-man tent into which the five of us squeezed, for Bryn mucked in like the others. Joe cut willow swatches and laid them on the wet mud under our groundsheet.

A grizzly bear had recently killed two young girl campers in their sleeping bags. We slept with four loaded pistols in the tent. 'A bullet woodn'a get far,' Jack muttered in the dark. 'The air's so thick with mosqueeters.'

At Fort Liard we were met by about a hundred local Sekani. There were also a handful of whites, including an eccentric French priest with a heavily pockmarked face, and a clean young Scotsman, who ran the Hudson's Bay Company store with a sign outside proclaiming 'HBC 1886'. The Scotsman told us the locals said this stood for 'Here Before Christ'. He warned us the mosquitoes would be far worse in Nahanni country.

'The upriver folk say the air is so thick with them, you canna starve. Simply keep breathing with your mouth open and you will get your daily meat ration.'

That night the two hundred village dogs sang to the moon. There were five dogs to every local man and they worked hard in winter, when the rivers became frozen highways through the white forests.

The French priest, Father Mary, gave us moose stew and carrots for supper and advice about the river. 'Your rubbaire boots . . . *Piff!* They never take you to the falls. You must have a flat-bottom rivaire boat like mine. Thirty feet long and solide. Hire one, pleeze, at Nahanni Butte. You have 140 miles of big fast rivaire. One mistake and *woosh*!'

I followed his advice as soon as we reached the butte, the point where the South Nahanni River joined the Liard. I hired a thirty-two-foot river boat made by a Sekani man for $50 and a bottle of our sponsored Black & White whisky. With two outboards, this craft would enable us to carry extra fuel for our two inflatables and a more solid platform for the BBC crew.

A hunter at the butte named Brian Doke told us to go carefully. A moose-hunter he knew had capsized only twelve miles up the Nahanni, lost his kit and twisted an ankle. They found him nine days later half-starved and demented by insects. The previous year another hunter friend had turned around in the bush to see a black bear, normally harmless to humans. The man's body, half-eaten, was found later alongside his loaded rifle.

Next day we entered the first canyon of the Nahanni. The towering walls acted as an echo chamber to every gush and twirl of the current, the sky above narrowed to a faraway strip of blue and we shivered in deep shadow, three water beetles struggling against the flow in a sheer-sided drain. The wiles of the river had to be watched at all times. There was no time to relax and enjoy the incredible scenery. To do so would be as suicidal as studying the Arc de Triomphe while driving round it.

High above us soared sheer red walls with successive pine-clad tiers of rock teetering atop the lower cliffs. The sun seldom touched us as we inched along the gloomy corridors of the canyon. Elsewhere, fighting for every inch of progress, we had to tug the river boat upstream on tow-lines with the eight of us hauling knee-deep in icy shallows. Policeman Ben, the strongest of us, was built like an Aberdeen Angus bull and, when he slipped, we all went under. The rope ripped away, tearing free of my numbed grip. On our next attempt we lined her, the jockey-light Stanley stayed aboard and cleverly nosed the boat upstream as we took in slack on the ropes.

Eventually we entered a region much favoured by the Canadian press due to its macabre associations. In Deadmen Valley, tucked between the Headless Mountains and the Funeral Range, three headless skeletons were found in the early 1900s. Canadian newspapers had been clocking up the unexplained deaths score in the area ever since and put the toll as high as thirty-two, but Ginny's research at the Royal Geographical Society and the Royal Canadian Mounted Police records confirmed only seventeen unexplained deaths or disappearances. Which might be considered enough. We did not add to those statistics and left Deadmen Valley with our heads intact.

In less than a hundred miles we had climbed over 1,000 feet. The final canyon was an impressive display of water force. A pocket of converging currents very nearly defeated us. We inched up the wall of water in the eddy-trap and water poured out of the butterfly valves in our boat bilges. Stanley zigged the tiller of our boat, shouting with relief as we crested the last rapid in an explosion of spray. Then the roar of pounding water intensified to an overall boom and from the heavens, or so it seemed from river-level, there appeared a waterfall of Olympian grandeur beneath a halo of high-flung spray. We had reached the Virginia Falls. Even the dour features of Constable Ben softened with pleasure at the majesty of the place.

The current whisked us back to Nahanni Butte, where Bryn and the film team caught a bush plane to Fort Nelson to film fire-fighting in British Columbia. The trial journey was over. We drove north-west to the Yukon border ready to launch the boats on our 1,500-mile attempt to transnavigate British Columbia.

No sooner had we been rejoined by the BBC film crew than I sensed an overtly hostile atmosphere. Earlier they had fretted about not having a more definite timetable and again about not having enough time to sort out their gear at the end of the day. But I had been able to ignore that. Now I could tell I was in for trouble.

The Hyland River took us gently over the Yukon border into the Liard River and all went well as far as the Cranberry Rapids, where the Jocks overturned and Stanley ripped our own boat open on a snag. Jack's morale was dented by the experience, for he was sucked below by undercurrents, despite his life-jacket, and battered against submerged rocks.

Not far beyond the Cranberry Rapids and above the Rapids of the Drowned, we entered the mouth of the Kechika (or Big Muddy) River. This tributary of the Liard was sourced from a high swamp in the Rocky Mountain Trench known as the Sifton Pass and every authority I had consulted assured me our inflatables would not penetrate very far upriver. When we could get no farther, I planned to canoe or to walk with rucksacks and had brought from England two portable canoes that, when dismantled, would be divided between our four backpacks.

The point at which we would have to give up on our inflatables was probably going to be a spot known as Skook's ranch. This was the kingdom of Skook Davidson, *skookum* being the Sekani word for The Tough One.

Skook ran a camp for big game hunters, with all his clients, guides and stores being flown in by floatplane. When the film crew learned that Skook had pack-horses for hire they approached me with, to them, the reasonable-sounding proposal that they hire these for their heavy camera gear. They could not see my view that the ethics of the expedition precluded outside support. Either we travelled the river or, where we ran out of waterways, we walked. But as far as the BBC crew were concerned I was being wilfully obstructive for no good reason. From that moment my fate was sealed. I would be the villain in their documentary film.

Skook was over eighty. Leaving Scotland as a teenager with £10 to his name, he became the finest rodeo rider in British Columbia and settled in his valley in 1939. Now he looked after twenty big-game hunters a year, specialising in grizzlies, bighorn sheep, cougars and mountain rams. The great man welcomed us from his bed, an old gnarled pioneer crippled by arthritis. He fumbled to light a candle.

'Sit down, darn you,' he barked. 'You folk from the old country never seem to know what the Lord gave you asses for.' Candlelight

revealed a row of medals nailed to a log. Skook had done a stint
as a sniper in the 29th Vancouver Battalion during the First World
War.

From Skook's the boats went back downstream with Ginny,
while the film team flew south to meet up with us at Fort Ware.

I asked Skook about the country to the south.

'When you can canoe no further,' he advised, 'you'll find my
old trail beside the river, all the way to Sifton Pass.'

The Rocky Mountain Trench and the Kechika both lie north–
south and, on the far side of the Sifton Pass, a new river, the
Tochika or Fox, flows south all the way to Fort Ware. Skook's
memories of his trail from thirty years ago were difficult to check
and I found it ominous that a surveyor whose book I had studied
described the trail, only six months after Skook had made it, as
'requiring much work every season if it is to be kept open, due to
washouts, rapid growth and windfalls'.

I consulted a Sekani guide. 'You'll be all right,' he said, 'so long
as you don't follow a game trail by mistake. They're all over the
place.' When asked how we were to recognise the real trail from
the game trail, he replied, 'Why, you just do. I been along that way
most years since I was a kid and you just get to know the right way
after a while. But you watch out for bears, man. Last month a
female grizzly came for me and I dropped her with my .303 not far
from Gataga Forks. You surprise a grizzly on the trail with her
kids and she can get real mean.'

The four Scots Greys left Skook's in fine weather and paddled
up to Gataga Forks. Then the stream became too narrow and too
powerful, so we collapsed the canoes we were then using, lashed
them to our 110-pound packs and started following a trail blazed
with old tree slashes, definitely the only trail within a mile of our
side of the river.

We were soon wet with sweat, and biting horseflies took advantage of our captive hands. Then Jack fell off a tree-bridge and
landed spreadeagled in a thicket of thorn and dead branches. He
lay there face upward and pinioned by his rucksack. I released

him from that predicament, but that incident alone cost us a half-hour delay.

After a frustrating afternoon, Jack and I came to three deserted log cabins by the Frog River. Little Stanley Cribbett, who was not much larger than his rucksack, stumbled along an hour later and tottered over beside us, his face pale and sweating profusely. He winced from a spasm of coughing and spat a gob of bright blood on to the grass. He said that his groin pained him and he had tasted blood for some time. He was our only trained medic.

Another hour passed before Joe arrived. He had fallen off a log and wrenched his back, which now hurt him badly. Unable to carry his load, he had tried hauling it on a two-pole 'sled', but fallen trees made this impractical. Reluctantly, but unanimously, we agreed that Stanley and Joe should return to Skook's ranch and radio for a plane to take them south to Fort Ware, to rest and recover with the film team.

This left Jack and me, but things got only worse. An hour later the track ran out altogether, so we followed a blazed trail that veered east away from the river, hoping we might pick up the correct southerly trail further along. We camped under a polythene sheet a mile inside dense forest. The trees dripped all night and heavy animals moved about in the undergrowth.

Next day we continued deep into the forest, hoping that the track would bend back towards the south. Instead it began to head north-east. Somewhere we must have overlooked a southerly turning. We had wasted eight hours but Jack never complained. We turned back, reached the Kechika by nightfall and drank thirstily, for we had long since emptied our water bottles.

In the morning, rain lashed the trees and our meagre cover. We coaxed some kindling into a fire and dissolved our daily ration of four oatmeal biscuits into two mugfuls of boiling water to form a glutinous porridge, which we laced with salt and gulped down with relish.

In the hope that yesterday's trail, the only marked route,

eventually returned to the Kechika, we wearily set out again, in the wrong direction but knowing there was no alternative. For three long, wet days we slogged through swamps, up steep hills and down slippery slopes. Jack missed his footing on the second morning and fell off the pathway down a muddy forested incline. I found him badly scratched and bruised. His ankle was sore and began to swell, so I bandaged it.

Rain fell all day and every day so that the trail became a stream and deep pools formed between the knee-high roots that criss-crossed our route. We trudged in silence, sometimes losing the trail altogether until one of us spotted another faint tree-slash or sawn-off branch.

Each night it seemed to get colder. We slept close together under our polythene sheet. However wet the forest, there was always moss and old bark to be found under windfalls, enough to kindle a fire and dry our skin.

With four days' rations left, for safety's sake we began to cut down our daily intake and decided to shoot anything edible that came our way. Twice the fresh spoor of a wolf showed on our path, but the foliage was too dense to see any game. Our morale was finally boosted when a Spruce or Franklin's grouse landed on a branch a few yards ahead. Jack carefully drew his 9mm pistol and took aim at the pretty dappled bird. He fired three shots, but he missed. The bird stayed put, clucking with indignation and fixing Jack with a stoney stare. So I grabbed the pistol from Jack and toppled the poor bird with my third and last shot.

On the fifth day the trail gave out in a region of many creeks, numerous wooded valleys and, immediately to the east, a high-walled canyon. We agreed to be bold and to cut due west by compass until we reached the Kechika; then, if there was still no sign of the trail, to wade along the river itself.

As we inched west, we climbed higher until we reached the tree line. At first we were pleased to be clear of wet leaves but, out in the open, the wind lashed through our wet clothes. A snowstorm caught us up on a high mountain slope, so we sheltered in a narrow space between rocks. Jack, his face gaunt and wan, shivered and rubbed his bad ankle.

When the snow stopped we climbed higher to a ridgeline, and for the first time in days we were able to take stock of our location. I clutched the map against the wind. Ahead, to the west, was an unbroken line of bald-topped mountains. To return towards the Kechika River in a direct line would mean climbing this western ridge which, by my map, was nowhere under 6,000 feet and was separated from us by numerous forested valleys. Depressing as it seemed, our only sensible choice was to return to our starting point, and this meant relocating our outward trail.

Descending to the tree line, we pressed on in the general direction of our earlier track. We waded through mushy swamps and climbed over tangled deadfalls. We could no longer see mountains or useful features, in fact nothing but the immediate tangle of vegetation. A few days later we struggled clear of the forest, but later that evening we ran out of rations. We had to find our way back quickly to Skook's, collect more food and try again. Jack was nursing septic ankles where his boots chafed against burst blisters, and my shoulders were raw in places where the pack had rubbed against them.

One swamp took eight hours to cross and we sank to our knees in the spongier veins. This sapped our will to keep going. We emerged on to a wide game trail and I remember thinking how strange it was to find footprints in this wilderness. We must have trudged along for a full five minutes before common sense began to assert itself through the fog of exhaustion and hunger.

'Hey, Ran,' mumbled Jack, 'd'ye think these bootprints could be oors?' They were. The relief was great.

We came to Gataga Forks on the last day of the month and paddled our canoe the thirty miles back to Skook's. He could not understand how we had missed the trail, but it was a long time since he had been on it. The Irish doctor strapped up Jack's ankle and we packed a fresh supply of rations. For a day we rested and feasted on moose steak and blueberry pie.

Next day, in ten degrees of frost, we set out again – this time without our canoe, rifle, ropes or radio. After three miles Jack was lagging badly. His ankle was worse than ever and we would only court disaster to tempt fate further. We argued the toss and Jack finally agreed. I could see he was crying in frustration. He gave me his pistol and we shook hands.

Route-finding continued to be a nightmare. I was ready to throw in the towel myself until the possibility occurred to me that the local Sekani, the nomads of these parts, might have moved Skook's trail across the river. I waded across and six hours later picked up a clearly marked triple slash, the sign in Sekani territory of a nearby trapline. Forgetting sores, hunger and blisters, I covered the next twenty miles in two days to the headwaters of the Kechika, high on the flats of the Sifton Pass, a cheerful place of flowering plants and berry bushes. This was good trapping country, flush with beaver, marten, mink and otter. Now the trail became easy to see, no longer a will-o'-the-wisp passage through undergrowth, but a trodden path with blaze marks every few yards.

Late in the afternoon after crossing the pass, I rounded a bend to find Jack and Joe hunting squirrels and they led me down to their camp at Fox Lake, where the film crew were also installed.

Everyone seemed rather subdued. There was no welcome for me. Jack brought me tea and a pot of stew and, when the others were out of hearing, I asked him what was going on. He said, 'I canna say for sure. My guess is that the Beeb and Ben have talked them into hating yoo's.' He explained how the film team had passed their waiting time prompting Stanley and Joe to complain about their treatment on tape.

They had pictures of the diminutive Stanley staggering about under the weight of his pack. They had film of Joe declaring that 'Ran couldna' organise a piss-up in a brewery', and by way of proof that I was an egomaniac glory-seeker, the suggestion that I had encouraged the others to drop out so I could cross the Rocky Mountain Trench all by myself. On top of everything else, I was plainly a lousy navigator. All that was needed now was for the journey to fail somewhere along the miles of violent rivers to our south. Then the BBC could make a fascinating in-depth study of leadership failure.

To select the perfect expeditionary team, in my opinion, is nearly impossible. There is no foolproof selection process and the longer, the more ambitious the endeavour, the more time there is for each person's failings to rise to the surface. The most I hope for is to find at least one true companion on each journey. In Canada I was lucky. Jack became a loyal lifelong friend, a man I would ask again on any expedition and trust whatever the stresses.

We launched ourselves back on the river at Fort Ware then followed the boisterous Finlay, the log-jammed, storm-tossed Williston Lake, the mosquito and black-fly-infested Parsnip, Pack and Crookford Rivers, until at last we reached Summit Lake.

One night Ginny, waiting to contact us in a thickly forested swamp beside the river, was surprised by a black bear. She lost her nerve and screamed. The bear came closer and she pulled her .38 Smith and Wesson out of her anorak pocket. Somehow she pressed the trigger before the gun was clear and a bullet passed through the outside welt of her rubber boot, within a couple of millimetres of her foot. The bear departed and so did a terrified Ginny.

Next time I met her she was furious. Why had I not made the rendezvous? Why did she have to wander through stinking woods and portage heavy gear? Nobody ever thanked or acknowledged her. I did, I pointed out.

'No, you don't. You just use me. You couldn't care less what happens to me so long as I'm in the right place at the right time.'

I did not try to argue as, by that time in our marriage, I knew it would be useless. Instead I thought of my favourite quote from Albert Einstein: 'Some men spend a lifetime in an attempt to comprehend the complexities of women. Others preoccupy themselves with simpler tasks such as understanding the theory of relativity.'

All the rivers we had travelled prior to reaching Summit Lake had flowed to an Arctic destination. Summit Lake was a dead-end, a high-altitude source of this Arctic watershed. To continue south we carried our boats nine miles along the ancient Giscombe Portage trail, over the Intercontinental Divide and down to the Pacific watershed and the biggest river of British Columbia, named after the great Scots explorer Simon Fraser.

We launched the boats on to the Fraser River late on 20 September and within minutes swept over the Giscombe Rapids wearing black frogsuits and life-jackets.

From Giscombe, the lifeline but also the grave of so many pioneers, the river flowed for 850 tempestuous miles to Vancouver and the sea. Between Prince George, British Columbia's most northerly city, and the Fraser-side town of Lytton the river drops 1,200 feet, four times the height of Niagara Falls and, within the canyons, it rises up to eighty feet in spring. Then the power of the whirlpools, boils and hydraulics is greater, but the danger of hidden rocks causing endless rapids and razor-sharp snares becomes less.

Seventy miles south of Prince George, it penetrates a deep trough many hundreds of feet below the surrounding land mass. The river responds to the new resistance of the enclosing walls by seeking a sinuous route through a succession of nightmare canyons, livid with foam and mad with the roar of boiling water to the exclusion of all other sound.

The uncertainty of not knowing the state of the river ahead wore at all our nerves. Each day the cataracts grew more powerful and more frequent. In a small rubber boat, even a twelve-foot wave can seem awesome. When they are legion and they explode from every side, some boiling up from beneath the hull, they can make any traveller edgy. In the back of my mind lay the fear that around the next corner, or the next, we would come without warning, and with no chance of extrication, to the impossible maelstrom of the bottomless whirlpool of some half-remembered nightmare.

Part of the problem was the team's awareness that the worst was still to come. Ahead lay the Moran Canyon followed by a series of awkward major rapids. For three days, based at the old gold town of Clinton in the Caribou, we tried to reconnoitre the canyon before embarking, but helicopters were beyond our means and no trails led to suitable vantage points.

To glean knowledge from the locals, we visited the Pavilion Reservation's chief who said that, not being crazy, he had never been into the canyon nor would a thousand spirits drive him there. He took us to see an ancient chief, who also advised us that many people had died over the years down in the canyon and we should avoid the place. There were whirlpools that stretched across the river and a steamboat had once been dashed to pieces there.

In Kelly Creek we visited the shack of Andy Moses, who had spent fifty years beside the river. 'Never been into the canyon,' he said. 'Too many guys drowned in there. Anybody who tries to boat through it is jest plumb crazy.'

After three days in Clinton I feared the men's morale was beginning to plunge so, although I hated to enter the canyon unprepared and ignorant, I knew we must go before further delay sapped our will.

We entered the Moran Canyon, a rushing, roiling cauldron squeezed between black walls 1,000 feet high. The underplay of currents was impressive. Huge surface boils, bubbling like hot water in a saucepan, twice turned us about completely and thrust us chaff-like against the granite walls. By nightfall we stopped a mile above the great killer rapid of the Bridge River confluence.

The press were waiting for us in Lillooet town below the Bridge River Falls: they sensed drama. Four months earlier, a muscular Frenchman had arrived in town. He had canoed every major rapid in North America, now he had come to tame the Bridge River Rapids. The Mounties retrieved his battered body from the whirlpool below the falls.

All of us rose early to preview the rapid and we agreed upon a likely route. We returned upstream to the boats and then fought our way through the remaining rapids of the Fountain Ravine. Nerves were tattered. Jack and Joe had a bad time in the ravine and, spotting an especially rough stretch not far above the main cataract, refused to risk attempting it, in the knowledge that a capsize there would lead to being swept into the turmoil below. I agreed that their boat should be lined through the rapids and then the two Jocks would continue in the boat of the film team, who were preparing to record the rapid-shooting from the cliff top.

Stanley took us through the last section of the Fountain Rapids without a capsize and we beached three hundred yards above the Bridge River rapid. One hundred yards upstream of the troubles, a rock ledge ran right across the river and sieved the water through shiny black teeth. Should a boat overturn here, there would be no time to re-right it before the falls.

The sun was pleasantly warm. I felt drained of energy and my stomach fluttered wildly. But I knew we must go *now*. Stanley was deathly pale and sweating profusely. He nodded at me and ground out a cigarette on a rock. He climbed on to our boat as though it were a tumbrel. Bryn and the film team waved from a high boulder. They were ready. Joe, idling on the bank, gave us a thumbs-up.

Stanley whipped the engine to life. I pushed the boat off and sprang aboard. Plucked from the bank like a feather, we plunged into the white water below the rock ledge. Twice the propellor crashed into submerged rocks and we scarcely dared breathe as the outboard burred unevenly, threatening to stall. If it did, there would be some twenty seconds in which to restart it or to man the oars before we hit the main falls.

But the engine did not fail us. The rocks were behind and now a short stretch of smooth racing water, too powerful to fight, sucked us straight into the maw of the cataract. Our previous plans were immaterial.

A roar like the thunder of doom rushed at us as we shot downwards. For a while I could see nothing. Then a scene of total turmoil. We became like sodden shirts inside a high-powered washing machine. We entered by way of a broiling flume to be engulfed by a huge hydraulic, in the grip of which we corkscrewed deeper and deeper. There was nothing to see or to feel but solid water; we were awash within a cartwheeling tunnel.

The craft keeled over, forced to the side of a monster wave by centrifugal force. It was a wall of death on the horizontal plane and our hull clung to the inner side of the spinning liquid tube. Almost upside down within this whirling tunnel, I could see only a confused kaleidoscope of moving water.

At the lower end of the cyclic action, the boat was gripped by an undertow, dragged around and around, then spat out into a whirlpool. Our outboard roared frantically as we swung around the sinkhole and the cliffs of the river disappeared as we sank deep within the river's bowels. Then the sinkhole closed and regurgitated us towards the left-hand cliff. Stanley, water gushing from his helmet, tried to steer away from the rocks. He failed and we dashed against a boulder. The hull screamed in rubbery protest and crumpled along one side as the tube split open. But we were through.

We shook hands and felt on top of the world. Our second boat also managed to defy the Bridge River Rapids.

After repairing the boats, we continued south to Lytton and Boston Bar. Here the river flows fast and furious through the Coastal Range to pound down a deep and gloomy gut called the Black Canyon. We fought through nameless rapids hidden from the world by the gorges they had forged. Then it was time to face the Fraser's final monster rapid, Hell's Gate. The whirlpools beneath the gate had recently sucked down two thirty-foot inflatable boats, folding them in half the better to accommodate them. The river descends through the rocky narrows at up to fifty miles per hour, but we navigated the Gate with ease, a simple affair compared to what we had already been through.

Finally the last confining ramparts of the canyon fell away and our three boats moved on through a gentler land of grazing cattle and fruit farms. Four days later we passed through the beautiful city of Vancouver with its backdrop of snow-clad peaks and into the river delta. A sea mist covered the marshes, so we navigated with care into the Pacific, until a police launch met us with a bullhorn.

'This is it, folks. You're in Yank territory now.'

The two BBC films that were made from this expedition led their sixteen million-strong British audience to believe I was a cruel and incompetent publicity seeker. The innuendoes that helped paint this picture certainly added spice and colour to the films, but did surprisingly little to discourage my sponsors in the future, and even helped me to develop a tougher skin when later expeditions were laid open to public scrutiny and criticism.

Jack and Stanley left the Army a year after the expedition and emigrated to Western Canada, where they both married. Jack called one of his sons Ranulph.

Monty Don
Horticulturist, broadcaster and writer

Sarah and I met Ran and Ginny Fiennes through a mutual friend, not long after they had returned from the Transglobe Expedition, who suggested that we might get on via a shared, slightly obsessive love of dogs and an equally compulsive love of the outdoors. We also had a slightly deranged terrier like Bothie and when their Arctic Black Dog had pups, we somehow ended up with two of them.

We had very good times, holidaying with a crowd of assorted children on Knoydart in Scotland, walking and climbing in the Alps, and above all visiting their farm Greenlands on Exmoor. Ran was always wonderful with the children when they were small. His public persona is that of the intrepid man of action overcoming insuperable odds to achieve feats of superhuman endurance and danger. But with the children he was gentle, patient and kind and they adored both him and Ginny. We all did.

Ran and Ginny got me to help them choose and plant scores of roses at Greenlands, in what was probably a vain attempt to soften the extremes of exposure and soil, but was also an act of great kindness and generosity at a time when I had little work and things were not going so well.

Ginny's cattle and Ran's tree-planting on Exmoor inspired me to do the same in the Black Mountains, where for the past twenty years we have had a small hill farm. As I go around weeding the growing trees, I always think of Ran.

I miss those doggy days at Greenlands when the children were little and there was a constant swirl of Black Dogs. It was all too long ago now. But some friendships can withstand time and distance. Some experiences and shared time can never pall or lose their lustre.

Ran (second from right) with the crew of his 70-ton Conqueror tank while serving with the Royal Scots Greys in Germany, 1965.

2

Germany

Serving as a tank troop leader in Germany
with the Royal Scots Greys
1963–1965

*R*an's *childhood ambition was to follow in his father's foot-*
steps and become Commanding Officer of the Royal Scots
Greys. He did not gain enough A-levels to get into Sandhurst, so
first he had to pass through a five-month course at the Mons
Officer Cadet School in Aldershot. Next he was sent to the Royal
Armoured Corps Centre at Bovington Camp in Dorset, where he
undertook further military training and courses in gunnery,
signals, tactics, vehicle maintenance and driving a Centurion
Mark VII battle tank.

After just passing the tank-training course, now a second lieu-
tenant, he was posted to join the Greys at Fallingbostel, near
Hamburg.

My father Ranulph had joined the Royal Scots Greys in India,
after Eton and Sandhurst. After a spell as aide to the Governor
General of Canada, he had risen to second in command when war
came. He was charged with disposing of the regiment's 600 grey
horses and training men as tank soldiers. The first major clash
with General Erwin Rommel, commander of the German *Afrika
Korps*, was at Alam el Halfa in August 1942, by which time

Ranulph was commanding the Greys. At Nofilia, he led a 'frontal cavalry charge' against the Panzer tanks from a turretless tank and was badly wounded. Altogether he was wounded four times, and he was awarded the DSO. I keep a letter written to my mother by one of his troopers: 'I knew Colonel Lugs as a sympathetic and understanding, fair and just, loyal and fearless, leader of men.'

At El Alamein, Ranulph led the Greys through two major minefields during the main attack. At one point he spotted two wounded Italians in no-man's-land and rescued them, although his tank was hit in several places. In June 1943, he came home on leave and I was conceived. When he left, my mother was never to see him again.

He commanded the Greys at Salerno and through southern Italy. Reconnoitring a bridge over the Pascara river unarmed and alone, he surprised three Germans in a cave and took them prisoner at the point of his briar pipe. Two Greys troopers, escaped prisoners, reported that their interrogators had wanted to know the correct pronunciation of the names of the three commanding officers of the regiment, Twisleton, Wykeham and Fiennes.

Not far from Naples, checking out a possible route of advance, Colonel Lugs trod on an S-type mine and, on 24 November 1943, four months before my birth and nine months after the death of his father Sir Eustace, my father died of wounds and jaundice in a Naples hospital. My mother never married again.

They were together for only ten years unbroken by war, but for her their love has lasted undiminished down the long years since. From childhood I have wanted to be as he was.

In February 1963, I made my way to Germany to join the Royal Scots Greys. I was eighteen and had just bought my first car, an elderly Peugeot 403, for £150.

Most of the Greys had still not arrived from Aden when I joined their advance party in the dismal barracks of Fallingbostel on the Westphalian Plain. The camp had been built for Hitler's Panzers twenty years before and was sited close by the main tank-training

ranges of northern Germany, the British defence sect
Army of the Rhine (BAOR).

My new fellow officers were Hamish Macrae and Thuggers
Kingston (the aggressive Earl of Kingston, whom I had met at
my prep school, Sandroyd), and three others I did not know.
Until quite recently, newly joined officers, like Victorian children, were supposed to be seen but not heard by their seniors,
meaning all other humans in the Officers' Mess. This practice
was still prevalent in some regiments, but not in the Scots Greys.
So long as you were not blatantly noisy or disrespectful, you
could get a civil answer to a sensible question. For this I was
thankful, since it was altogether a new world and I had plenty of
questions to ask.

Regimental Sergeant-Major Rowan, a big man with a bristling
moustache, swagger-stick and high blood pressure, patiently
taught his new officers the Scots Greys' drill with swords and
submachine guns. We were also instructed in the regimental
customs, history and taboos.

A month later, the bulk of the regiment turned up in dribs and
drabs, including the CO, Colonel Jack Balharry, an entirely
unfrightening sort of boss. As in my father's day, the lion's share
of the officers were Scotsmen, as were over 90 per cent of the
troopers and NCOs. Only two Greys remained who remembered
my father from eighteen years earlier, but the fact that he had
commanded the Greys and that Fiennes, pronounced 'Feens' by
all the Jocks, was thought to be a Scottish name, saved me from
most of the mickey-taking suffered by a number of the more obviously English Greys.

Few officers were wealthy but most were comfortably off, with
a private income to supplement their wages. My allowance was
£200 per year and most of the 1963 dollop had gone on the
Peugeot. After regimental deductions, my monthly wage was
between £15 and £25, which left little for extra-regimental activities. I was to find this more and more irksome, especially when
fined for misdemeanours.

, who joined with me, Paddy Earp,
…er than most twelve-year-old boys.
…np it seemed as though his car was on
…as invisible through the rear window. His
…rew, since this is the very smallest item in a
…aying cricket in the bedroom block corridor
tennis ball and coal shovel, I missed the ball. The
…ad flew off its wooden handle and shot down the
cor… …ddy Earp, emerging from the Gents doing up his flies,
was stru… … in the mouth by the shovel. There was much blood, but
the Grubscrew was brave and told nobody.

A while later, with helicopter pilot Louie Parsons, I was engaging in a .22 rifle practice in the same corridor when an NCO crossed the passage without warning. Frightened by a bullet that missed his torso and ricocheted off the wall, he told stories in high places. I was summoned before the adjutant, Prince Edward, Duke of Kent, who gave me a serious warning with a pointed reminder that a few years previously a friend of his had been thrown out of the regiment for shooting his brother officer in the backside with a .45 revolver.

Keen to play polo, I struck a deal with Peter Loyd, one of the other troop leaders in my squadron, that we would each pay for half a pony and share its use. Unfortunately the two of us went to Hamburg in my Peugeot to a farewell dinner for our squadron leader, Major Brian Booth. The party, at the fabulous Vier Jahrezeiten Hotel, included a great deal of alcohol and operatic performances by officers on the tabletop. One Baron Franckenstein, who had followed me from Eton College to the Scots Greys, sang *Figaro* to the music of the Four Seasons orchestra.

Disorientated by fine wines and port, neither my passenger nor I could remember where my Peugeot was parked. After two hours of useless wandering and reports to the *polizei*, we took a taxi back to camp. By selling my half of the pony I managed to purchase an ancient Citroën from an older officer, and took up singing in the garrison choir, a less expensive hobby.

Germany

There were no girls in Fallingbostel. Years of incide...
the local *Fräuleins* and the garrison incumbents had caus...
parents of all pretty, and most plain, girls to shut them up out o...
working hours and to resist all attempts at familiarity by British
males with short haircuts. In four years at Fallingbostel, the only
officer who ever succeeded with a local *Fräulein* was the Grubscrew
and he probably managed it by sneaking underneath the parental
radar.

The local dearth left only in-house attractions and they were
few and far between. A handful of Army education teachers lived
in the garrison, but they were singularly unattractive and known
by all as screachers. Our regimental paymaster's daughter, Susan,
came to stay from school in England. She was dark, sixteen and a
classic beauty. I played tennis with her and took her to one or two
dances, but nothing came of it. Her voice was as intoxicating as
her looks, so I joined the choir to listen and watch. Baron
Franckenstein was another keen attender, but I never found out
whether he came for love of Susan or the sound of his own voice.

My then girlfriend Ginny's parents would not allow her to visit
me, as she was still at school, but another friend Maggie Rayner
came out for one or two weekends. Driving her back from
Hamburg in a borrowed Mercedes, I went to sleep at ninety miles
per hour on the *autobahn*. Maggie screamed a warning as we
homed in on the tail end of a truck. Somehow I swerved in time.

On other occasions, seven or eight of us went at weekends to
the notorious David, Herbert or Winkelstrasse and paid ten
marks apiece to watch two ladies performing naked rites with
bananas. Few if any of us spent time with the prostitutes who
beckoned from ill-lit windows in the sin-streets. Whether this
abstinence stemmed from moral inhibitions or fears of syphilis I
could not say.

Senior officers told us there was a Hamburg nightclub where
the ladies made love to well-endowed mules and another where, if
you left coins on the corner of your table, naked waitresses would
remove them entirely by adroit application of their thigh muscles.

.eated his coin with a lighter and sent
pite numerous weekend sorties to see
ves, we never located the relevant dives –

JR's existence, as for the American and French
outh, was to defend Western Europe against
Wᵤ ᵣvasion. Since an attack could theoretically be
mountᵤ ₐ only a few hours' warning, all BAOR personnel
and vehicles had to be in a permanent state of war-readiness. To
test this without warning, regimental commanders held 'crashes'
from time to time and woe betide the troop leader who did not
get his three battle tanks, fully crewed and armed, to their pre-
designated battle positions within the allotted six-hour period.

Indicative of NATO's strategic intentions, the drill was to position each tank in a snug protective hollow with the vehicle facing
west in readiness for retreat and its gun pointing east to knock out
a Soviet or two before fleeing. For four years, almost without
exception, our training concentrated on withdrawal practice
except when acting as 'enemy'.

Each squadron consisted of four troops with three tanks each.
Three troops manned standard fifty-ton Centurion tanks and the
fourth, of which I was troop leader, crewed the great seventy-ton
Conquerors, which were unwieldy but lobbed their shells a good
deal further. The Conqueror Jocks referred to the Centurion
tanks as 'bubble cars'.

Immediately after the war, tank-training was conducted in
cavalier fashion, with little respect for the vanquished farmers,
whose crops were crushed and barns destroyed with impunity. By
the 1950s, 'Huns' were being referred to more often as 'German
citizens' and, after the Berlin airlift, as 'our German allies'. Year
by year, training rights were curtailed until, by the early 1950s,
training areas were barely large enough to cope with more than
two tank regiments at any one time.

For brigade or divisional exercises, which moved over whole

areas of German countryside outside the designated
complex scale of compensation was laid down and upgraded
year. Slight damage to a twenty-year-old pine tree could earn its
owner £100 and a crushed gatepost £50. Often enough smiling
farmers would stand by open gates waving invitingly at oncoming
tank commanders. A poor crop could be turned into a small fortune
if a British tank could be persuaded to drive over it once or twice.

The main training zone, a quagmire of muddy couloirs, criss-
crossed the pine forests of Luneberger Heide, the flattish region
between the Elbe borderline and the main cities of Hamburg,
Bremen and Hanover. The tanks of a good troop leader moved in
slick orderly fashion, never getting lost or bogged down, and
leapfrogging so that one always covered the progress of the others.

In most American tank units, and we trained with a number,
the troop leader did the map reading and his NCOs went wherever he led, quite unaware of their location. All British tank
commanders used their maps at all times and often were told to
take over as troop leader for a given exercise or cross-country
movement. This led to a testing time for young officers whose
map reading was slow or uncertain, but often enough their troop
sergeant or corporal was an old hand on the Luneberger training
zones and knew most of the area by heart.

There are few more embarrassing situations known to military
man than to take a wrong turning when acting as lead tank for a
squadron move. Twelve steel monsters lumber behind you, each
with a commander who is aching for you to make an error. When
you discover you have gone wrong, panic takes over. There are
many dead ends on Luneberger Heide, and the experience of
having all the other tanks turn round in a forest of narrow lanes
just wide enough to take a single tank is the stuff of nightmares.
The fault may have resulted from a muddy blotch on the map as
one squinted through blinding rain or choking dust, but try
explaining that later to an angry troop sergeant.

As a rule I found the troopers and most of the corporals good
solid characters and easy to get along with. However, as soon as

ᴣ and therefore competitive, the sparks

first two troop sergeants as bitterly as

the sentiment.

ged a private war with my own sergeant,

on his co-sergeants, Scabby Harris and Big

of the other troops. For reasons I have never

ad feelings seldom extended to the other squad-

en the smallest matter concerning efficiency in the

field st to the mill of the sergeants. They always maintained outward politeness in terms of addressing me as 'Sir',
saluting and obeying outright orders, just as I never shouted at
them and always called them 'Sergeant'. But underneath this
necessary veneer we loathed each other and scored points whenever possible. Sadly, I lost at nearly every turn, for I was a novice
and a slow learner.

There were many incidents on many exercises, but the one that
hurt the most was on the Night of the Shovels. Every year a squadron CIV (Central Inspection of Vehicles) took place, when every
tool was checked and those that were lost were charged against
the wages of the man responsible. Naturally a good deal of thiev-
ing took place prior to each CIV, mostly between different troops,
but sometimes, in desperation, within a troop.

The week before the 1964 CIV was spent on exercise and my
troop was on guard duty within the squadron leaguer position the
night before return to camp. My tank crew had identified themselves with me as unfairly treated underdogs, endlessly persecuted
over the last two years by Barchi, Scabby and Big John.

They were a colourful bunch and I loved them as brothers, even
lapsing within the steel confines of the turret into their Glaswegian
effing and blinding against the injustices we jointly suffered.
Certainly there was no stiffness between officer and men. The
radio operator, tall and ungainly, was called 'Scratch' Sherville
owing to an intermittent crutch-itch. 'Zeebo' Stevens, the gunner,
had lank spiky hair and was always dirty, while Ian Durrand, the
driver, was canny and by far the best mechanic in the squadron.

Our tank's tool supplies had dwindled during the nights of exercise, not because we had carelessly lost them but because of silent raiding parties while we slept. 'The worst items,' grumbled Stevens, as we scraped the evening's bully beef and peas from our mess tins, 'is the shovels and picks. We've none left.'

'That's no' yer fockin' problem, Zeebo,' said Durrand. 'The shovels are on *my* fockin' signature.'

Scratch poked the log fire with his fork. 'The bastards did it on guard duty, the theevin' fockers . . . they must a' done.' He looked up and added, 'What's sauce for the fockin' goose, d'ye ken?'

At this the others glanced up too. They were all looking at me. I nodded. There was no alternative.

The next dawn, when Durrand woke me up with a cup of tea, he muttered, 'We're OK, Mister Feens, I put the fockers under the turret floor.'

As I finished the morning check on the gun's alternator, meta-dyne and Mullins ejection gear with Zeebo, he squinted up at me from his gunner's seat. 'Don't you fret nay mair aboot the shovels. I fetched us two fra' Scabby's tank.' His white teeth glistened in the turret gloom.

This meant we now had four shovels hidden in the ammunition bins. I began to sweat.

Scratch Sherville's long legs dropped through the other turret hatch. He said nothing, but squashed out a fag end on the C42 radio and then laid a single finger against his long nose and winked with a look of evil satisfaction.

All around the leaguer, invisible in their mantles of cut foliage, the Morris generators and main engines of the squadron tanks coughed into roaring life. Blue smoke belched in the crisp air of late autumn. I stuck my head out of the turret to check the readiness of the other two tanks and saw, with a sick feeling of imminent doom, a cluster of green denim and white NCO stripes. A deputation of sergeants had brought the squadron leader, Major 'Horsey' Anderson, to see me. That had to mean bad news.

...derson, his neat moustache a-bristle
...ing the knees of his boiler suit like the
...il. 'I am told there is reason to suspect
...their role as squadron guard . . . They have
...irst, Second and Third troop.'
...n alarm, I could only stare, mumbling, at the
...der clasps on the sides of my tank.
...Mister Feenes, not there.' The gravelly tones of
Scabɒ, ...s. 'They will be inside your tanks.'

Barchi Leader, loving every moment of it, glared at me in right-eous indignation. I had besmirched the honour of his troop. Big John Audis, whose nose was a scaled-down model of Mount Ararat, lowered his bulk beside Scratch Sherville.

'Out, Sherville,' he said, as though addressing a dog.

The Conqueror's gun barrel traversed slowly left and right as the sergeant gained access to one after another floor bin. As he did so, shovels appeared one by one, handed up to the smug Scabby Harris and down to the squadron leader. Burned into the handle of each shovel was the tank number of the previous owner. My crew had not had time to rebrand them with our own number.

I was severely admonished and given extra orderly officer's duties, but the shame for the four of us was much worse. The taunting went on for months – indeed was still remembered with much laughter over leaguer fires five years later. We were dubbed Ali Feens and the Fourth Troop Thieves.

Each winter, regimental boxing championships were held in the garrison gym to a capacity audience. It was after all a rare chance to watch troopers smashing officers to the floor. I had grown since Eton days to six feet two inches and weighed twelve stone, so I entered the Heavyweight class and fought through three bouts to championship finals. To my genuine horror I was woken one morning by the Grubscrew, who usually knew everything before anyone else did. 'You're up against "The Beast",' he said. 'Trooper Reid 66.' (Since there were many Reids in the Greys, the last two figures of their Army number were always appended for differentiation.)

The Beast was not a true Grey. He was a REME mechanic attached to the regiment. Nor, in my mind, was he a true human. He weighed over fifteen stone and stood taller than me. Worse, he was notorious as the most dreaded fighter in Fallingbostel.

I contemplated 'flu, but there was none about. Or falling off my tank turret – but that seemed too obvious. Somehow the time ticked by until the awful moment when I entered the ring to the deafening howl of the assembled Greys, their appetites for violence whetted by the previous bouts of lesser weights. I hardly dared take a look at the grinning bulk of The Beast, fearing I would disgrace myself then and there.

The first round was awful. Twice a glove like a moon rock contacted my head and my vision exploded in starbursts. Once a sledgehammer swing caught my chest and I hit the floor determined I was done for. Then, realising the roughhouse tactics could only favour The Beast, I cast my mind back to my long years of boxing training at Eton and the feint-and-cut tactics of my school instructor, Reg Hoblyn. This paid off and The Beast began to bleed. His bulk made him tire in the third round, his guard dropped and I was able to damage his face. I won by a narrow margin.

I grew to love the Greys as much as I had loathed public school, but for all the wrong reasons. In lieu of a war, the Army provides excitement, and therefore hopes to hold on to its more venturesome members through the medium of adventure training. A certain budget is made available for journeys away from the garrison at times when no tank exercises are anticipated.

Since many of my fellow officers were avid polo players or hunting fanatics, there were few contenders for adventure training and sporting activities. I joined the cross-country running team and when Sergeant Ernie Newport, our leader, slipped on ice down Minden Hill and suffered a nasty compound fracture, I took over the team. The training often involved dragging a scented sock across country and over hedges instead of a fox for the regimental draghunt to follow.

Since many of Europe's great rivers flowed within easy reach of Fallingbostel, I asked our colonel if I could form a canoe club. He agreed and forty-two Jocks each paid 165 Deutschmarks at a rate of 10 Deutschmarks per week in order to purchase one quarter of a two-seater canoe. I ordered twelve fibreglass Gmach canoes from England. They weighed sixty pounds each and were soldier-proof, since they could be endlessly repaired *in situ*.

Each week the entire regiment was paid cash wages in the main canteen. By closing all exits except one, beside which I sat with a millboard and cashbox, I extracted the money over a period of six months. Then the Canoe Club thrived.

For three months each summer, I took two separate groups of Jocks down different rivers. An Army lorry with a driver and a cook drove ahead each day to an agreed spot to set up a night camp. Over the years, we descended the Elbe, the Oste, the Weser, the Rhine, the Danube and the Rhone. By the time each summer was over, the best four canoeists sported calloused layers on their hands and backsides and invariably won the BAOR Canoe Cup for the main touring canoe section.

I soon discovered that some Jocks had joined merely for the women and wine to be found in riverside towns. Since canoeing 100 miles a day is tiring, I instituted a rule that each canoeist had to sign out after the evening meal and be back again by 10 p.m. or forego a week of camp leave. This was very unpopular and the stronger characters determined to buck my system. A war of wills followed and several Jocks on return to Fallingbostel asked for their 165 Deutschmarks back. I sold their shares to other applicants and gradually weeded out the troublemakers, but not before the aggrieved ex-canoeists had passed the word around the regiment that the club was in reality 'Mister Feens's Concentration Camp'.

In the village of Oste where we camped, one trooper dropped a thunderflash into the cistern of the newly opened village toilet and blew it to bits. I gave the local mayor eight boxes of Army tinned food to soothe his feelings, but the next night my canoeists drank too much at the annual Oste *Schutzenfest* and went on the rampage with broken-off chair legs. They emptied an entire marquee of 300 villagers and a brass oompah band clad in *lederhosen* and leather bibs.

My corporal came back in a taxi to warn me and together we cajoled eight drunken Jocks, complete with chair legs, out of the marquee and into the taxi. That cost six more food boxes and, subsequently, a hefty cheque from the regiment for the damages. Our colonel took the matter at face value and I escaped reprimand. But later that summer he had another reason to be unhappy with me.

On a windy day off the Danish town of Snaptun, I took twenty canoeists to the lee shore of an island to learn capsize drills. Some of the men started to shiver in the cold offshore wind. Soon the sea between the island and mainland was rough with spray and tossed spume. Two canoes went missing for an hour and a well-meaning Dane at Snaptun, misunderstanding some of the Jocks, telephoned the Danish Emergency Service. A well-practised, slick and very expensive operation followed, involving two motor launches, a helicopter and the Press.

Somehow the reporters learned that a canoe was still missing. This was after a launch had picked up one canoe, despite the protests of its perfectly safe occupants, and in lifting it aboard had smashed the fibreglass shell in two. It made for dramatic photographs and erroneous stories of wreckage. The international Press, including the *Scotsman*, picked up the story, alluding to a missing canoe. Anxious parents phoned the regiment, which of course knew nothing. The absent canoe was in fact mine, for I had returned to the island to search for the canoe that had been picked up by the launch. The colonel was not amused. But a month later there was even more mayhem.

After the Denmark camp, I had obtained four weeks' training rights for forty canoeists and twenty trekkers in Schleswig-Holstein. The agreed training zone was along the Schleie River above Eckernfjörde but, for a major night exercise of sixty men, it was a useless area. We had four Army lorries and two jeeps, so we drove south to the Kiel Canal, strictly forbidden for Army training but, since it offered an ideal series of easily controllable checkpoints, by far the best place for an exciting exercise for the Jocks. Besides, the authorities were unlikely to find out about our trespass since the exercise was to begin and end the same night.

The men were dropped off in two groups fifteen miles apart, half with canoes on the Kiel Canal and half on foot in a forest. Their goal was a ruined house with a crate of Carlsberg upstairs and a web of trip flares below. To get there, each group of two trekkers had to locate their designated canoeist partners and cross the canal by midnight. Although there were only eight 'enemy', including myself, the canal made it easier to locate the Jocks. Identification meant disqualification.

Being crafty, some of the canoeists waited for a merchant ship or tanker to pass by them. Then, braving the powerful wash and backwash between hull and canal banks, they tucked in close behind the stern of their chosen host vessel, which sucked them along, making for less work and good camouflage from the watchers on the bank.

I had forbidden my 'enemy' Jocks to fire Very flares close to any ship but, keen to identify canoeists glimpsed in the wash of a giant tanker, one over-zealous corporal landed a red phosphorus flare on the ship's rear deck. He could not have chosen a worse target, for it later transpired to have been a Soviet tanker with a liquid chemical cargo so volatile that the crewmen wore rubber soles so as not to risk causing a single spark.

Our flare hissed and burned away fiercely on the boat deck and in a short while the klaxon and red light system, which is installed along the Kiel Canal banks right across Europe, began to honk and flash as if World War Three was about to erupt. Loudspeakers crackled and a disembodied male voice spoke to us with British Rail-like lack of intelligibility. I understood only two words with crystal clarity: '*Englander Soldaten*'. A British-style beret or cap comforter must have been spotted on a canoeist.

I contacted the lorry drivers and the other enemy posts and ordered the immediate end of the exercise. Somehow, within two hours, all but four of the men were assembled by the ruins. All grey berets were removed and mud smeared on the number plates. Those soldiers who were temporarily with us from other regiments were told to keep their black berets on and sit prominently beside the drivers.

We sped on our way north back to our own training area, but the driver of my open jeep (or *champ* as they were known) grew sleepy so I told him we would change places. Officers were forbidden to drive MOD vehicles, but I felt sure I was doing the right thing to avoid a possible crash. A short while later I woke from a drowsy trance to find myself driving straight towards a German pine tree. I jerked the steering wheel around but it was too late. I sheared the off-front wheel clean from its axle, flung both my passengers into the dark undergrowth and generally redesigned the shape of the jeep. I seemed to be unhurt but for a bruised ribcage and forehead. The Jocks were bloody but healthily voluble.

Back in Fallingbostel, I was ordered to report to the divisional commander, General Miles Fitzalan-Howard, shortly to become the Duke of Norfolk. For my misdemeanour, the crash, I was fined £25 and given a stern warning. Luckily there seemed to be no MOD central filing system that cross-checked the growing number of incidents I had accrued and, more fortunately, the Russian tanker mishap had not been blamed on the Greys.

Telegrams had flown to all regimental commanders. My own had quite rightly protested innocence. It appeared that because of the flare, all canal traffic across Europe had stopped for five hours, an expensive delay. Six months later, some busybody forester found a Greys' beret by the canal and handed it to the *polizei*, who gave it to the local Army liaison officer. Within twenty-fours my CO had summoned me and this time I saw a different general, received a heavier fine and a dozen extra orderly officer duties.

Did I realise the possible consequences had the Soviet tanker exploded? I assured the general that I did, but I had acted in innocence and with only the interests of training in mind. I persuaded myself that the matter would be forgotten and that I had as yet done nothing that might slow down my progress towards command of the regiment.

One odd side effect of the canoeing journeys was that I ended up, after a couple of years, as the possessor of some two thousand of Her Majesty's Forces contraceptives, rubber-male-for the use of. Each journey, by Army orders, I drew from the quartermaster an exact number of contraceptives (the number of canoeists multiplied by the number of days' travel). This was to protect the locals from an outbreak of wee Jocks and to protect the Jocks from collecting hostile pox.

After 100 miles of paddling and with only four hours' local leave per evening, canoeists had little chance to utilise the contraceptives, so they rarely signed them out. The quartermaster's accounts were happier without quantities of returned prophylactics, so they mounted up month by month in my bedroom.

Macrae and others learned of my collection and from time to time 'borrowed' a dozen or so. These would be filled with water and left in more senior officers' rooms as cunningly placed booby traps. The most annoying application of these limp water balloons was prior to squadron tank parade. Once a week every officer would don his smart khaki service dress and drive from the Officers' Mess to the tank park. Then he would march to his position in front of his men prior to squadron inspection.

On one such morning, leaving breakfast at the last moment as usual, I leapt into my old Citroën and started up. Without warning a grey jellyfish-shaped UFO slid from its hidden perch on the driver's sun flap and landed on my lap, where it burst. There was a great deal of suppressed mirth among my troop as I halted in front of them and saluted, the area all about my crotch sodden wet from Macrae's flying jellyfish.

When I left the Scots Greys, I took the johnnies home in a suitcase and left them for years in my mother's attic. One day a plumber found them strewn all over the place by mice, who had used them for several generations of nest linings.

For three months every winter, I trained the regimental cross-country (or *langlauf*) ski team, six men including two reserves, in the mountainous country around Wertach village in Bavaria. We lived in a *gasthaus* or cooked for ourselves in a farmer's cottage.

As with the canoeing, there were no competing claims for the post of *langlauf* officer, because those who did want to ski made up the downhill team. During the early 1960s, the Royal Scots Greys ski team included Prince Nicolas von Preussen, the Baron Franckenstein and Charles de Westenholz, but this did not stop some of the onlookers at the annual Oberjoch Championships from shouting, 'Go it, Jock', as our heroes flashed by.

Cross-country skiing was hard work and held none of the glory of downhill skiing. During our first year in Bavaria, no one in the Greys could *langlauf* except a stocky English corporal named Jones. He was a sadistic fellow. Six days a week for three months he took half a dozen of us around cunningly sited ski circuits through forests, down giddy gulleys and up sharp inclines. And always against the clock. The last man to complete each circuit would do twenty press-ups in the snow.

The start of each day saw us parade in blue cotton jackets, knickerbockers, Noddy hats and skis at the shoulder. Then we marched through Wertach village with one of our number playing the bagpipes and 'Jonesey' railing at us from the rear. The piper, then Second Lieutenant Jameson, became CO of the regiment in 1986. But in those days he sweated and froze alternately like the rest of us at the whim of the gimlet-eyed Jones. We hated him, but we did become above-average *langlaufers*.

One August, I spent my three-week leave on an unusual project in Norway. An old school friend, Simon Gault, was keen to try a journey in the rugged Jotunheim. Our plan was to follow an ancient cattle trail or *drift* over Europe's largest glacier, the Jostedalsbre, in Central Jotunheim, then to canoe down the glacial wastewaters to the east. Three Scots Greys officers agreed to accompany us, and so did a former girlfriend named Vanda Allfrey.

To start the journey we agreed to save valuable days of leave by cheating. We would hitch a lift on a charter plane and parachute on to the 8,000-foot-high glacial plateau with all our gear. Sergeant Don Hughes, a founder member of the SAS freefall parachute team and a pioneer of the sport in Britain, agreed to 'throw us out at the right moment' so we would stand a good chance of avoiding the 6,000-foot cliffs that rim the plateau.

The drop went as planned: although no one was injured, the experience was decidedly hairy. But other aspects of the journey failed. We did not follow the complete course of the cattle trail because the combination of heavy packs, altitude and thick snow proved too much for some. Only Simon accompanied me on the thirty-mile hike down the Faberg Glacier and on to the fount of the eastern river system. Finally the rivers were too rough for our canoes, which were all smashed to bits.

I learned on that little journey to lead by physical example rather than rhetoric and also to choose, for challenging endeavours, a selection of leaders and followers, not a gaggle of the former. A by-product of the trip was a good deal of coverage in the Norwegian press, all of it favourable to the British Army. I was awarded the brigade Tie of Merit, a sure sign of forgiveness for my previous sins.

However, they would never be forgotten. My Whitehall file was marked in indelible red for caution. I might wriggle my way up to major over the years, but it was clear I would go no further. So I made up my mind to call it a day as soon as my contracted service was up.

I was not to know it then, but all the months of dedicated ski training for the Greys were to serve me well for the future, just as the years of preparation in battle tanks in Germany subsequently proved about as useful as learning Latin.

Dr Mike Stroud
World authority on human endurance

When I met Ran for the first time in 1986, it was with considerable trepidation. Only a few days before, I had been trying to sort out my return to work as a hospital doctor after more than a year away, overwintering in Antarctica with the Footsteps of Scott expedition. Then came a call from Ran's wife Ginny.

Ran was in the high Arctic, waiting for the first, post-winter sunlight to attempt the first unsupported sledge journey to the North Pole – 600 miles across Arctic pack ice without the help of other men, animals or machines. His partner for the journey had to return home at short notice, for personal reasons. Ran needed a replacement. Could I drop everything and go?

Ran's reputation was formidable. He had undertaken numerous major expeditions and especially the Transglobe – an accomplishment which I held in awe. He came from a military background and so he expected loyalty and adherence to orders. How would I, an easy-going individual with a very civilian temperament, cope with it?

It turned out that his reputation, at least to my mind, was far from the truth. He welcomed me with open arms and open thinking, never showing his disappointment at my small physique, which was not ideal for manhauling incredibly heavy sledges to the North Pole.

Once out in the brutally cold, semi-darkness of early Arctic spring, we found that we could work together – facing hardship with equanimity and setbacks with humour. We chatted, laughed and got to know each other in our tiny, ice-encrusted tent.

We failed on that first endeavour together, but it was the most successful unsupported attempt at the North Pole yet, and it would not be long before we came back to try again.

Roger Chapman, Bob Powell, Ran, Geoff Holder and Patrick Brook after their successful descent of the Briksdalsbre Glacier in Norway, 1970.

already over the western end of the ice cap,' he told us, 'and heading this way fast.'

He checked our parachutes and gear minutely, fixed smoke cannisters to Roger Chapman's ankles and then taught us one by one how to jump out of the Cessna's side door on to one of the floats. Once there, we had to throw ourselves sideways and outwards, in order to fight the fierce inward drag of the slipstream. Then Don marshalled the first group of four into the fuselage, glancing as he did so at the approaching screen of cloud that already filled the sky to our west.

As the Cessna's engine roared, I licked my lips. My stomach felt furry-lined as squadrons of butterflies free-fell within it. I would be first to jump and did not relish the idea. However, the other three men looked unconcerned as the alloy floats surged out over the lake, so I put on a mask of nonchalance. I found myself staring at Patrick's fingers, drumming on his knee, but he noticed my glance and was still. Stiff upper lips but thudding pulses were the order of the day.

The *Sunday Times* described the occasion as 'The World's Toughest Jump', but then they had paid £1,000 for coverage rights and wanted their money's worth. Their photographer, an ITN cine-cameraman and other media people were already hovering high above the ice cap in press helicopters.

I had seen no area suitable for a drop zone, only cliffs and serrated crevasse fields. The ice-cap surface was 6,000 feet high and we would drop from 10,500 feet, a safe height that would enable us to get well clear of the Cessna, orientate ourselves and steer towards the drop zone.

We levelled out 2,000 feet above the ice and the pilot set a circular course over the target area. Don taped a pair of clear-glass goggles into place and thrust his face into the doorway. One hand jerked out and deftly released a furled streamer that jinked away, its orange fabric tail unrolling as it fell. Its flight path acted as an anemometer, telling Don the speed and direction of the various wind currents between us and the ice.

Although the drop would take place from this noted position along the oval of the Cessna's course, we must first climb another 2,000 feet. From that height we would jump and count each second out loud, up to fourteen, as we fell. Then, at the height where Don had ejected the streamer, we must pull our ripcords. From there to the ice cap we would behave like the streamer, unless the wind currents had changed.

Awkwardly, careful not to brush our packs against each other, we levered ourselves into kneeling positions facing the door. This was the moment of truth from which there could be no honourable withdrawal. My greatest fear was not so much the act of jumping as the thought that one glimpse of the black peaks below, or the cold space beyond the aircraft door, would activate the vertigo I invariably experienced.

A rough hand shook my shoulder. Don was shouting at me, his words whipped away by the wind and engine roar. He prodded his finger meaningfully at the exit as though to say, 'Get the hell out.'

I forced one arm through the slipstream and grasped the wing strut. Then I lunged my legs outwards, tightly clenched together, aiming for the float. As my boots scrabbled for a foothold, my hands lost their grip on the strut and I was sucked bodily into space. Out of control, I passed close by the fuselage and struck the side of the float with the back of my hand.

'One thousand and one. One thousand and two . . .' I heard my voice inside my helmet churning out the seconds and I opened my eyes. Then came fear as I recognised the early signs of body-spin. I stretched my arms and legs out and back and thrust my stomach forward . . . but the spin became more, not less pronounced. 'One thousand and five, one thousand and six . . .' I craned my neck to the side and spotted the cause of my instability: my left leg was running, kicking out like a trapped rabbit. Only through an effort of will did I control and force it to remain rigid. 'One thousand and nine.' Five long seconds still to go.

For a moment I sensed neither movement nor urgency. I was floating in a void, a most pleasant sensation I would have liked to prolong. I was now flying 120 miles an hour, my terminal velocity, and every limb must remain perfectly positioned in a star-shape for my body to remain stable. Without warning, I began to keel forward into a nosedive. 'One thousand and twelve . . .' Then sudden panic.

Both my arms snapped inwards to locate my ripcord, but my camera had come loose inside my anorak and lodged itself against the ripcord bar. Now my body position was bunched and beginning to tumble.

Grabbling in the folds of my anorak, I found the red handle and ripped it outwards. Then I snapped both arms back to the star position to arrest a rapidly materialising somersault. A second or two later, with a whipcrack sound and a breathtaking jerk, my orange canopy deployed fully, a beautiful sight from my point of view.

Down between my legs, the icescape passed by at twenty knots. Reaching up I tugged on a steering toggle. I tacked across the wind and swung towards a high peak, the Lodalskapa, which I knew to be a boundary marker to our drop zone.

Two fissured crevasse fields passed beneath my boots. Rock and ice rushing up now, everything close including crevasses. I braced my legs, knees bent for the impact . . . but when it came, I hardly knew it as my landing was cushioned by the softness of a snow-bridge spanning an old crevasse.

Surface winds caught at my parachute and dragged me over the ice. I hauled in on a single cord until the wind spilled out of the canopy. Then the adrenalin dispersed and I suddenly felt cold.

Patrick and Peter picked themselves up from different corners of the drop zone. Patrick planted flare sticks – markers for Don's next drop. Clouds already obscured the mountain ranges to the west and south.

Don and the Cessna pilot worked fast, dropping the rest of the team without preliminary streamers to save time. To aid the photographers in the press helicopters, Roger ignited the smoke flares attached to his ankles and Geoff, jumping next, used a camera installed in his helmet to film Roger as they dropped. Geoff landed seventy-five yards from the edge and was dragged by the ever-strengthening surface winds to within eight yards of a sheer precipice. He cracked two ribs and split open the bridge of his nose on the steel aiming-sight of his helmet camera.

We spread around the perimeter of the drop zone and when Don began to drop the equipment loads soon after dusk, we rushed hither and thither, grabbing at the billowing silk canopies as they careered towards the cliffs. Nothing was lost and none of the survey gear broken. Separating into groups of two, we bedded down on the parachutes with blocks of snow for windbreaks around our cotton tents.

At dawn we loaded our two sledges with 200 pounds apiece of survey gear, inflatable rubber boats and 1,800 feet of rope coils. Personal kit and tents filled our rucksacks and our skiing expert Henrik Forss gave us each a pair of *langlauf* skis and sticks.

To the south-east of the drop zone and some four miles distant, the ice cap poured down, via two steep canyon glaciers, to the Faberg Valley below. Our task was to survey the northernmost of these glaciers, the Fabergstolsbre, and we needed to pitch our camp at its crest by nightfall. At first the metal sledge-runners ripped hissing over firm crust. After four hours Roger stopped, frowning. 'By my reckoning we should have reached the top of the Faberg Glacier half an hour ago.'

Not everyone agreed and a heated discussion ensued. All ice sloped downwards to our front and, if we took the wrong route, we would sooner or later have to climb back up with full loads. A compromise route was selected, down which we slid at an ever-increasing pace. Henrik stopped and so, with difficulty, did the two skiers harnessed to the sledges.

We fixed rear-retaining ropes as brakes to each sledge and continued more warily towards a cluster of rocks that marked the upper crest of a glacier. Reaching this feature, we peered downwards and, sure enough, found it to be the hinge point of the northern side of a glacier. But the memory of the Faberg Glacier that Simon Gault and I had briefly glimpsed in 1967 was different from the ice now ahead of me.

While the others rested, I went north-east with Patrick, a strong skier, and forty minutes later we breasted a rise above another, very similar glacier. I scanned the far, northern cliffs of this new ice-tongue and knew for sure that *this* was the Fabergstolbre. The others were now at the top of the Nigardsbre, a glacier that earlier in the century had surged down its captor-valley crushing houses and homesteads in its path. To cross in a straight line from where we were to the far, northern side of the Fabergstolsbre would entail crossing a wide crevasse field. Yet our camp must be on the northern side of the glacier's crest for survey purposes.

When the others reached us with the sledges, we debated for or against a long uphill detour around the crevasses. Exhausted by the heavy work, nobody could face the thought of the safer but more tiring way, so we set out to cross the zone of fissures. Our route zigzagged around open holes and cracks by way of 'gang-planks', where the snow from last winter's blizzards still bridged the gaps. The problem was knowing which of these bridges were several feet thick and which were on the point of collapse.

Patrick went ahead to lay a trail. Geoff, in harness, fell through a snow-bridge and his sledge very nearly followed him. Two of us hauled him up by his jacket, fully aware that he could have been crushed had the sledge broken through. We became adept at avoiding the weaker snow-bridges and took long detours in order to find gangways of snow not yet rotted by summer rain and sunshine.

By late afternoon, only a steep slope of blue ice separated us from a rock cluster that marked the northern side and summit of the Fabergstolsbre, where we hoped to camp. The sledges would not budge up so steep an incline nor could we climb it on skis, so we detoured around and above, unladen, and then hauled the gear up with ropes.

By six, the four two-pound tents were staked into a snow patch among the rocks. I jammed the pole of our Union Jack between two rocks above the camp. From this point, over the next few days, groups of two or three must establish commanding points on the surrounding heights and equip them with survey gear. The work must be finished by 21 August, since there were only two available guides who knew our desired descent route and they could work with us only on specific days.

Although two of our control points were on the ice cap within three hours' march of our camp, the third was on a separate mountain range four miles east of the Fabergstolsbre and separated from it by the main Faberg Valley, in which Johnny Muir and our road party were camped. Geoff and one other surveyor decided to descend to the valley right away and I left with them to help carry the gear.

We passed the night in Johnny's campsite and left at dawn for the eight-hour climb up the far side of the valley. I parted with Geoff at an existing Norwegian Trig Point, marked by a stone cairn. He was in pain with two splintered ribs, but he knew, as I did, that the map could not be made without him.

I returned again to Johnny's camp 3,000 feet below, collected radio batteries and rations and trudged back up the Fabergstolsbre by way of its northern rock flank. Halfway up I switched on my radio and listened in to a lively exchange between Roger and Geoff – the supervisor of the survey programme – as to the exact location of their respective positions. Glancing up, I was not surprised. Sheer black cliffs reared to the north and south, their upper walls invisible in mist.

From somewhere up on my side of the glacier, Roger spoke frustratedly. He had picked up the distant flares of Geoff's location and marked the azimuth on his chart, but the position of Henrik, Patrick and one other – directly across the glacier – had eluded him.

'You must be blind,' radioed Patrick. 'We have erected fluorescent panels on a back bearing of ten degrees from your location.'

I moved on, weary from the heavy pack, as thunder rumbled continuously along the valleys. Storm clouds burst over the ice fields with a spectacular show of lightning and, three hours later, the weather reached the cliffs up which I inched towards our camp. The whole glacial valley was now awash. Ankle-high water rushed between the rocks and boulders and the entire valley rumbled to the roar of the deluge.

Two hours after dusk, slightly disorientated, I reached the uppermost rocks. The sleet lashed at my face in the dark and I came quite by chance on the Union Jack lying in a puddle. I replaced it as a marker and slithered down to the camp. It was a sorry sight. The original snow patch was now an incline of grey mush. The tents had blown down and, worst of all, sleeping bags and clothes were strewn sodden about the ice.

This was alarming. Two teams were still out in high-exposure risk conditions without their safety gear. Without moonlight, I could scarcely see five yards. There was little sense in mounting a solo-search, so I re-erected two of the tents, wrung out four sleeping bags and anoraks as best I could and hung my torch from a tent pole. I fired three flares into the storm. I listened but heard nothing except my own teeth chattering and the enormous sound of rushing water. I crawled into a wet sleeping bag inside a tent and switched on my radio. I called but there was only silence.

What had happened to them I learned later from their diaries. The northern survey group, Peter and Roger, dismantled their theodolite as the mist reached them. It dawned on them that they had made a stupid mistake. The golden rule in such a place, given bad conditions, is to stay put, erect a shelter, and crawl into it. Since the weather had been excellent when they left camp and the weight of their gear had been crippling, they had dispensed with the tent and sleeping bags.

Now they must try to reach safety and warmth, but there was one large snag. Between them and the camp, along the direct route they had used on the outward journey, lay a 600-foot gorge. There was, however, an eight-kilometre ice-traverse flanking this gorge; their only chance of survival.

The glacier surface was melting at an unbelievable rate. On level ice they walked through slush up to their calves but, on any slope, black streams rushed by at torrential speed. One cataract moved so fast that to have slipped and fallen into it would have taken them straight over the cliff edge.

Sometimes they fell over in slush pools and disappeared up to their waists. After two and a half hours, according to Roger's calculations, they should have reached camp. They had not. Both began to wonder if they had made an error. If so, they were in deep trouble. At 8.30 p.m. they hit rock. They left their compass bearing and cautiously groped across boulders, not knowing where the cliffs dropped away. There was no sign of the camp . . . Roger wondered whether it had been washed away.

Then they saw the dim light of my tent. Numb with cold they awkwardly stripped off each other's clothes, and crawled into a single bag to benefit from each other's meagre warmth. I produced a flask of brandy.

They knew nothing of the other group. 'Henrik can't possibly have tried to lead them across the crevasse field: not in this blizzard,' said Peter. 'It would be suicidal . . .'

With Henrik were Patrick Booth and Bob Powell, a tough Territorial parachute officer. At 6 p.m. the weather on their part of the ice cap had deteriorated with no warning. They agreed to return to camp with haste. Thirty minutes later they were in sight of the glacier, but by then the conditions were appalling. Mist covered the ice cap, so they tried descending the cliff to the glacier itself. But they could not traverse the deep *bergschrund* that dropped away between rock and ice.

They had fallen into the same trap as Roger. The morning had seemed so bright and clear, they had left without protective gear or rations. Now, in the blizzard, they faced the prospect of either huddling together under groundsheets or blindly traversing the Fabergstolsbre crevasse field.

Bob favoured locating some shelter but Patrick argued that, with no tent and a freezing wind, they must attempt the crossing. Henrik, undecided, was swayed by their lack of gear and food, and agreed with Patrick. For four hours they crept through the crevasse field in the white-out. Only a few safe crevasse bridges remained.

Bob began to get stomach cramps, possibly through having drunk mineral-free glacier ice-water. But he could not stop, being roped behind the others. The cold was biting and they could not risk a halt.

Bob could see only the line of his rope leading forward into the dark and he marvelled at how Henrik kept to his compass course, since they spent most of the time in crazy detours around crevasses. He lost all sense of direction.

Towards midnight they came to a steep gradient. Could this be the final slope? They shouted . . . no answer. About 100 yards up the slope they screamed again and heard my faint answering cry followed by the gleam of my torch. As they turned, elated, Henrik plunged through a snow-bridge to his armpits. The last 100 yards took fifteen minutes to traverse.

We all drank whisky in the tent. Bob shivered uncontrollably for the five hours until dawn; nominating that night as the most miserable of his life.

Two days later the storm cleared and the survey work began in earnest. In four days many hundreds of theodolite readings were recorded. The work was cold and boring, but allowed no lapses in concentration since even the slightest slip could render the resulting figures unacceptable and the whole project a failure.

Geoff finally announced that the survey was complete. Peter Booth and one other left us to commence geological work further down the valley. They took the survey paperwork and as much gear as they could manage. All being well, our Norwegian guides would lead us to the Briksdalsbre, down which we would lower our gear, since it was very different from the Fabergstolsbre — steep, narrow and straight. From its snout we would place all the gear straight into our inflatable boats and paddle down to the roadhead. No porters. No sweat.

The only niggle in my mind was our failure to reconnoitre the Briksdalsbre or its glacial river due to having jumped a day early. Still, we had 1,800 feet of rope, enough to see us over even the worst icefalls. I told the others that they should leave with Peter if they did not like the idea of the descent, but no one volunteered to drop out.

In promising me the very best Jostedalsbre guides, the Norwegian Tourist Board had described David Mindresunde and Jan Mickelbust as 'superb'. They knew the ice cap better than anyone. At the time of our rendezvous, the guides were nowhere to be seen and when they did turn up, four hours late, their clothes were wet through and they shivered as they unstrapped their skis. Neither spoke English, but Henrik translated for us.

Geoff woke me at 4 a.m. A thick mist lay over the ice cap, tamped down by rain. Henrik talked to the guides as they packed their gear, then he came over to me, frowning. His words shocked me. He said that they had spent a poor night and were not prepared to take us, in dangerously thick mists, on the forty-kilo-metre ice-cap journey to the top of the Briksdalsbre. On skis with light packs they could do the trip in eight hours. Pulling heavy sledges, they reckoned we would take two days, if indeed we could get that far, overloaded as they deemed us to be.

Henrik said, 'Mindresunde has skied the entire Jostedalsbre, but never in such weather. The only safe route is to zigzag along the upper spine of the ice cap and that can only be done in condi-tions of reasonable visibility. Mickelbust says the Briksdalsbre has never been descended and, in these conditions, will be riven by tons of melting, falling ice. He says we must abandon the gear and descend by the Faberg route.'

I tried to cajole the guides. I could see they were loath to let us down, but their inborne sense of caution, their respect for the nature of these ice fields, held them back from what they consid-ered to be sheer folly. They knew that none of us except Henrik had previous climbing experience.

At length we reached a compromise. They would ski along the ridge for thirty kilometres, at which point they would leave one of our ice axes pointing in the direction of the Briksdalsbre. They would then veer north to descend a little-known track to the Kvamme Valley.

Following the guides' tracks we toiled at the sledge traces for five hours. Up and down had no real meaning in such white-out conditions; the heavy sledges were dead weights and slid neither forwards nor backwards if left untended.

At midday the mist lifted and the plateau stretched mile after mile into the western glare. Towards evening, mist and falling sleet slowed us up again. The guides' tracks snaked on, becoming increasingly hard to detect, for a wind had sprung up and blew the sleet over the spoor. After eleven hours of non-stop haulage, we came to the ice-axe marker.

Henrik grasped my arm: 'From here on it will be downhill, so the five of you will easily manage the loads. I will give you my medical gear for I will follow the guides' spoor down to Kvamme. I will make sure Johnny makes camp at the base of the Briksdal and keeps the radio open. Take great care.'

Later he gave his reasons for ducking out of the descent as appalling conditions and maximum avalanche danger, poor equipment (we were using Dexion shop-shelving instead of ice ladders) and the considered opinion of the guides that our descent plans were suicidal.

Roger asked him to stay as far as the top of the glacier, but he was determined. We watched him ski off into the mist.

The wind blew sleet horizontally and I regretted the loss of my goggles the previous day. It was too cold now to stop, with an icy blast coming up from the massed crevasse fields between us and the cliffs to our right flank. Explosions of falling ice sounded close by, and I knew the sloping shoulder that we traversed fell away to plummeting cliffs somewhere in our immediate vicinity.

As it grew dark, we entered our first crevasse field and gingerly threaded a maze-like route through wicked-looking fissures. We knew we should be roped up, but were too tired and cold. Each new chasm forced us off our chosen bearing. We advanced between the cracks in the ice along a narrow but solid isthmus. From every side now came the booming echoes of avalanches. With numb fingers we erected two tents and pegged their guy-ropes to ski sticks. Next morning the mist cleared at dawn and we saw the first icefall of the Briksdals Glacier directly below us.

The descent was sudden and, in minutes, one of our laden, boat-shaped pulk sledges slid out of control and careered into a crevasse. Alarmed, we donned helmets and roped to each other. About 100 yards further down the yawning incline, our second sledge turned turtle, dragging Roger and Patrick behind it. Using a sawtooth sheath-knife, Roger slashed through the harnesses and saved their lives. The pulk disappeared down a crevasse. All our skis were lost for, minutes earlier, we had donned crampon boot spikes. Our only remaining gear was in our backpacks, including one two-man tent between the five of us.

I winced at the thought of thousands of pounds' worth of lost gear, of angry sponsors and the effect on my future expeditions. But there were more immediate worries to hand: 3,000 feet of near-sheer ice. Most of it was as yet invisible from above, but immediately beneath us lay a great field of jagged ice-blocks; a nightmare in blue and white.

Our packs weighed sixty pounds each, so, descending narrow rock chimneys, we lowered them ahead of us on ropes. We reached the base of the rock at noon and stopped beside a waterfall. Just above the waterfall a chance ledge of ice-blocks formed a temporary causeway from rock-face to ice. Since the entire glacier was moving slowly down within its *bergschrund* sheath, the gap between rock and glacier, the causeway was liable to be dislodged at any moment. Clearly, there was no other route onwards and downwards save via this unstable ledge.

Roger viewed the teetering bridge alongside me. 'Any further movement from above will remove that, you know.'

Roger switched on the radio and this time Johnny's voice came through at once. The news was bad. He could not understand why no one had warned us before, but the Briksdalsbre was generally known to be a killer. Of the twenty-eight glacier tongues that pour off the Jostedalsbre, it was the only one as yet unclimbed by Norway's ace glacier-climbers.

'You must go back up and come down the Kvamme trail as Henrik did,' Johnny told us. But getting this far had involved a steep rock descent with ropes, which I knew we could never reverse. Since none of us was a climber, we needed gravity on our side. Downwards lay our only chance. Then I thought of a helicopter.

'No,' said Johnny, 'we've thought of that. There are helicopters but Jan Mickelbust here warns against their use. The noise and downdraught will dislodge avalanches all around you. You must understand this is the worst week of the year. Everything's melting. From down here it's like listening to Tchaikovsky's *1812*. Through binoculars I can see whole areas of face break off and fall away. If you can't go back, at least take care.'

Roger switched off the radio and I edged warily over the causeway. In places only thin wedges spanned the gap with nothing between them save a glimpse of rushing water far below. Twice I froze as lumps of ice, disturbed by my passing, fell away like rotten planks from a foot-bridge.

Once across, I made a rope firm and one by one the others joined me.

I noticed blood on the ice and discovered that my fingers were bleeding. There was no pain, for my hands were numb, but the coarse-grained ice had worn away both the wool of my gloves and the skin from my fingers. The others found the blood-trail a help when we passed through piles of loose ice-boulders.

The ice plateau was riven by the biggest crevasses I had seen, but we crossed twenty by leaping across without rucksacks and clutching our axes. A twelve-foot crack that stretched across the entire glacier finally foxed us. We were forced back on to the rock-face deep inside the *bergschrund*, difficult because the ice ran very close to the rock at that point and the latter was polished smooth as glass. Streams of icy water ran down our backs and a knife-like wind whistled down the dark cranny. The roar of subterranean currents rushed below us in the nether regions of the *bergschrund* and I prayed I would not slip from my fragile holds on the wet rock.

When we emerged from the cavern, we had bypassed the crack, but evening stars were already visible. We must quickly find a flat ledge away from ice movement and big enough for our tent. Patrick, I noticed, had collapsed and he refused to respond to my shouts to hurry. I swore at him and this set off ice falls further up the glacier. This did chivvy the exhausted Patrick, who rose teetering under the weight of his pack.

Geoff found a ledge at the very point where our *bergschrund* rock route reached the level of the glacier ice. Uncertain how we would cross from rock to ice, a distance of twenty feet, we agreed to camp on the rock ledge.

With bloody fingers we erected the tent, designed for two six-foot soldiers, and the five of us crawled in. We melted ice and made weak tea. There was only one twenty-four-hour ration pack to be shared by all. This worked out at a single spoonful of curry gruel each and two 'sips' of tea. Patrick was allowed two spoonfuls and three sips after he announced that it was his birthday.

Breakfast was exactly three-quarters of one Army biscuit and one gulp from a tin mug of steaming hot water boiled with yesterday's teabags. If anyone's Adam's apple jerked more than once as they drank, Bob's large hand descended at once and removed the mug.

Bootlaces, zips and rope coils opened up the raw patches on my fingers. Blisters squelched and Bob's lips bled. Geoff nursed his ribs, but did not complain. Once the tent was packed, he lay along the ledge and decided our only escape must be by rope down the cliffside. He fed out a 300-foot coil, secured to a boulder, and we slid down one by one. I had wrapped socks round my hands, which were blood-soaked by the time I finished the descent.

Next we faced a wet rockface that descended sixty feet to a possible causeway over the *bergschrund*. When Patrick saw the rock route, he snorted his reluctance. I must have spoken angrily, for I sparked off a tirade. He accused me of being totally unaware of the perils of our situation and of having abused his friendship by falsely luring him into the team with promises of fishing, a little skiing and minimal discomfort other than a night or two in a tent.

There was an element of truth in his charges, so I said nothing and moved off down the wet rock. We clung like limpets to every tiny hold, cursing the outward pull of our packs and sweating at the thought of what lay below. We were not roped up at that point for fear of one man unseating the rest.

We made the causeway and regained the glacier. Avalanches sounded every few minutes and the ice under our feet kept sliding away. For an hour we were forced to climb over temporary platforms of avalanche rubble. At some point I heard a scream from behind. Roger and I could not move due to loose ice underfoot, but we could see the others fifty yards behind. Patrick had fallen through the platform and hung dangling unseen somewhere below. Bob held fast to his rope while Geoff tried to remove the ice-blocks that had fallen into the hole above Patrick.

Geoff's urgency disturbed many heavy chunks, a further risk to our hanging colleague, but at length he re-exposed the hole. Bob and Geoff hauled together on their ropes and Patrick's head appeared in the 'plughole' between them. He was numb with cold but unhurt. There was no time to rest, so we continued over the rotten platform until, two hours later, we reached the top of the glacier's bottleneck. Here all avalanches from above were channelled into a 100-yard front.

We surveyed the bottleneck with dismay, looking down its length to the final ice falls and terminal lake. Not a minute passed but some part of the tongue was temporarily covered by an avalanche.

Geoff fixed our longest rope, a 400-foot coil, to an ice bollard, and threw it downwards. Henrik's voice came over the radio then. The rope had snagged. Geoff tried again. This time it fell clear to its full length, spanning the most lethal stretch of the glacier. We abseiled down wearing rucksacks. Bob joined me after a safe descent, but flying rubble caught the others halfway down.

Geoff lost his grip and slid 100 feet, saved only by the friction of the rope against his waist clip. One of Patrick's crampons raked down Geoff's leg, scraping along the bone. Roger, who was unhurt, tore off his shirt tail and bound up the wound. We knew we could not delay in this volatile spot and Geoff, despite this new injury, was as keen as the rest of us to hurry on.

Again Henrik's advice by radio proved critical. We were now no more than fifty yards from the final ice-cliff that ended in the lake, but cut off from it by a group of wide crevasses. A sheer gulley ran down between the left-hand cliff and these crevasses and Henrik bade us cross it.

'It is your only way, but go one at a time and watch above you as you traverse. Every few minutes since midday an avalanche has crashed down the slipway.'

Alluvial mud oozed slowly down the slide like lava flow. We grouped beside the gulley and tensed as several tons of ice hurtled by with the effect of a passing express train. One by one we cramponed across this skittle alley as fast as the loose surface allowed. Bob came last and, hampered by one broken crampon, lost his grip and hung for an edgy minute held only by his ice axe and our side rope. Within moments of his crossing, the whole grey slipway shuddered under a deluge of ice-spoil.

Our very last rope, another 400-foot length, took us down the rock cliff to the lake where Johnny, Peter and Henrik awaited us in a spare Avon boat, which they had carried up from the roadhead far below.

We had made it.

Anton Bowring
Oceanographer and explorer

Ran relishes confronting the elements – the tougher the better. In contrast, I don't. Maybe that is why our friendship has endured for over forty years. There is no competition between us.

When I first met Ran in 1977 as an applicant to join his polar ship on the Transglobe Expedition, he told me that there was no ship nor were there any other applicants. In his unique, unassuming but entirely compelling way, he suggested that if I could find a suitable ship, recruit the crew and acquire all the supplies, equipment and services to keep it running for three years at no cost to the expedition, then he had no objection to me becoming a deckhand.

God knows why he put so much trust in me, but I am eternally grateful that he did, despite the pressure of trying to achieve the seemingly impossible. In two years we secured everything we needed, all of it sponsored. Best of all, we attracted fifteen fully qualified, volunteer crew members from captain and chief engineer to cook and steward, all of whom became enduring friends to this day.

On behalf of all of us who served on the expedition ship *Benjamin Bowring*, I can confidently convey our heartfelt thanks to Ran and to Ginny, of course, for giving us the opportunity to take part in a record-breaking journey that opened up new horizons, not only for us, but also for all those who were inspired to follow.

Above all, nothing gave me more pleasure than the knowledge that Ran was somewhere out on the ice, struggling to pull his sledge against the cold, harsh wind or trying to cook a dehydrated meal in a flapping tent, while I was sitting in my heated cabin with a hot mug of soup listening to gentle, pastoral music and reading a good book, which I have to say is my preference.

Simon Grimes cooking in front of their Land Rover with Charlie Burton and Oliver Shepard in the Sahara on the Transglobe Expedition, 1979.

4

Sahara Desert

*Driving across the Sahara from Algiers
to Abidjan on the Ivory Coast
1979*

*E*arly *in 1972, Ginny Fiennes said to Ran, 'Why don't we go around the world?' Following the Greenwich Meridian, they would start in London, head south to Antarctica, then up the other side of the planet, over the North Pole and back to Greenwich. The first surface circumpolar journey around the Earth: the Transglobe Expedition.*

By 1979, after seven years of unpaid full-time work, they had acquired 1,900 sponsors from eighteen different countries and £29m worth of goods and services, a team of fifty-two unpaid individuals giving their time and expertise, an expedition ship named the MV Benjamin Bowring, and HRH Prince Charles as their patron. It would take them three years to complete the global circle.

From London, Charlie Burton, Ollie Shepard, Simon Grimes, Ginny and I were planning to drive overland through France and Spain, across the Mediterranean to Algeria, into the Sahara Desert, then straight on south to Abidjan on the Ivory Coast with two Land Rovers, a Range Rover and three trailers. We hoped to stop in Paris and Barcelona for trade shows and expected to meet up with our ship, the *Benjamin Bowring*, in Barcelona, Algiers and Abidjan.

On 1 September 1979, we left the Duke of York's Barracks in Chelsea in sheeting rain. Ollie and Charlie came to a sudden halt in Parliament Square when one of their trailer wheels went walkabout without warning and a split pin in the retaining hub was found to be missing. Our hopes of catching the midnight ferry from Folkestone to Dunkirk were dashed. What a beginning . . .

The British commercial attaché had arranged for our Paris export exhibition to be held in the heart of Montmartre on the first floor of a lovely old house with a circular marble staircase, ornate ceilings and extravagant chandeliers. But the passers-by stumped along in an urban trance, ignoring the furry dummy we had stuck on the pavement to advertise our presence; some even risked death by detouring on to the road to avoid the dummy. Despite minimal attendance, more items disappeared off our stands, including a large quilted sleeping bag, than at all our subsequent seven shows put together.

Depressed, we repacked the exhibition into some 400 crates and loaded these on to four railcars bound for Barcelona. Then we drove south through France.

Charlie left us and headed in the Range Rover for St Tropez, as he'd decided to meet a recent girlfriend there for a few days' holiday. When we met up with him again at Perpignan near the Spanish border, he announced his intention to marry Twink, a most shapely and attractive girl, who was also an executive of one of our sponsors, Berlei. The wedding, he said, would take place in Sydney after we had crossed Antarctica. However, I noticed that thoughts of impending marriage did not dull his perception on the beach that afternoon, when a lively little English girl with bared supercargo parked herself beside us. Simon also developed a squint.

One night a rainstorm washed Ollie downhill on his groundsheet and lilo and jammed him under the sump of his Land Rover.

Being a remarkable sleeper, he did not wake but looked rough next morning. The next night, determined to keep off the ground, he strung a hammock from the rear of his vehicle to the tow bar of his detached trailer. Charlie, not to be outdone, curled his bulk up inside the trailer. Whenever he turned over, the tow bar tipped up and Ollie shot down to the far end of his hammock. Woken, he would work his weight back up again, which sent the trailer down with a bump and Charlie briefly into orbit. Both were grumpy at breakfast, which raised the humour and the spirits of the rest of us, such was the way of our land team.

Barcelona had suffered severe storms before we arrived, ten people had been killed and the roof of the hall where our exhibition was to be held had partially collapsed, so our display was cancelled. In many ways this was a great relief, though very bad luck on our valiant sponsors, because it meant that we would not have to load the ship in a rush.

The *Benjamin Bowring* was waiting for us in Barcelona. Originally a Danish ship, the *Kista Dan*, she had been built in 1952 to transport lead from Greenland to Europe. Later she was used for sealing and then sold to the Canadians, renamed the *Martin Karlsen* and used as a survey vessel. The ship had been bought especially for the expedition by Peter Bowring, chairman of the insurance brokers C.T. Bowring, whose son Anton was in charge of our Marine Office. Ginny, plus a champagne bottle, officially renamed the vessel the *Benjamin Bowring*, in memory of the company's founder, and we soon called her the *Benjy B*.

The ship was in Barcelona's prime berth, right opposite the port's main bar, so I expected to find everyone wreathed in smiles when I arrived, instead I was met with moans and groans from our crew of unpaid volunteers. The atmosphere was tense. Our skipper, retired Admiral Otto Steiner, seemed hurt, the Canadian first officer looked utterly bemused and Terry, the bosun, appeared apoplectic.

Troubles had evidently arisen the moment we'd left England. I would soon be off the ship for three months driving across

Africa, so I realised I had to patch up differences right away, but luckily the Admiral had a forgiving nature and Terry calmed down. I then held a meeting on deck for everybody, during which I talked of our future plans, outlined the likely problems we would all face in living together during the years ahead and suggested some guidelines. These I admitted might not work; only time would tell.

With that over, we nosed out of Barcelona at night and headed for Africa in a dead calm beneath a cloudless sky. Jill, the cook, served baked mackerel.

I *hate* fish. All fish. But knowing that normal people like it I had jumped at the chance when a sponsor offered us five tons of fresh mackerel. One freezer was full of the stuff. By the time the crew reached Barcelona, they'd had a surfeit of it and also of ravioli, another commodity I somehow seem to have over-ordered.

I took one half bite and drowned it with tomato sauce and pepper. But the evil salty tang came through. Struggling, I noticed a silence in the saloon. Some fifteen pairs of eyes were on me. I attacked the mackerel at once with relish and switched on a more appreciative smile.

'Nice, isn't it?' said Eddie Pike.

I nodded.

'Shame you'll miss it in Africa but, never mind, we'll save you a few hundredweight.'

Cyrus, the Indian officer, sprinkling his with tabasco sauce, offered to pack a freezer full of mackerel to take on the Land Rovers.

'Help you to get on with the locals – instead of coloured beads,' suggested Terry.

'More likely start a revolution,' muttered Jill.

Dave Peck, the second mate, seemed to be making all the running with our pretty cook, though I noticed other eyes cast in her direction. But there were plenty of ports to call at for the competition.

The next meal was ravioli.

On the second day we came to Algiers, where a clutch of officers came aboard. All had gold pips or stripes on their uniformed shoulders. Customs, port officials, police, sanitation and other unguessable authorities.

The Admiral came into his own with his white uniform, monocle and conquistador beard; he fascinated our acquisitive visitors and quite put them off what was doubtless their normal custom of demanding goods for favours; or it almost did. An hour later with voluminous wads of forms signed and stamped, Otto saw the port junta off his ship with a mere half-dozen bottles of whisky and some rather passé boxes of teabags.

'You'd better disembark before their brethren come for a second visit,' said the Admiral and without more ado Terry and his deck crew winched the vehicles on to the quay, whilst Jill parcelled up a delicious joint, uncontaminated by mackerel or ravioli. Our chief engineer Ken Cameron ambled up to inform the skipper that the variable pitch control for the propellor was jammed in reverse. So we stood on the quayside and watched the *Benjy Bowring* depart backwards into the clammy darkness: we would not see her again until we'd crossed the Sahara.

A British attaché arrived to take Ginny, Simon and Charlie away for the night, but he warned us that light fingers were everywhere, so Ollie and I decided to sleep in the vehicles. To ensure greater security for all three cars and the trailers, Ollie spun a web of cotton around our line-up and attached tins at intervals. I slept in the cab of the first Land Rover but Ollie decided he could only guard the rear from 'outside', so he set up his lilo and mosquito net in the gutter.

Around dawn the cacophony was indescribable: it sounded like the local foxhounds arriving in full cry. I shot out of the cab, cut my ear on one of Ollie's tins and was almost garrotted by a cotton line. Ollie struggled out of his sleeping bag and mosquito net wide-eyed.

'Christ,' he exclaimed. 'The hounds of the Baskervilles at full moon.'

No dogs to be seen. Instead an impressive mosque overlooked the harbour security fence, from which issued the muezzin's dawn chorus to the faithful. The local verger must have set his loud-speakers on full volume. An appalling noise beat the humid air, unlike any I had ever heard in Arabia. Even the mosquitoes fled.

'Just as well,' said Oliver, pointing.

A wave of black sludge advanced along the gutter in which he had slept, complete with fish bones, half a bowler hat and the remains of a cat.

For two full days I struggled with customs formalities and an alarming complex of bureaucrats. I got nowhere fast until I met the Chief of the Port Authority himself. For the sum of 1,000 dinars, some $250, he cleared the way with three phone calls. This left me with exactly £80-worth of dinars for the rest of our stay in Algeria.

Our last night in the capital was spent in the British ambassador's house. He was a charming bachelor with a subtle sense of humour. As Simon Grimes wrote in his diary: 'One of the nicest houses I've seen. Airy French style, slight Moorish influence, old English furniture and books, with oriental rugs and carpets. Beautiful garden with tennis court and pool. Had breakfast served on a tray by my window looking down the Embassy gardens to the port of Algiers.'

Ginny set up her thirty-foot antenna in the embassy garden and spoke to HRH The Duke of Kent at a communications exhibition in Bayswater, London. Then we drove south on good tarmac with heavy oil tankers for company. Flat-topped mesa straggled away through the roadside haze. It was 43°C at noon. I travelled with Simon, followed by Ginny alone and the others behind in the Range Rover. There was as much a sense of exploration as on a motorway trip out of London. But it was good to be free in wide open land.

At dusk we stopped beside the rolling sand dunes of El Golea, immediately christened 'El Gonorrhea' by Ollie. A few miles to the south lay Khanem, where Ollie was commissioned to catch sand lizards or skinks for the Natural History Museum. While we made camp, Ollie went off to set his traps, baiting them with corned beef.

The sun rose huge and orange next day and all the traps were empty. Clouds of large flies which tickled and little flies that bit attended us all day as the sweat ran down in rivulets. We wore next to nothing. Ollie recorded 50°C in the afternoon. We could not decide whether it was less unpleasant inside or outside the tents.

After two skinkless days, Ollie decided we must be more aggressive. Perhaps this particular sand bowl was bad news for skinks. So we trooped out into the dunes with water bags, compass and skink traps.

Two hours of dune-trudging later, Ollie had picked up no spoor, although he assured us that the five-inch lizards did leave identifiable tracks, and decided to call it a day.

'Are you sure you can track them?' I pressed him.

'Of course I can. I have all my notes and my training from the Natural History Museum.'

'Yes, but that was on the museum lawns at South Kensington.'

'Don't fuss.' Ol's confidence was undented. 'These things always require perseverance. Skinks don't grow on trees, you know.'

'Just as well,' muttered a hot and weary Charlie, 'there don't seem to be too many trees in El Gonorrhoea.'

Everyone was a bit touchy by dusk when, almost to order, the mosquitoes began their familiar whine.

The food naturally had a fair amount of sand additive. Simon was the cook and much resented the fact that his private knife, fork and spoon had disappeared. It could only be one of us. But everyone denied the theft. 'I don't see why people have to lie,' said Simon and went off into the dark in a huff.

Next day I joined him in our Land Rover to hunt skink-catchers. In fly-blown El Golea they speak French and/or Arabic. Simon spoke French and I spoke Arabic.

'What do we request?' I asked him.

'*Un homme qui peut attraper les poissons-de-sable,*' said Simon without thinking. 'What about in Arabic?'

'Ah.' I did not want to be outdone. 'The Latin form is *Scincus scincus cucullatus.*'

'These Arabs may not learn Latin at school,' he said evenly, as we passed by a row of mud and brick hovels.

I was ready for him.

'The colloquial for lizard is *dhub* or *zelgaag*. Since skinks are lizards, that should do.'

Much investigation led us to the mud home of one Hamou, the local 'guide'. Inside there was a freezer full of Coca-Cola beside a colour TV set. Hamou assured us he was *the* skink-catcher of the region, but he must warn us it was a dangerous and therefore expensive business. Did we realise that sand vipers and scorpions, which lived under the same sand where skinks must be sought, were in abundance? During the last year alone, he assured us, 128 people in town had been treated for scorpion stings and three of them had died. Sand vipers were deadly poisonous.

'Twice,' he added, 'when hunting skinks, I have plunged my hand into the sand and brought out sand vipers gorging on skinks.'

I was glad Ollie was not present.

That afternoon, with Ollie watching closely and three *bedu* boys to help him, Hamou led us into high dune country, not a mile from our camp, and within minutes he had captured two prime skinks. By evening he had a third and we took him home to enjoy the tinned fruit and tomato purée with which we paid him.

For two days Ollie applied Hamou's tactics and added to his collection of pickled lizards. Each time he popped a new catch into his formaldehyde bottle, he sighed and swore he would never again become involved in anything so cruel. Later Ollie received a letter from the Natural History Museum, thanking him for his work:

Previously, the nearest known localities for the two widespread forms of sand skink were some hundred kilometres apart . . . your specimens narrow the gap to twenty-five kilometres and, as they show no tendency to resemble the other form known from El Golea, it is likely we are dealing with two full species and not just subspecies. One cannot be a hundred per cent sure, but your specimens make it much more likely. Thank you for helping to solve the sand skink mystery.

Pleased to leave the El Gonorrhoea sauna, we went south to Ain Salah, which means 'salty well', where we replenished our water supply with salty water. Warm winds from the western dunes fanned our camp that night in the Jebel Moujdir. Pretty Walt Disney mice called jerboas hopped about and overhead a lanner falcon wheeled on dusk patrol.

Then on to Tamanrasset, self-styled tourist centre of the Hoggar Mountains. South of the ugly sprawling town we drove off the gravel track at the Ain Tahadet, to Jo-Jo spring, as generations of hippies have dubbed it. The proprietor, who looked more Italian than Arab, was introduced to us as Spaghetti by a German tourist already camped there.

'Three dinars for each jerry can of my water,' said Spaghetti in passable French. We filled all our cans and paid with Marmite and honey. Below the spring was a dry wadi, which the German told us had been a roaring vent fifty metres across only a week before. So we camped beside it instead of on it.

Our next step must be south-west across the dry wastes of the Tanezrouft, for our second task was bat-collecting on either side of the Mali border. Papers for such a journey must be signed by the Wali of Tamanrasset and the Police Chief, which took several hours. I then visited the hotel with Charlie, who discovered to his horror that one beer cost the equivalent of £1.50 and a shot of gin £2.50.

Finally I located a desert guide who spoke French. 'Due west to Bordj Mokhtar. The track has not been crossed for five years.

Much bad sand, no piste.' My Michelin map indicated a good piste to Bordj Mokhtar, but perhaps the guide was more up to date: after all, sand does shift about.

'Best you go Gao by way of Timiaouine,' said the guide. 'Then I will take you.'

I explained we only had food to pay him with. This disgusted him; obviously an urbanised *bedu* who dealt only in dinar. 'You go without a guide. It is possible. You may not get lost.' These encouraging words seemed to absolve him of all feelings of responsibility. I then asked where we might find colonies of bats.

He sat up and frowned.

'*Les chauves-souris*?' He pondered awhile. 'Ah, those are west. Maybe you look in the wells of Silet.'

I was dismissed.

Ginny and Simon both wished to see the local hermitage of the remarkable French monk Père Charles de Foucauld. We had a day to spare whilst Ollie and Charlie practised their bat-hunting techniques in local caves, so we drove for fifty miles along an excellent rocky track into the Hoggar peaks. At 8,000 feet we came to the pass of Asekrem and walked up a well-worn mountain path to a little rock chapel, which had as its sole guardian an elderly French friar, Petit Frère, to whom, as was customary, we carried water and food.

The friar, of Father de Foucauld's order, had lived there twenty years. On the plateau above the chapel was a set of meteorological instruments with which he kept meticulous daily records. The view from that lonely chapel was an experience to be savoured. A cool breeze plucked at mountain flowers, rare and tiny, whilst beyond the silent hanging void, great mountains soared to spires and pinnacles of dizzy height. The rock road took us back to Tamanrasset through another pass and dusk fell about us with sudden indigo gloom.

Back at camp, Simon lit a fire of roots to cook over for we were hungry. Charlie gave a shout, 'Come and have some curry, it's still warm.' Ginny and Simon prepared to wait for their own stew, but I went over to the others and Ollie spooned out some curry.

'How was the bat hunting?' I asked.

'Not a sausage all day. There was a storm in the afternoon which knocked the tents down.'

I thanked him for putting ours up again and took a heaped mouthful of curry.

Without a doubt it was the hottest I have ever tasted either side of Shiraz. My eyes and tongue bulged out.

'Water,' I croaked.

Thoughtfully and with no hesitation Charlie passed me a glass of water which I gulped down in great swallows. The world seemed to come to an end. I was in hell: red hot sandpaper rasping my throat as I gasped for air.

'Hey, Charlie,' said Ollie, 'that was my last gin and tonic and we're on the last bottle.'

I threatened vengeance through watering eyes, but my words were drowned by their cries of mirth.

From Tamanrasset we drove west on worsening tracks to a place called Tit. Here there was a fork not shown on my map. There was no sign *at* the fork, but I found one 300 yards from the current track. Abalesa and Silet lay to the left. The vehicles rattled like peas on a drum as the track leapt from scarred black basalt steps to sand-filled ruts. Storm clouds, dark and massive, massed behind in the unseen Hoggar Mountains. We sped over wadis green with *gai'sh*, *kfeeter* and the ubiquitous *ghadaf* dwarf palm, rousing clouds of dust; a dust so fine it reflected the very sheen of the sun, an orb of spectral orange. Dusty as ghouls, we emerged to slake our thirst at the well of Silet.

Simon, master-of-water, flung our roped canvas bucket down the stone-rimmed hole and drew up a gallon or so. This he poured into a jerry can through a filter.

'Little bastards,' he muttered, blowing at the filter's gauze.

I peered over his shoulder, not difficult for Simon is Ginny's height. A dozen miniature hook-tailed tadpoles writhed in alarm as the warm air struck their horrid little forms.

'Hook worms, liver worms, toe worms, every sort and kind of disease carrier and those are just the visible ones.' Simon seemed delighted. 'Imagine what a drop of that water would look like under the microscope. The locals here must be eaten alive from within.'

I watched Simon apply sterilisation and purification tablets to our bottles once he had pumped the water into them through lime candles: even then I doubt I would have drunk any but for my thirst.

One of the vehicle starters gave up the ghost. For five hours at 40°C Simon struggled to fix it. He burnt his fingers on the hot metal but to no avail. Ollie, disapproving of Simon's methods, ended up shouting at him in exasperation and finally vented his ire in his diary. That night he recorded, 'S. very set in his ways. He never wants to listen.'

Ollie, despite the lassitude we all experienced, decided Silet looked good for bats. I went with him to interpret. We found the village elder, who spoke French of sorts. At the mention of bats he showed alarm. 'Not in this village. We have no bats. But outside in the wells . . . maybe many.'

He tried to explain the location of the wells, but without a local map it was useless. Reluctantly he agreed to come, and four miles from Silet showed us some gravel pits where shafts had been sunk between twenty and fifty feet deep. We lowered Ollie down on a rope where the elder indicated. We tried four, but found nothing other than pigeon feathers and the foul odour of dead animals. In one well there was water and slime. We watched fascinated as a thin green viper over five feet long surfaced and raised its head to stare at us. Then, as Ollie approached, it submerged with frightening speed.

Allah willed that we should find no bats here, but to the west, across the wasteland, we would see countless bats in the wells of Tim Missao: of that the elder was certain.

We gave him at least a year's supply of tomato purée for his pains. Weeks later I discovered from a Frenchman that bats are thought to be sons of the Devil, whose main desire is to steal the souls of young Saharan villagers. No one wished to annoy the local bats by giving their presence away to foreign bat-catchers, so the best policy was to keep us moving on to ever-new bat pastures well away from wherever we were at the time.

For three days Simon rationed our water as we edged south and west over featureless wastes. Violent dust storms raged, blotting out the trail. For hour upon hour we drove through yellow gloom with our lights on, following a compass course, trying to keep to the old blurred tracks. It was often necessary to get out and verify we were on a known path: sometimes we seemed to be meandering about on our own.

On 15 October, in a shallow wadi far from any track, we happened upon three lonely saddles. Close to burial mounds of black rock, the three camel saddles lay in the dust; beside each was a neat pile of utensils, of cast-iron cooking pots, carved wood spoons, metal fire tongs and heavy clay gourds. Why? We wondered in silence.

I went off on foot to reconnoitre, to pick up the long-ago piste of twin camel trails. These led south and west and by evening we had rejoined clearly defined vehicle tracks from the north. The wind stirred sandstorms all night, which lashed our tents like driven sleet.

Crossing wadis, the vehicles bogged down in the soft loose sand. Once we came upon a scene from some surrealist film. Two juggernauts overladen with goods and people appeared fleetingly between surges of the storm. They had sunk in up to their axles, as we had. A giant of a man, turbaned and robed in white, gestured king-like as figures swarmed down from the loads to push and pull in unison. Blue-clad Touaregs from Mali and dusky desert nomads bent in two long lines under the will of the great bearded Moses, their robes whipping and billowing in the screaming dust clouds as we watched from our cosy cabs.

We made camp only one hundred miles north of the Mali border, sticky with dust and our own salt, tired and thirsty. Next day we came to Timiaouine, where we found a guide who took us across the unmarked border soon after dusk: then left us without a word.

Somewhere north of the path that runs from Bouressa to Tessalit, we reached a more attractive land with no wind, no sand and a pleasant dry heat. Sometimes our 'track' disappeared altogether over stone, but never for long. We climbed through high gravel hills, strewn with boulders, the northern rim of the Adrar des Iforas, where camel and goat herds roamed under the watchful eyes of wiry Touaregs. At night, moths beat at our mosquito nets and the sky was littered with brilliant stars. It felt good to be alive and loose.

Trailer springs fractured, tow bolts snapped and tyres punctured, but nothing serious impeded our progress south from the Adrar and down the lovely vale of Tilemsi where, for much of the time, there is no water. Our camps became more interesting, filled with scorpions, spiders and the nocturnal music of frogs, crickets and nightjars. Insects of fascinating shapes and hues, rabbits, foxes, lizards and gazelle now appeared. The Sahara was behind us. Some parts were as green as an English spring garden and spattered with indigo where tents of nomads sprawled by herds of grazing camel.

In the low bush land south of Anefis, a trailer chassis fractured. Simon assembled our welding kit, but his results were not satisfactory. At dusk a Tamachek with wife and child came into our camp. He wanted medical treatment. Doc Ollie satisfied his needs, in return for which service he did a superb job on our trailer, for he turned out to be a skilled welder by trade.

At Tabankort we met four Frenchmen nursing a group of tanned French girls, who wore as little as possible. They had somehow lost their trucks. Thereafter, every policeman from Tessalit to Gao stopped us, looked hard at our Land Rover and asked if we had seen the 'having gone absent lorries'.

Camel skeletons, some still furnished with rags of dried and hairy skin, lay about the trail especially where zones of sand caused mini deserts. In one such arid place, a wizened nomad waited. He made no gesture but we stopped. He offered us camel milk from a brass bowl and when we had drunk, he proffered his empty goatskin for water. Another, searching the sands for a lost camel, was obviously parched. He drank deeply; his dust-caked eyes closed tight. I could only guess how wonderful that feeling of relief must be to him; the feel of the water in his throat, a satisfaction which urban peoples, in their comparative sufficiency, can rarely savour.

At Gao we reached the wide, fast-flowing Niger River and followed its westerly curve for 400 miles to Tombouctou. This was a paradise for Ollie, always a keen ornithologist, and we stopped many times for him to identify this or that species from his bird book. From the Camargue to our camp at the Torro Bravo, from Algiers to Timbuktu, he noted everything with feathers. His entries included the Egyptian vulture, the shirka, the mouse-bird and the bee-eater, the bru-bru shrike, the cut-throat weaver, the white-rumped blackchat and the hoopoe.

The bird I remember most vividly was a Timbuktu chicken. We arrived in that town, famous for epitomising the back of beyond, at dusk and discovered a 'restaurant'. The set menu for that evening (and every evening) was 'Sardeen, beer and dead hen'. The beer was cold if you drank it quickly and the sardines, if you got them down before the indigenous flies did, were excellent. Our chef, a man with indescribably dirty hands and dish-dash, entered the dark room with a proud air of 'now for the *pièce de résistance*'.

The *pièce* was, in fact, one of the scrawny black chickens harmlessly cleaning up our crumbs and it put up a great deal of verbal resistance when cookie grabbed it by the neck and plucked it nude. Only then was the pitifully squawking bird put out of its misery by having its neck wrung. Our appetites dispersed more quickly than the feathers.

On the northern side of the town, stinking dunes piled themselves up against lanes of flyblown kraals, where children with distended bellies lolled in the shimmer of noon. The town's southern flanks sported concrete tenements and tarmac rimmed by dry forest. Timbuktu is indeed the end of the desert. Not far to the south, flood plains and vast shallow expanses of Niger water spanned the horizon. We planned to spend four days bird-watching in the lakes of Goundam, before crossing the Niger River south of Niafounké and heading through the Upper Volta to the Ivory Coast.

Camping in the Forest of Timbuktu is not to be recommended. We woke wet from a clammy sleep to the maddening call of thousands of doves and multi-coloured hoopoes in the pango-pango trees about our tents. Whether that was what the trees were really called, I don't know, but Simon, the only one to have travelled to West Africa before, called them that, so we all followed suit. The sand around us was soft and it was hard to get the vehicles and trailers going whenever we stopped, while if we inadvertently touched the rough dry grass, we found ourselves beset by marble-sized burrs, which clung to our clothing and made us itch.

There was little improvement on the piste to Goundam where we often got bogged down, struggling to free ourselves by means of our 300-foot tow rope. Progress was slow and we were passed by many hundreds of donkeys with outsize ears, which tripped along in dusty cavalcades followed, rather than led, by little barefoot donkeymen in sampan hats, with skirts hoicked up round their muscular thighs. They shouted happily when we finally managed to free ourselves and roared past them, trying to keep up speed so as not to sink in yet again.

Goundam turned out to be a pleasant village of hilly bumps round which snakes a Niger tributary, fringed by gardens and palms. We drove on for about four more miles to camp in a peaceful spot. From here Ollie journeyed upstream in our foldaway boat to a great reed-covered lake rich in bird life. Close by, in some ruins, he found his bats at long last.

In London, he, Charlie and Simon had been injected against rabies in readiness for bat-bites: nonetheless they wore leather gloves for the hunt. With bird-catching nets stretched across all exit points, they roused the dormant bats and trapped six of them, none bigger than a sparrow. Ollie's initial delight at this long delayed success soon turned to gloom when he had to pickle the little dears. Charlie made an especially hot curry to cheer him up. Then he located a Senegal fire finch and forgot all about his pickling traumas. That night a powerful wind whipped the river and dismantled Simon's mosquito net while he slept. He was bitten all over and was a miserable sight the next day.

I was sorry to leave the river camp, a happy place of chattering fire finches, hovering hawks and lunging kingfishers. Skulls and carcasses of cows littered the brush around us; probably the site of an abandoned charnel house, but there was no smell and we ignored them. As the others zoologised, Ginny washed clothes on the river bank and I began the detailed plans for unloading in Antarctica. By the time we reached Cape Town, some 200 pages of kit lists must be checked and allotted priority groupings.

Leaving the river, we passed a troupe of long-tailed monkeys on a watermelon hunt. Secluded pools flashed with bird colour. Simon was by then incubating malaria, but didn't know it. In Niafunké we learnt that the floods were so extensive, ferries were unable to cross the swollen river and our route south was barred. To skirt the flood waters, we would have to make a 700-kilometre detour through wild nomad country before we could get back on our original road south. It was a rough area and at Léré the lieutenant of police who checked our papers told us that we were the first foreigners to pass in four months.

My memories of our journey south of the Niger are fractured. A camp with a new moon outlining giant ant hills and cicadas that chirped through the silver night. A once great forest of dead and dying trees, where no birds sang and too many cattle had for too long churned the undergrowth into pig-pen mire. A pueblo village, where it seemed every inhabitant came out at our approach and followed us jogging and clapping along their only street, until the last child and yapping dog dropped away beneath a dusty halo.

A nomad encampment, where black Arab-speaking Mauritanians sang at sunset, the men with spears, shields and knobkerries, the women with bare breasts and rings of coloured beads. Soft orange lights etched the scene on my mind, dugout canoes beached high among the reeds, groups of smiling girls stomping and chanting in time as they flayed heaps of millet to flour dust. And lowing herds of African long-horns jostling behind thorn corrals, each with a series of long branded scars on its flanks.

For the next three days we drove south-east through damp forests and the irrigated rice lands of Kourouma, until we reached tarmac again by the thundering Niger barrage at Markala with its Coca-Cola sign scenery. Wild Africa is shrinking day by day.

Now our camps were in forest not savannah, under coconut palms and baobob trees. One moonless night I heard Ginny moaning outside our camp area. She was lying on her back. There were ants on her legs but she ignored them. For some years she had experienced slowly worsening stomach pains; tests had indicated a spastic colon but all the normal pills she tried gave no relief. I gave her painkillers and by morning she felt well enough to drive.

Simon's eyes were badly bloodshot from the dust and irritation of the past few weeks, made worse by his contact lenses. In Loulouni, close to the Ivory Coast border, he bought yams and guavas and cooked a delicious meal over a log fire. We dined in an elephant grass clearing whilst lightning forked and thunder burst in the rain forests all around.

Beside the guava market, Simon told us he had found a sign in French saying, 'Trade-in Western clothes for sale' and under it the English translation, 'Dead White Men Here'.

At the Mali border I took our five passports to a big black officer, who not only spoke English but came from Goundam. He was proud when he heard that we had stayed in his city, but extremely baffled when he spotted the word 'Traveller' in Charlie's passport.

'But dis man cannot have traveller for job. No man can make money from travel!'

He went out to the Range Rover to inspect Charlie in silence. Then he burst into laughter and proclaimed. 'So it is indeed a lazy man we have here.' An irate Charlie, suspecting me of putting the officer up to it, made threatening gestures from his cab. In exchange for much tomato purée, we filled our cans with fresh water and drove on south to the Ivorian frontier of Ouangolodougou.

On 4 November we reached Tiassale and stopped in a restaurant for beer and biscuits. We were a bit high from weeks without baths. I hoped to find a bank beside the Bandama Rouge river where we could swim as well as snail hunt, for Ollie still had one last task left to perform in Africa, to collect bilharzia-bearing water snails from stagnant pools in this jungle area.

Seeking access for our vehicles through the forest to the riverside, I found a smart bungalow overlooking the river. Parking outside, I walked gingerly over a well-trimmed lawn, flanked with exotic flowerbeds. A kitchen boy with an apron appeared and I asked to see *le propriétaire*. The kitchen boy fetched a houseboy with secateurs. He called a uniformed butler who produced a spectacled and thickset secretary. Was there anywhere my vehicle could reach the riverside, I asked.

He shrugged. '*Monsieur le Président est à l'église.*'

An hour later, Monsieur le Président, who turned out to be the local judge, arrived in a Mercedes with a white wife and kindly sent his houseboy, Jean, an Upper Voltan, to guide me. After an hour's drive through the forest, our muddy track emerged by the river bank where two dugout canoes were beached beneath giant jungle trees.

That night we set up camp in a space cleared of bamboo and undergrowth. Charlie found a nine-inch black scorpion, which Ollie promptly pickled 'in case it's interesting to the museum'.

Simon cooked over a slow log fire of mahogany and procured a chicken from Jean, whose village was only a mile downriver. Using a Land Rover starting handle for a spit, he fried the bird with yams. Together with stewed onions and aubergine, dinner was a feast. As well as being my co-driver, Simon had purchased all our fresh food from London to this, our last African camp. I now asked him how much we owed him, knowing his barter system had not always worked. 'A pound each should cover it,' he replied.

Ollie led us on a snail-hunting foray into the nearby forest. Fifty yards from the camp, we came across an apparently endless file of black ants, some half an inch long. They packed a shocking bite, as Ollie discovered when a couple became lodged between his shirt-tail and pants.

Simon spotted a snake curled up in a rotten bamboo cane. On its neck, a death's head symbol was elegantly fashioned. Ollie and Charlie refused to get friendly with it for the sake of my camera, but Simon prodded it gently and initiated a disappearing trick of unbelievable speed. There were black and yellow spiders of great beauty and everywhere dappled light falling in laser beams from the black canopy so far above us. Tree boles were massive, the vegetation underfoot deep and rich with decayed matter. Butterflies, moths and dragonflies graced the speckled gloom till dark when gyrating fireflies took over.

Happy with his slimy plunder, Ollie took us back to camp. Ginny, clad only in dusk, was bathing on the sandspit, her towel and soap at the ready on the end of a mahogany canoe. As I joined her by the twilit river, a native, silent as the current, arrived in a second dugout and beached on the spit.

Ginny whipped round and grabbed her towel, all two-foot square, and faced the visitor. He stared back entranced and not at all embarrassed. My camera and flash were sadly not at hand, so

I could not record Ginny's expression of outrage. In a while the fisherman grinned and went into the jungle.

After two long bird-watching patrols, Ollie was satisfied and we left the forest. Three hours' drive to the south brought us to the coast and the capital city of Abidjan, a place of skyscrapers on hills rich with foliage, fashionable hotels and suicidal orange taxis.

Anton Bowring came to meet us in the northern suburbs and told us that the *Benjy B* was already waiting for us at berth in the harbour. A few days later, the ship moved out of Abidjan's wide lagoon into the Atlantic, carrying us on the next leg of our Transglobe Expedition to Antarctica.

Oliver Shepard
Explorer and Transglobe team member

Ran was an excellent leader on the Transglobe Expedition, although he was slightly aloof from us at the beginning, as I don't think he really trusted Charlie Burton and me completely. However, once we started to progress across Antarctica, we kind of got our polar feathers and Ran's leadership qualities really shone.

Ran was always in front in terms of leading, whether it was skiing or on a skidoo, Charlie was in the middle and I was at the back to pick up the bits. We worked well together, because Ran was a pessimist, Charlie was about average and a very good mechanic, and I was an optimist. So we never had any arguments.

We also had code names for each other on the land party. Ran was called Padre, because he used to take the Sunday church service in the tent, and he called me Hudson as in the butler from *Upstairs Downstairs*, because I was in the middle of our tent, sleeping next to a knight.

We made it to the South Pole without any misdemeanours, but then we had a slight problem, because wherever you go from there you have to go north, and Ran couldn't work out how to do this at all.

We charged off going in one direction and fairly quickly our expedition Twin Otter aircraft took off, flew over us and chucked out an empty tin of baked beans, inside which there was a message saying, 'Ran, you are going in the wrong direction.' So we turned around and the three of us completed our crossing of Antarctica.

At this stage, very sadly I had to leave the Transglobe, as I was getting too much grief from my wife at home, so I came back to England. But I hope Ran accompanies me on my final long journey.

Ran and Charlie Burton become the first men to travel around the surface of the world via both Poles on the Transglobe Expedition, 1982.

5

North Pole

The first men in the world to travel the
Earth's surface to both Poles
1982

*A*fter *the* Benjamin Bowring *had dropped off the Transglobe*
team and their supplies in Antarctica, Ran and Ginny
Fiennes, Charlie Burton and Ollie Shepard spent the next eight
months living on the ice sheet in four cardboard huts during the
extreme polar winter. Then in October, the three men set off to
travel 2,200 miles across Antarctica, arriving in January 1981,
sixty-seven days later.

Ollie Shepard had to return home, but the Benjamin Bowring
carried the rest of the team across the Pacific and up the west coast
of North America to Alaska. From there, Ran and Charlie Burton
navigated up the Yukon and down the Mackenzie rivers by boat to
reach the Arctic Ocean, then traversed 3,500 miles east through the
infamous North West Passage to the remote outpost of Alert, on
Ellesmere Island. The most northerly such huts in the world, long
uninhabited and once used by Canadian scientists, this would be
the base for their attempt to cross the Arctic Ocean and complete
the first surface circumpolar journey round the planet.

Five days before our arrival at Alert, Ginny had flown in with the
winter equipment, our old Antarctic skidoos and the two dogs.

The three of us spent the next four months of permanent darkness in the Alert huts preparing equipment, completing a new series of scientific research tasks and training on the local pack ice.

In mid-January, Ginny received warnings from her Canadian met contact that his sea-ice recordings showed a thickness of 87cm, thinner than that of any previous January on record, the average being 105cm.

The true cold, which crackles the nose and ears like parchment, congeals the blood in fingers and toes like rapidly setting glue and fixes the sea ice slowly into a precarious platform to the Pole, finally came in late January. Better late than never. The camp thermometer hovered around −51°C with a fresh ten-knot breeze. One night a fox outside the hut awoke me and I noticed Ginny's hot-water bottle lying in between her bedsocked feet − frozen solid.

We received a radio message from a Californian friend. Walt Pedersen, the American aiming to reach both Poles, had given up his impending attempt on the South Pole due to stonewalling by the US National Science Foundation. We could still become the first people in history to reach both Poles. Prince Charles radioed through to Ginny and mentioned that he had heard rumours of a Norwegian team racing us to cross the Arctic. 'No racing,' he said to me with a stern edge to his voice.

By the last day of January I must decide when to set out to cross the Arctic. To start prior to the first appearance of the sun would be to lay myself open to accusations of irresponsibility. On the other hand, it was imperative that we reach the North Pole before the annual summer break-up. Once at the Pole, we would at least be in the zone of currents, which float their ice cover in the general direction of Spitsbergen or Russia.

If we delayed our departure from Alert until after sun-up in March, as Ollie, Charlie and I had done on our first attempt to reach the North Pole in 1977, we would again risk falling short of our target and have to be extracted from the ice by ski plane.

Whenever we set out we could not be certain that success was attainable, for the simple reason that no man had ever crossed the Arctic Ocean in a single season.

On 13 February 1982, I said a quick goodbye to Ginny. We had spent the previous night in our hut closing our minds bit by bit to reality. Over the years we had found it better that way. The wrench of departure was worse than in Antarctica, for we both knew the southern crossing was a mere nursery slope compared with the Arctic.

The weather was clear, although the day was as dark as night, when we pulled away from the huts. I glanced back and saw Ginny clutching her two dogs closely and looking up at the passage of darkness by which we had left. At such moments we both wished she had never conceived the idea of the journey.

Charlie Burton and I sat astride the open, heavily laden skidoos, each towing 600 pounds of fuel and gear. Our beards and eyelashes were ice-laden within minutes, for the chill factor was −90°C when stationary, increasing with the speed of our advance. We followed a wild, zigzag way along the dark and ice-girt coast. I remembered our 1977 travels, which helped me not to get lost, although that year we had travelled in daylight. Crossing a high pass somewhere on the Fielden Peninsula, Charlie turned his sledge over on a steep slope above sheer cliffs. He managed to extricate himself some yards from a long drop into the dark.

On 17 February we came in twilight to a canal of newly open water from which emanated dark clouds of frost-smoke. In the depths of winter, long before sunrise and at a point of maximum coastal pressure, this was an ominous sign.

We had not expected open water so early. With extra care we skirted the canal and entered a narrow corridor of blue ice, emerging a short distance east of Cape Columbia, that coastal point off which the southerly sea currents split west and east. This makes the cape a sensible jumping-off point from land ice to sea ice. After axing ourselves a ramp of ice-blocks, we took the skidoos for a twenty-foot slide over the tide-crack. We were now 'afloat' at sea.

We camped 300 yards out from the coast in a field of broken ice. In a way I was glad of the darkness, for it prevented a wider and therefore more depressing view of our route north. I pressed a mitt to the raw end of my nose and was silent as I recalled what had transpired the first time we tried to pit our wits against the power of the Arctic Ocean. We had learned a lot of lessons then about what not to do.

During the first day of twilit labour with our axes, we cleared 800 yards of highway through the pressure rubble. Our axed lane was precisely the width of a skidoo and it followed the line of least resistance, which unfortunately added 75 per cent of extra distance to the straight course we would have taken were it not for obstacles. To gain the Pole we must cover 825 miles – then much further again on its far side to reach a potential rendezvous point with the ship.

There were two dangers: failure to reach the Pole – and therefore the Spitsbergen current – by summer floe break-up time, and the subsequent worry of failing to reach the *Benjamin Bowring* before the end of summer when the ship must retreat to more southerly waters. We could not hope to achieve either goal without air resupply with food and cooker fuel from the Twin Otter ski plane, which was to fly out from England with the specialist maintenance engineer Gerry Nicholson and a skilled Arctic pilot called Karl Z'berg, a Swiss Canadian who had flown our chartered Otter in 1977.

We axed our skidoo lane through 200 yards of twelve-foot-high ice-blocks. With a total of 1,000 yards cleared, we went back to bring in the skidoos and sledges up to our new front-line point.

Charlie and I both weighed 185 pounds, so together, by using our joint weight as a fulcrum, we could just shift the 800-pound laden skidoos and the 600-pound sledges over any insufficiently axed blockages. Damage to equipment was inevitable, as the only way to negotiate the switchback lane was at full tilt, bouncing off walls and over iron-hard slabs. On 19 February, my drive axle snapped. That did it: I determined to switch to manpower and abandon the skidoos – at least for the first hundred miles where the pressure rubble would be at its worst.

The previous winter at Alert, preparing for this eventuality, I had tested two lightweight eight-foot-long manhaul pulks and it was with these fibreglass sledges, carrying 190 pounds each, that we pushed north on 22 February. After eight hours of haulage, our underwear, socks, facemasks and jackets were soaking wet or frozen, depending on which part of the body they covered and on whether we were resting or pulling at the time.

My haemorrhoids became worse day by day until I could think of little else. The constant vicious tugging of my shoulder and waist harness, as the pulk jammed against snags, exacerbated the discomfort. Charlie's lower back and his knees pained him constantly, but, by the end of four dark days, we had logged eleven northerly miles. This would not sound very impressive except to someone who has also pulled a load in excess of his own body-weight over pressure rubble in the dark and at a temperature of –40°C.

Charlie plodded on at his own pace and, unable to slow down, I stopped every hour for twenty minutes or more for him to catch up. I attempted to avoid freezing solid during these long waits by cursing the Arctic in general and Charlie in particular. Sheer exhaustion overcame any fear of bears or indeed of falling into the sea.

Charlie and I saved time daily by never cooking breakfast. We merely drank a mug of coffee from our vacuum flask, heated the night before. This gave us the courage to unzip our bags and climb into our frosted clothes and boots. For seven months we were to remain in precisely the same clothing without washing.

We dragged behind us, man for man, the same weight as Captain Scott and his team. Their aim was to be first to reach the South Pole, ours was to be first to reach both Poles. Like them, we were racing the clock. On 3 March, at –49°C, the blood-red ball of the sun slid briefly along the rim of the sea. Sunlight, although welcome to improve visibility, was our number-one enemy. Ultraviolet rays would now begin to eat at the structure of the pack ice and, by mid-April, so weaken the ice that the least pressure from the wind would crack up the floes and halt our progress.

At 4 a.m. on 4 March, at −40°C, a fire broke out in our stores hut back at Alert. Ginny rushed out with an extinguisher, but: 'It was just one big fireball inside with smoke issuing from the seams in the walls and flames filling the windows . . . There were forty-five gallon drums of fuel stacked by the wall. They had been there for years and were frozen into the ice.' While they watched, eight drums of gasoline exploded, as did fusillades of rocket flares and 7.62 FN rifle bullets.

Until that point the world's press had ignored the expedition. Now newspapers and television screens all over the world carried headlines such as 'Conflagration at Polar Base' and 'Polar Expedition in Flames'. After the night of the fire, every action we took – and one or two that we didn't – became news from London to Sydney, from Cape Town to Vancouver.

Seven years beforehand, Ginny had argued that I should lay an equipment cache at Tanquary Fiord as well as at Alert – just in case. With the generous help of the Canadian Coastguard's ice-breaker two years before, we had done so. This meant that the expedition need not now be abandoned. Spare radios, generators, ice rations and skidoo gear were available for our Twin Otter to collect from Tanquary as soon as the weather allowed. I made a mental note to tell Ginny once again she was not just a pretty face.

With enough food for eight days, we digested the news of the fire – about which we could do nothing – and concentrated on northerly progress, yard by painful yard. Our shoulders and hips were raw from the rub of the pulk harnesses. My nose, weeping blood and fluid for the last two weeks, was now frost-nipped as well. The rough and frozen material of my facemask chafed the wound and I could no longer wipe away nose-dribble with the back of my mitts, so a sheen of ice, constantly growing in size, covered the bottom half of my facemask, punctured only by the small hole over my mouth.

At night the act of breathing caused the worst discomfort. Generally speaking, polar travel would be quite pleasant if it was not necessary to breathe. When we tried to snuggle down inside our sleeping bags, our breath formed a thick rime of frost where it met cold air. The resulting frost layers cascaded down our necks whenever we moved. To avoid this I blocked both nostrils up with plugs of Kleenex and tried to position my mouth to breathe out of the bag's hood-hole. This worked well, except that my frostbitten nose remained outside the bag's warmth and, unprotected from the tent's average temperature of −40°C, was far colder than a deep-freeze.

A storm blew up and shattered the ice pack. All about us were vast areas of open sea where, for at least the next two months, the ice should have remained largely solid. On the coast behind us, the five-man expedition of our Norwegian rival Ragnar Thorsketh, which had announced its intention to beat us across the Arctic, were astonished to find open sea and no ice at all in sight. They made camp on the land and waited.

Simon Grimes and Karl Z'berg located the two skidoos we had abandoned along the coastline and managed to land the Twin Otter beside them. Later they delivered the skidoos and steel sledges to us on a flat floe. Overjoyed at shrugging off the harnesses, we continued by skidoo and were blessed by a patch of good going.

Still travelling at dusk, I swerved to avoid a sudden canal and drove straight into a trench full of *shuga* porridge-ice. I was flung clear and watched my skidoo sink out of sight within a minute. The steel sledge slowly up-ended, but I caught hold of its lashing strap. Charlie ran over in response to my yelling. He attempted to save our tent by removing his mitts in order to undo a lashing buckle. In seconds his fingers began to freeze and, before we could loosen the tent, the sledge disappeared underwater. We saved only our radio and theodolite.

Charlie's hands were in immediate danger. I erected a make-shift shelter from the tarpaulin with which Charlie used to cover the vehicles and started up the cooker. He spent an hour forcing blood slowly back into his hand and so saved his fingers from anything worse than painfully nipped ends. We passed an extremely uncomfortable night at −40°C under the tarpaulin with one sleeping bag between us.

Two days later Karl found a landing floe half a mile from our location and brought in a skidoo, sledge and gear from Tanquary Fiord. 'Don't sink any more skidoos,' he advised. 'That's your last.'

Forty-knot winds battered the pack and we headed north in a semi-white-out. With no visible sun, I followed my compass needle. On 16 March, with millions of tons of ice on the move all about us, we camped and lay listening to the awe-inspiring boom and crackle of invading floes. The anemometer rose to fifty-five knots and weaker pans fractured all about us, nipped and flaked by their larger jostling neighbours. One crack opened up twenty yards from our tent and cut us off on an island for a day.

Ginny warned me that the press were turning critical. In England the *Daily Mail* stated that the Transglobe sponsors were considering finding a new leader since our chances of success were looking bad. One reporter interviewed the cameraman on our 1970 Canadian expedition, who said the soldiers on that journey had mutinied and threatened me with knives. In Vancouver, a reporter pointed out that SAS members Fiennes and Burton had cleverly cut themselves off in the Arctic beyond all possible recall by their regiment for service in the Falkland Islands war, which was raging at the time.

When the storm died away we packed up in conditions of total white-out and moved off into a curtain of brown gloom, a certain sign of open water. Within minutes I narrowly missed driving into the edge of a river of moving sludge.

Charlie and I took a deep breath and spent two perilous days pussyfooting through a sludge swamp, often crossing lakes of half-inch-thick ice that writhed under our skidoos and broke under the sharp runners of the sledges. God was good to us on both days. The next two days passed by in a haze. We pushed on our bruised bodies and mutinous minds and craved more sleep.

My chin was numb one evening when I came into the tent. I must have pulled my frozen facemask off too hard. When thawing the garment out over the cooker and picking ice-bits from around the mouthpiece, I found a one-inch swatch of my beard complete with skin implanted in a bloody patch of iced wool. It took a while to detach this from the mask. Where the skin had torn away from my chin, there was an open patch of raw flesh the size of a penny. In a while my chin warmed up and bled. Then it wept liquid matter, which froze once the cooker was turned off.

On 22 March, I shot the sun with my theodolite and found the loose pack had drifted us many miles too far east. I applied a 15° westerly correction and we moved on at a good rate. My chin throbbed like a tom-tom by nightfall and, running out of antibiotic cream, I applied some pile cream.

'He's got piles on his chin,' Charlie shrieked with mirth. It was lucky we shared a weird sense of humour. Unlike during the latter part of our Antarctic crossing more than a year ago, there was now no tension between us. I hugely respected and admired his ability to suffer and keep going.

During a long axe session I cut through one of my mukluk boots, the blade slicing through the nail of my big toe and deep into the flesh beneath. Charlie bound it up with gauze liberally daubed with pile cream.

For a week we averaged fifteen miles a day, sometimes travelling for sixteen hours at a time in what we called a double-shuffle. Charlie was frost-nipped along the length of his nose and one of my eyelids puffed up with wind-burn. Navigation was becoming more or less instinctive, with or without the sun.

On 27 March, at −41°C with twenty-three knots blowing in our faces, we had to stop frequently to restore blood to our extremities. Fingers were quickly numbed by axe work. My neck glands puffed up. The whites of my eyes were blood-red. I could not navigate wearing protective goggles and the glare was intense.

A memorably evil day was 29 March, during which we pushed to the limits of skidoo travel. Streamers of brown vapour wafted through the overall fog and soft squeaking, grinding sounds emanated from the moving sludge banks we passed. To check each apparently weak section, before charging it on my skidoo, I went ahead gingerly on foot with my ice-prod. Charlie advanced halfway between me and the sledges, calling from time to time when I lost sight of him in the gloom.

When we made it at last to solid ice I felt elated. If we can cross that, I thought, we can go anywhere. We stopped at 87°02' North, within nine miles of our most northerly camp in 1977, but forty days earlier in the season. If our aim had been solely to reach the Pole, we could have felt reasonably confident.

As we crept north in early April the movement and noise of the floes increased. It seemed as though we were rushing pell-mell, caught in an unseen tidal race, towards the maw of the world, Edgar Allan Poe's 'Maelström'.

For three days the troubled fissure zone of the convergence, the area where the Beaufort Gyral current ends, slowed us to a crawl. For some time we crossed a no-man's-land where floes spun around in limbo, uncertain which way to go. Then the fringe of the transpolar drift began to take hold of all surface matter and we entered a new gyral with a strong north-easterly pull. A great deal of rubble was piled up in pyramidal heaps within this convergence and at 87°48' North we were stopped by the bulkiest wall I had ever seen in the Arctic. Rising to thirty feet high, the barrier was well over 100 yards wide. It took us four hours to axe and four to cross.

After the convergence we entered a sixty-mile region of fissures and high barriers. On 8 April we crossed sixty-two sludge cracks, often by shovelling snow into the water and then ramming the resulting weak bridge before it sank.

Twenty miles short of the Pole the going improved dramatically. At midday on 10 April, I carefully checked our noon latitude and each subsequent mile until we were at 90° North. I had no wish to overshoot the top of the world. We arrived there at 11.30 p.m. GMT and passed the news to Ginny early on Easter Day 1982. We had become the first men in the world to have travelled the earth's surface to both Poles.

Apprehension about what lay ahead overshadowed any sense of achievement that we may otherwise have felt, for the *Benjamin Bowring* was still many cold months beyond our horizon.

I aimed south along a line some 15° east of the Greenwich Meridian. We changed to a routine of travel by night and sleep by day so that the sun would project my body's shadow ahead and prove a natural sundial.

As we left the Pole, the Transglobe crew steamed from Southampton harbour *en route* for Spitsbergen. Over 1,000 miles still separated us from the latitude to which the *Benjamin Bowring* might, with luck, be expected to smash her way in August, when the pack was at its most penetrable. The *Benjamin Bowring* would not be able to penetrate heavy Arctic pack, being merely an ice-strengthened vessel, but if we could reach as far down as 81° North, she might – through the skill of her skipper and the eyes of Karl in the Twin Otter – be able to thread her way into the pack's edge.

From the Pole all went well for four days – in reality, nights – during one of which we achieved a distance of thirty-one miles in twelve hours over a freakishly unbroken pan of floes. From 88° down to 86° the conditions deteriorated slowly with an increasing number of open leads. I had grown accustomed to keeping an eye ever open for potential Twin Otter landing strips. But for the last forty miles there had been neither a single floe flat enough for a landing nor a pan solid enough to camp on safely during a storm.

The temperature rose to −20°C and stayed there. New ice no longer congealed over open leads within twenty-four hours, so wide canals with no crossing-points became permanent stoppers, not mere hold-ups. Tedious foot patrols to find crossing-points became increasingly necessary. Following a brief storm on 23 April, we axed for two hours through a forest of twelve-foot-high green rafted blocks and reached a series of winding couloirs of new ice packed with black pools of sludge.

Alongside this marsh I tripped and fell. My hands shot out to ward off a heavy fall. My axe disappeared and sank. My arms pierced the surface up to the elbows and one leg up to the knee, but the snow-covered sludge held my body weight. Seven miles later seawater cut us off in all directions except back north, so we camped. The wind blew at thirty knots and chunks of ice, floating across pools and along canals, all headed east.

That night I told Charlie I would begin to search for a floe on which to float south. He was horrified, feeling we would never reach the ship if we did not make much more southerly progress before beginning to float. Stop now, he feared, and the expedition would fail. I argued with him that wind and current should take us to 81° before winter, providing we could only locate a solid enough floe to protect us during storm-crush conditions. If we waited one day too long before locating such a floe, we could easily be cut off on a rotten pan and then there would be no answer to our predicament. Better safe than sorry. Charlie agreed to disagree. But, he reminded me, in the future – whatever happened – I should remember the decision to risk a float from so far north was mine alone.

Two days later we escaped from the weak pan and managed to progress another five miles south on increasingly thin ice before having to camp. After four days I thought the river-ice had congealed and attempted to cross by skidoo. To my surprise, my sledge runners broke through the sludge at a point where I had safely walked an hour earlier. Thereafter this sludge-river remained at the same tacky consistency, insufficient for sledge weight. The temperature rose towards 0°C and we ground to a halt.

I told Charlie we should stay on the floe and try to find the safest spot. He searched for cracks and weak points and eventually decided upon a line of hummocks along the impact point of an old pressure ridge. We flattened out the top of this high ground with axes and made a camp there.

During the first week of May, I asked Ginny to send us two light canoes and rations for a long float. She flew with Karl and Simon from Alert to the north-east corner of Greenland and at remote Cape Nord set up her last radio base. She told me that the remnants of the Norwegian expedition racing us to cross the Arctic had reached the Pole too late to continue and had been evacuated.

On 11 May, without a sound, our floe split apart 500 yards east of our tent and we lost a third of our original real-estate. Bending over the edge of the newly opened canal, I saw that our two-thirds was some five or six feet thick. I had hoped for a minimum of eight feet but – too bad – we were committed to this place.

Our tent floor of axed ice was uneven and daily became more sodden with water as the surface of the floe melted down. Soon, all about our slightly raised platform, the floe became a floating pool of vivid blue salt-water, five feet deep in places.

Late in May, two members of our London committee travelled to Spitsbergen to visit the ship. Karl flew them over the pack and, horrified at our overall predicament, they returned to London and warned the committee that our chances of success this summer were minimal. We must be airlifted out at once while such a course was still possible, or any subsequent disaster would be on their hands. Ginny queried the committee's follow-up message, a direct evacuation order, and rallied those in London who were against such a course. Only when the order had been softened to a recommendation that we abort the float, but that the final decision should be mine, did Ginny inform me.

I felt, and Charlie agreed, that there was still a strong chance of success without risking an international search-and-rescue operation, so we continued to float at the mercy of wind and current.

For five days a southerly storm blew us back towards the Pole and for several days our southerly heading veered sharply towards Siberia, but overall we continued south at a steady rate towards Fram Strait, between Greenland and Spitsbergen.

Karl managed to land on a rare mist-free day. He dropped us off two tents, two canoes and a two-month supply of rations. He warned us that in another week he would no longer be able to take off from our increasingly soggy floe. We were on our own.

On 6 June in thick fog our floe was blown against its northerly neighbour and, where the ice fronts clashed, a fifteen-foot-high wall of broken blocks reared up.

The sense of smell of the polar bear is phenomenal: they can detect a seal from ten miles away. Large males weigh half a ton, reach eight feet tall and tower to twelve feet when standing. They glide over ice quietly, yet can charge at thirty-five miles per hour.

One night in my sleeping bag I was woken by loud snuffling sounds beside my head on the other side of the tent cloth.

'Ran?' Charlie called.

Since his voice came from his own tent, I knew with a sinking feeling that he was not snuffling about outside my tent. It must be a bear. Grabbing camera and loaded revolver, I peered outside. So did Charlie, whose eyeballs grew huge as he spotted – behind my tent – a very big bear. I craned my neck and three yards away saw the face of the bear, which was licking its lips with a large black tongue. We photographed the fine animal and after a few minutes it shuffled away.

A week later another bear would not leave and showed signs of evil intent. We fired bullets and even a parachute flare over its head, but the bear only grew irritable. We agreed to shoot if it approached closer than thirty yards. It did, so I fired a bullet at its leg. The bear hesitated in mid-stride then broke sideways and loped away. There were blood splashes but no sign of a limp. Over the next few weeks many bears crossed our floe and eighteen visited our camp, tripping over our guy-ropes. This kept us from getting bored by our inactive existence.

The uncertainty of our situation, especially at times when communications blacked out, was a great strain on Ginny. She had a long history of migraines and spastic colon attacks and her life at Nord was full of pain and stress. She had no shoulder to cry on and no one from whom to seek advice. She hated this part of the expedition, but kept steadily on at her job. Late in June she made contact with the *Benjamin Bowring*. The sooner she could remove us from our floe the better, for the remnant of our floe was fast approaching a danger area known as the Marginal Ice Zone, the ice pulverisation factory of Fram Strait.

Two million square miles of the Arctic Ocean are covered by pack ice and one-third of this load is disgorged every year through Fram Strait. Very soon now our own floe would enter this bottleneck, where currents accelerate by 100 per cent and rush their fragmenting ice burden south at an incredible thirty kilometres a day. Keenly aware of our danger, the skipper and crew agreed to take a risk. Arctic pack ice is far more hazardous than the Antarctic equivalent.

On 2 July, after a game attempt, the ship was forced back some 150 miles south of our floe. On 10 July the mist cleared at noon long enough for a sun shot. After seventy days on the floe we were at 82° North. That night a chunk of two acres split off our floe. The next-door floe rode up over a forty-yard front and 80 per cent of our pan was covered in slush or water up to seven feet deep. New ridgewalls rose up daily and noisily where we struck our neighbours.

Off our seaside edges, humpback whales sang at night and huge regattas of ice sailed by before the wind. There was seldom any sign of the sun and the low-hung sky reflected the dark blotches of great expanses of open sea to the south and north of our floating raft.

Hardly a day passed without a bear visit, sometimes two. For a while they came at us from our one remaining dry side but, as this narrowed, they took to swimming across the lake that hemmed us in. At night I would awake, my heart pounding. Was it a bear close by or a new breakage of the floe? By way of an answer, more often than not came the plunging roar of many tons of ice breaking off from our floe-rim, followed by the rushing of waves striking the lead-banks.

As we approached nearer to Fram Strait, we began to gyrate like scum heading for a drain. To remind us that summer here was short, the surface of our melt-pools began to freeze over.

The *Benjamin Bowring* tried a second time to reach us in mid-July and again they failed, this time putting themselves in considerable danger. Anton Bowring recorded: '. . . hurling the ship at six- to seven-feet thick floes which are breaking without too much difficulty. But the ice is more solid and further to the south than before . . . Evening: We are stuck solid at 82°07' North, 01°20' East, 82 miles south of Ran . . . Jimmy has spotted a cracked weld.'

Cleverly the skipper rammed a low floe and managed to lift the damaged bows clear of the sea. Two engineers worked, squatting on the ice, to effect temporary repairs with welding gear.

During the last week of July our floe was daily buffeted and diminished in size. Charlie had chosen our camp spot with great skill, as it was about the only part of the floe still uncracked. But on 29 July he showed me a widening seam close beside his tent. We had been on the floe ninety-five days and our entry into the crushing zone was imminent.

I told Ginny and she spoke to the skipper. They decided to make a final dedicated push northwards. Karl flew Ginny from Greenland to Longyearbyen, where she boarded the *Benjamin Bowring*. They set out on the first day of August, our seventh month out on the pack ice, and – within twelve hours of smashing a straight route through medium pack – they reached a point forty-nine miles to our south.

Late on 2 August, after a twenty-four-hour fight north-west through heavy ice and thick fog, the skipper reported sinister signs of a wind change. The pack would close about the ship if the wind rose. Throughout the long night the skipper and crew willed the ship north yard by yard in a potentially suicidal bid to reach us.

At 9 a.m. on 3 August, Ginny spoke on my radio. She sounded tired but excited. 'We are seventeen miles south of your last reported position and jammed solid.'

Charlie and I packed basic survival gear into our two canoes. We had hoped the *Benjy B* would smash her way to our floe, but this was clearly impossible. For us to attempt to travel from our floe might easily prove disastrous, for everything was in motion about us: great floating blocks colliding in the open channels and wide skeins of porridge-ice marauding the sea lanes. At noon I took a sun shot which put us only twelve miles from the ship. A southerly wind or current could easily widen this gap. We left our bedraggled tents and I took a bearing south-east to the probable current position of the *Benjamin Bowring*. The wind blew at twelve knots as we paddled nervously through the first open lead.

Having lain in our bags with scant exercise for so long, we were unfit. Charlie was nearly sick with the sudden effort. Every so often I filled my water bottle from a melt pool and we both drank deep.

Makeshift skids attached to the canoes snapped off on rough ice and then we dragged the boats along on their thin metal hulls. Trying to negotiate a spinning mass of ice-islands in a wide lake, I glanced back and saw two high bergs crunch together with an impact that sent a surge of water towards my canoe. Luckily Charlie had not yet entered the moving corridor and so avoided being crushed.

At 7 p.m., climbing a low ridge to scout ahead, I saw an imperfection on the horizon along the line of my bearing. I blinked and it was gone. Then I saw it again – the distant masts of the *Benjamin Bowring*.

I cannot describe the feeling of that moment, the most wonderful of my life. I jumped high in the air, yelling at Charlie. He was out of earshot, but I waved like a madman and he must have guessed.

For three years I had always known our chances of overall success were heavily loaded against us. I had never dared allow myself to hope. But now I knew and I felt the strength of ten men. I knelt down on the ice and thanked God.

For three hours we heaved and paddled. Sometimes we lost sight of the masts, but when they reappeared they were always a little bigger.

At fourteen minutes past midnight on 4 August at 80°31' North, 00°59' West, all but astride the Greenwich Meridian, we climbed on board the *Benjamin Bowring*.

Ginny was standing alone by a cargo hatch. We hugged each other as though we would never let go. Her eyes were full of tears, but she was smiling. Between us we had spent twenty years of our lives to reach this point, the fulfilment of her dream.

Revelry lasted well into the night. There was no hurry now, which was just as well because the ship remained stuck fast for twelve days, until the wind changed.

From the lonely islands of Spitsbergen we steamed south through the Greenland Sea and the North Sea. On 29 August, Prince Charles joined us on the Thames and brought the ship back to our starting-point at Greenwich, almost three years to the day since we had set out. Ten thousand cheering people lined the banks. Our polar circle around the world was complete.

That night, when all the crew and our friends had gone, Ginny and I slept in our old cabin. I watched as she fell asleep and the lines of stress fell away from her face. I felt as happy as I had ever been.

Erling Kagge
Norwegian polar explorer and author

I have heard sensible people compare risky expeditions to playing with death and I can understand why they think that such undertakings are meaningless.

After all, it can seem absurd to expose oneself willingly to extreme cold, hunger and uncertainty – but to go on an expedition to the North Pole as Ran has done so many times is not to play with death. It is the opposite. It is about willingly making life more difficult – and living a little more fully.

Somehow Ran is in a paradise, with each step, when he walks towards the North Pole. He is being moved when he is moving. Ran seeks out dangers because the experience of intense situations such as' facing a polar bear or a heavy snowstorm, and his ability to overcome them, feels like a confirmation of his own vitality.

Suddenly you are present in your own life, in your own strange paradise, unlike Adam and Eve's paradise, which must have been the most boring place ever.

A few dozen seconds stretch out like an eternity. Only the present moment matters when you are freezing cold, hungry and worried about the pack ice breaking apart. The present moment and eternity are not necessarily opposites. Time ceases, and both can be experienced at once.

What I like most of all with Ran is his attitude – he keeps on putting one leg in front of the other until he nearly collapses. The pleasure, the exhaustion and the absurdity of walking towards the North Pole are all blending together in one man. Ran wears himself out because he wants to, not because he has to.

He is a moving reminder of the fact that a practical *I walk* prefaces the Cartesian statement, *therefore I am.*

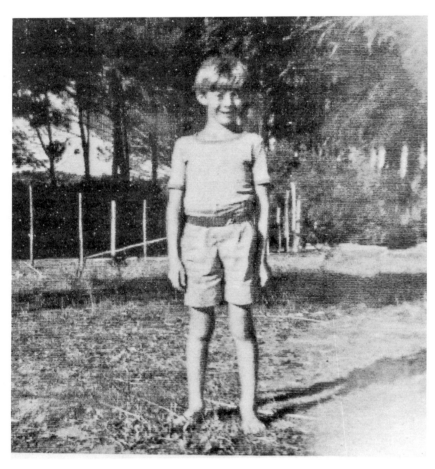

Ran aged about seven in Constantia Valley, in the Western Cape province of South Africa, where he spent his childhood from 1947 to 1954.

6

South Africa

*A childhood in Constantia in the
Western Cape province
1947–1954*

*R*anulph *Fiennes was born in Windsor, Berkshire, in March
1944, nearly four months after the death of his father,
Lieutenant-Colonel Sir Ranulph-Twisleton-Wykeham-Fiennes,
2nd Bt, from his war wounds in Naples, Italy. Ran inherited his
father's title, becoming the 3rd Baronet of Banbury. At first he
lived with his mother, Audrey, and his three elder sisters in
Sunningdale, Berkshire, at the home of their grandmother
Florrie, who had grown up in Constantia, Cape Province, in
South Africa.*

*After the end of the Second World War, during which Florrie
had lost both her husband and son, she made the decision to leave
England and return home, taking her daughter-in-law and four
grandchildren with her.*

In her eightieth year, when I was two and a half, Granny Florrie
decided to return to South Africa. There was nothing left for her
in England after my father and grandfather had gone, and
perhaps she wanted to die in her homeland. But she did not
mention this. All the talk was positive – a new house, a new life.
The idea rejuvenated Florrie and my mother was carried along

in her wake, as were all the furnishings from Sunningdale and we four children.

We crossed the Line on board the good ship *Capetown Castle*, passing the voyage in deck quoits, gin rummy and bingo sessions. An extremely smart widow of Granny Florrie's acquaintance, Mrs Hambro, happened to sail with us. One day, when I was left unattended in her cabin, I located her resurrection box, removed a porcelain pot of scented rouge and liberally rouged everything within three feet of the ground – clothes, shoes, bed, carpet and toiletry. My mother had a deal of explaining to do and must have regretted leaving our old Nurse Wells behind in Surrey.

We arrived in Table Bay at dawn on 23 January 1947. Apart from Granny Florrie (who always wore voluminous apparel), we looked like refugees direct from Belsen, or so my mother was told later: obviously rationing had been very much a reality back in post-war England.

A tall, handsome man wearing a small suit and a bow tie welcomed us to our new country. This was Richard Butters, the first of a great many cousins we were to meet. Turning to me, he asked Granny, 'And what is her name?' Granny exploded, for she was proud of her only grandson. 'But,' protested the cousin, 'how can you blame anyone for mistaking his sex when you doll his curly hair up with these long blue ribbons?' The ribbons, the height of Sunningdale kiddies' fashion, were removed that very evening, never to be worn again.

Richard Butters, who became a friend for life, drove us from Cape Town to Wynberg through avenues of oak and creeping plumbago, past wide suburban gardens bright with mimosa, hibiscus and oleander. Every bungalow seemed to have a pool, with children who splashed, shouting, in the rainbows of garden sprinklers. Beyond Wynberg the gardens gave way to vineyards and to pine woods with a strong whiff of resin. The soil was rich and the horizons bounded by wild mountains.

The Brommersvlei Road led us deep into rolling vine country, through narrow friendly lanes, some of tarmac, some of dirt. Richard turned round and smiled at our wondering faces. 'This is Constantia, the Valley of the Vines, where our family lives – the most beautiful place in the world.' And it was.

He took us to a white homestead on high ground at the head of an oak-lined drive. Les Marais was 100 years old or more. Rock doves murmured from a cote in the cobbled stable yard and sun birds whistled in mulberry trees around the parched lawn. The walls were thick, busy with columns of ants that followed long cracks in the mortar and with darting predator lizards. Inside, behind the red-tiled stoeps covered in grapevine and the heavy lace curtains, it was drowsy cool.

There were thirty-three cousins, most of whom lived, in happy harmony, in or near Constantia. All were descended from the marriage between Johannes Rathfelder, of Prussian descent, and a Scottish lady, 'Miss MacFarlane'. His butcher's shop in Wynberg had earned a handsome income from the British Army during the Boer War. With the proceeds they bought the valley of Constantia, which Johannes first put to the vine and later divided between his brother and his children.

Brother Danny owned a magnificent pub in nearby Diep River and had never married. Then came Aunt Ethel, who had married a Mr Marais, after whom she named the white homestead where we were lodged on our arrival. Between Ethel and Florrie there was Stenie, once known in the Cape as a beauty, who had married an English millionaire named Taylor. Finally there was Otto Rathfelder, whose wife, Aunt Evie, lived at the crown of her combe with one unmarried daughter. In the yard of her dark homestead, Belle Ombre, stood a slave-bell that still rang on special occasions, though no longer to call slaves in from the vines.

Aunt Evie was still feuding with Aunt Ethel over an ancient water rights quarrel, and, although they were neighbours, the two women would not speak to each other. Now that Florrie had returned to the valley with her daughter-in-law and grandchildren, the clan decided to hold a Great Tea Party at Les Marais to welcome the prodigal home. Aunt Evie and Aunt Ethel were both invited, and at last resolved their differences over suckling pig and trifle.

A Great Business Meeting followed the Great Tea Party, and Granny Florrie was given three acres of Aunt Ethel's vineyard not a mile from Les Marais and close to the Vlei, the marshy land around the valley's stream where the Cape Coloured folk lived in small shacks under a clump of pine trees. The Cape Coloureds were the largest ethnic group in the Western Cape, with ancestral links that included European settlers, indigenous Khoi, San and Xhosa people, and slaves from the Dutch East Indies.

Granny took us to her new plot and, with a great deal of gesturing, described her plans for the house, which was to be called Broughton, the name of the Fiennes family castle back in England. Until it was built we had no home and we soon moved to St James, a quiet resort on the Cape coast, where we rented a house belonging to one of our cousins.

My sisters were sent to school, so I was the sole charge of our English nanny, Nurse Ella Ritson. At just three years old, I was known as the naughtiest boy at St James. We went for afternoon walks on a sandy beach where there were pretty shells and bewitching rock pools, and I would scream when the time came to go home. When Nurse Ritson took my hand, I would go limp, forcing her to drag a dead weight. When she lifted me up, I would scratch at her face, even bite her hands. At other times I loved her dearly and told her so.

Sometimes Granny drove us to watch our Constantia home taking shape on the hill above the vineyards. Broughton cost £17,000 to build – a great deal of money in 1948 – and Granny Florrie was immensely proud of it. When we finally moved in, she entertained almost daily, serving tea and fine-cut brown sandwiches to every relative or past acquaintance she could summon.

Granny Florrie advertised in the Vlei for a staff of three full-time servants: cook, housemaid and gardener. Mary the maid and Christine the cook, both local Cape Coloureds whose families had at some stage settled in the Constantia Vlei, stayed with us from the beginning. The gardeners, who lived in a small summerhouse-cum-toolshed in the garden, either died or disappeared.

The first was John, who wore a tweed cap day and night. As a four-year-old, I would listen for hours to stories of his travels around the Cape. In the pine woods beside Broughton he stashed an old cooking-oil container in which he fermented grapes. This he called *dagga* and said I should tell no one of its presence. John never washed, and he smoked homemade tobacco in an old briar. The sweet, pungent smell lingered in the summerhouse long after he had left us, suddenly and without collecting his pay, never to return.

Abner appeared the very next day, a tall Xhosa from Transkei, not a Cape Coloured at all, which was rare in those parts. For a year he stayed with us, but one hot day when the dry Berg wind withered lawns and flowers he failed to appear as usual. I found him curled up on the summerhouse floor under empty potato sacks, his black face shining with sweat. He seemed frightened of me, his lips curled back in snarling rictus, and he ignored me when I poured water into his mug from a clay pitcher.

I fetched Mary the maid, who first spoke to him, then shouted. He muttered a reply, not looking at her. His voice was quite changed from its usual deep, proud Xhosa tones, more like a febrile old man. Mary took me away abruptly, one firm hand around my wrist. 'You *not* go back in there.' Later my mother called a doctor and, on his advice, the local priest. 'There is nothing I can do,' he said after visiting Abner. 'The witch doctor has said that he will die, and *he* believes it. I have seen this many times before.'

Abner's mysterious illness cleared up as suddenly as it had arrived and he remained at Broughton until two years after we left the house, though the new owners later told my mother that he had once again received a witch doctor's curse and died in hospital of an indeterminate sickness.

When children from the Vlei came up to Broughton with messages for Mary or Christine, I waited at the end of our drive to intercept them. There were no white children of my age in the valley except cousin Bella Rathfelder, who cried all the time. Soon the Cape Coloured boys took me to their homes and showed me how to play Pooh sticks under the plank-bridge by their stream.

Over the next four years our gang often roamed the valley together, avoiding the Tokai Forest, with its baboons and packs of wild dogs. Bamboo spears and short leather straps to whip the dirt were *de rigueur* and I became co-leader of the gang along with a one-armed lad named Archie. For some reason, Granny Florrie called me 'Bay' not Ranulph, and whenever I appeared at the Vlei my friends danced out of their homes, shouting rhythmically: 'Bay, Bay, Stick fer may' – 'Bee, Bee, sting me'.

At Christmastime Granny Florrie gave everyone from the Vlei a present and the children sang carols in the shade of the stoep with its halo of coral-blue agapanthus and red-hot pokers in place of snow and stars.

From Broughton we could see west across the vineyards to Les Marais and Belle Ombre, and north to the ramparts of Table Mountain, Devil's Peak and Lion's Drift. A sandy lane wound through the vineyards behind the Vlei and I loved to walk along it with my mother – preferably without my sisters, because then I had all her attention. Sometimes these walks took us to Les Marais where Cookie, as old as Auntie Ethel, would bring us lemonade in a jar beneath a beaded lace square, and delectable cinnamon crumble.

I began to go daily to the Little People's School in Wynberg, which was mainly attended by Boer children. The dreadful Alan Read and his cronies chased and beat me with bamboo canes, no matter how much I tried to maintain a low profile. Eventually, I was removed to a school called Forres, run by two dear old ladies who did 'not *tolerate* bullying of any sort'.

In fact, there was as much bullying as there had been at the Little People's School, but the Forres monster, Lionel Gertz, warned his victims that, should they tell, their lives would become one long nightmare. Unable to tell my mother or the headmistresses – I was as mesmerised by fear as the next boy – I began to give Gertz my prize marbles, catapult, biltong sticks, anything to placate him. Eventually Gertz left and I have only happy memories of Forres after that. Apart from standard academic lessons, the school emphasised handicrafts. I have long been thankful for the lessons in raffia-work, egg- and teapot-cosy making and, above all, darning and sewing.

Mark Charnock, a Forres friend and fellow six-year-old, often came home with me at weekends and joined in the patrols of the Vlei gang. The Cape Coloured children were skilled at hitting moving targets with their bamboo spears and, although not up to their standards, Mark and I would practise on the lawn, away from others. Taking turns, one of us would throw six spears at the other as he ran across a fifty-yard patch. The 'target' would hold a dustbin lid for protection as he ran.

One Sunday after church, I hit Mark in the eye with a sharpened bamboo. I was horrified. So was my mother. I was locked in my bedroom and my mother beat me with a cane, as my father would have done – but, I suspect, rather less effectively. Two weeks later, we breathed again. Mark's sight had been saved, and in time his scars improved.

Gillian, my third sister, was five years my senior, and at twelve was already showing great talent on a horse. Cousin Richard and his wife Joyce across the valley owned a popular riding school, where their daughter Gonda was the star attraction. For the next twenty-five years cousin Gonda Butters, as Gonda Betrix, was to shine as South Africa's top eventer and showjumper, outperforming even Britain's Pat Smythe in the days before South Africa was banned from competing in international events. But my sister

Gill, on her Anglo-Arab named Quita, was Gonda's equal at local gymkhanas, and I idolised her. I was given a Zulu pony named Zimba, but I preferred to run barefoot in the sand, so the neglected pony was resold.

Celia, my middle sister, was eight years older than me, and Susan an impossible ten years older, so we could hardly play together. Aunt Evie often asked us down to Belle Ombre to swim in the homestead pool. Although the pool was cleaned every few years, the water was ink green and the sides of the pool slippery with slime. My sisters happily swam in this fetid tank, but I went along to catch toads in my butterfly net.

All around the pool were gazanea, wild nerine and white moon-flowers. Clusters of weaver-bird nests hung from bamboo groves. Birds chattered, frogs croaked, and sisters splashed, so nobody heard when I took a swipe at a crouching toad and missed. Unable to swim, I struggled and sank into the wet murk. By chance Susan saw my hair surface and shouted to the others. She then plunged in and rescued me.

Through the early Broughton years, Granny Florrie went from strength to strength. One of her chief pleasures was family feuding. When Aunts Ethel and Evie both died, Florrie became quite senior in the valley. There had long been talk of relatives who by night removed boundary markers between the vineyards, and one cousin, Joy Packer, had written a colourful novel, *The Valley of the Vines*, encapsulating the various intrigues. The apparent equivalents of Aunts Ethel and Evie were given disguises as thin as cling-wrap, and well-publicised controversy amused the family for many months, doubtless boosting the book's sales locally.

At midnight one New Year's Eve an especially spirited cousin, Googie Marais, whose land lay to the north-east, conducted the traditional 'Beating the Bounds' ceremony by firing his rifle at our roof. The impact was intended to arouse Florrie's wrath, but Googie hit the wrong end of the house and panicked a temporary nanny, who packed her bags and left us the very next day.

In October 1950 Florrie suffered a stroke, and a nurse watched by her bedside for eight weeks. She died quietly in the house she loved and was mourned by everyone in the valley. The funeral was held in the Anglican church in Constantia, although our normal place of worship was St Saviour's in Claremont, where the priest, Canon Wade, had two skinny little daughters. The younger, Virginia, later became an English tennis star.

With the wonderfully strong spirit of Florrie Fiennes at rest, there was nothing to keep my mother in South Africa. The call of England was strong, but the family's funds were partially tied up in Broughton. Susan was studying for her degree at Cape Town University and my other two sisters were preparing to matriculate. My mother felt it best that we stay in South Africa four more years.

My mother was fervently involved with a then relatively docile anti-apartheid movement known as Black Sash. She drove into Cape Town and helped collect 90,000 signatures on behalf of black people's rights. She also gave her entire personal wealth to a project called Cafda Village towards rehousing 2,000 poor blacks from the Windermere district.

When Granny was alive, we had never travelled far from Constantia. Now my mother decided the family should see the Kruger National Park, so, with a couple of friends and all the girls, she headed north-east. I was too young for the long journey and spent the holiday with a schoolfriend, James, by the sea. The memory of an incident at that time will remain etched in my brain as long as I live, as clear a vignette as that painted by Camus with his seaside murder in *L'Etranger*.

Making castles in the hot white sand at Betty's Bay, I watched a fat man rise sweating from his beach chair and trudge slowly into the breakers with his surfboard. He ducked and porpoised to less broken water further out, and I forgot him until his wife awoke and found him missing. I can see her homely face now as I pointed for her. Her husband was by then only a dark speck in the sea.

A rescue boat was launched but they brought the man back dead, for he had let go of his board. Perhaps he had suffered a heart attack. When I smell seaweed or feel the heat of a long white beach, I sometimes hear the racking sobs of the woman as she knelt by the sandy body of her man.

Once away from school, James and I were no longer friends. We fought and threw rocks at each other, so his mother telephoned my aunt in nearby Kommetie Sands. This Aunt 'Utcha' was Granny Florrie's daughter by her first marriage, to an Englishman who fell off his horse while hunting and died in her arms. Utcha lived with her thirty-year-old son Michael on a chicken farm, and I went to stay with them.

Michael would wake me at 5 a.m. and let me hold the kerosene lamp as he moved about fascinating sheds full of the weirdest chicken smells. The woods above Wenga chicken farm were wild and tangled all the way down to the empty dunes beside the Atlantic. Sometimes, resting on hot afternoons, I could hear the thunderous boom of breakers above the happy cluck-cluck of the free-range hens.

The girls, back at Broughton after their holiday, bubbled with stories of hippo, impala and kuda, of lion and elephant. I sulked, for nobody cared a jot about the wonderful Wenga chickens, nor even how I had hit James's head from ten yards with a rock and made him bleed. Susan was the worst, for she had entered the boyfriend stage with a vengeance and made it plain that little brothers were to be neither seen nor heard when her men were at Broughton – which was most of the time. Two of her boyfriends, probably on her instructions, rolled me all the way down the stairs in a linen-basket and, one afternoon, locked me in the upstairs bathroom.

Down in the Vlei, I exhorted the valley gang to ambush these boyfriends, but even one-armed Archie, who feared nothing, failed to react. At only seventeen, Susan became the youngest student on record to obtain a Bachelor of Arts degree from Cape Town University. She left home for a tour of Europe with a

Rathfelder cousin and then to stay with family friends in England.

In 1952, when I was eight, I became a boarder at Western Province Preparatory School. My cousin Nicky Taylor went with me. In later years he became the Elvis Presley of South Africa, though he was not popular with the government because of his political lyrics.

At school it is best to conform and try to blend in with the herd, as any individualistic trait is a red rag to the bullies. I found it immensely embarrassing that, by parental order, I was to study Latin while my peers learned to chatter away in Afrikaans. The school was proud of its cricketing record, but I soon found that my eye was almost as slow as my reactions. Mathematics were utterly beyond my grasp, but I excelled at Divinity and I could fight rather better than most of my contemporaries owing to my Vlei experiences.

I enjoyed the weekly official game of *Skop die Blijk* or Kick the Can, in which two large teams attacked each other inside a forest adjacent to the school. The school staff also organised an indoor, nocturnal version called 'British Bulldog'. All the boarders were divided equally between two classrooms at either end of a long concrete corridor. Each team formed offensive and defensive patrols and, in the pitch dark, attempted to imprison in its room as many boys from the other team as possible. After thirty minutes, the masters switched on the lights and congratulated the winners after a head count of prisoners.

During the nightmarish half-hour, all side-doors were locked to prevent reluctant boys from creeping into a haven. This vicious struggle in the dark produced an impressive crop of cuts, bruises and worse, and was intended to be character-building. Had he but known of it, Kurt Hahn would doubtless have included the activity in the Gordonstoun programme.

For a treat on my ninth birthday, I was allowed a gang battle in Tokai woods, using the great sticky fir cones called donnerballs as ammunition. One boy was struck at by a rat-snake, but we all agreed it was the best party we could remember. Afterwards at Broughton my mother arranged a more normal celebration with an iced cake and candles.

Despite Mark Charnock's eye, my mother was patient with the valley gang and my rowdy schoolfriends. However, she was allergic to guns of any sort. Three times during our Constantia years she caught me pointing a toy gun at someone and without ado beat my backside with a cane. But the worst occasion did not involve a cap-gun.

One day, annoyed with Christine the cook for withholding a chocolate cake, I took my father's wartime pistol and threatened her: her life or the cake. Instead of complying, our plump cook backed up against the Aga, her eyes bulging. Ella Fitzgerald would have been proud of her sound effects. Shocked, I escaped to the woods, where a posse of women – my mother, Celia, Gill and Christine – quickly brought me to justice. The penalty for this armed hold-up was six hard strokes of the cane and no supper, let alone chocolate cake. Also 500 lines: 'Never, never let your gun pointed be at anyone.'

With Archie and the others from the Vlei – eight in all plus two mongrel dogs – I often wandered for aimless hours through vineyard and wood. We called ourselves the Mealie Gang, because our favourite meeting place was in a high field of Indian maize or 'mealies'. If anyone in Constantia objected to our ethnically mixed and barefoot band of local boys with their curious customs, they showed no sign of it. Apartheid did not seem to touch pre-teenagers, at any rate not in the valley.

One afternoon at grape-picking time, Archie ran into the clearing by the Vlei huts where the gang played marbles. 'They are taking the dead thief to your mum, Bay. You'd better go quick.'

My sisters were out riding, but I found my mother, flanked by Christine and Mary, near our boundary gate listening to a large Cape Coloured man with a knobkerrie stick. Beside him a colleague held the bloody neck of an unfortunate Zulu man in an

120

arm lock. Blood welled from the open wounds on their prisoner's head and cheeks. Each time the knobkerrie man's voice rose, his colleague dashed their prisoner's head against our wrought-iron gate as though to emphasise the point.

Christine told my mother that the man had stolen clothes from a nearby hamlet and that all the inhabitants had gone out into the countryside to find the thief. These two had just caught him hiding in our wood. My mother must call the police. This she did and the thief was taken away, still bleeding freely. My mother must have been shaken by this glimpse of the valley's less serene face, but she never admitted her concern in front of us.

Every century in Cape Town a magnificent festival is held to celebrate the founding of the Dutch Cape Colony under Jan van Riebeek in 1652. I was taken to Cape Town in 1952 to see the exhibitions and funfairs. A Scottish friend of my mother's, a stout-hearted widow who brooked no feebleness in life, devoted her day to giving me a good time but was disgusted when, terrified, I refused to take a ride in a rickshaw pulled by a giant Zulu clad in ostrich feathers, cow-horns and beads. Afterwards the good lady had serious words with my mother. I was obviously spoiled or over-cossetted and, as a result, of a timid disposition that would do me no good when the time came to face the world beyond my mother's apron strings.

In 1954, Celia matriculated with the highest possible grade and my mother took us all on a holiday within the Cape. She drove our battered Chevrolet through the dusty Karoo and the dark mystery of the Titsikama Forest. We stayed for a while in picturesque spots called Allan and George, and spent the first week of May in and around Ceres, the most beautiful countryside I have ever seen.

Streams and rocks, fern and oakwood graced the mountain valleys. There were hidden pools rimmed with canna and arum lilies, where bees droned and honeybirds darted. On the lower slopes, glades of glorious protea bloomed above a mat of morning glory. The distance south to the sea was blue with haze and green with vines. Inland the Drakensberg range underpinned the huge sky with its western ridges.

We idled east to Assegaibosch, the lowest valley in the country, where the mechanic's wireless in a roadside garage announced that Dien Bien Phu had fallen the previous day and that food rationing was about to end in Britain. At Outshoorn, where the land was Karoo dry and the air clogged with dust, we gaped at the burly Boers who could carry 300-pound tins full of honey around the Bee Farm. Next door at the Ostrich Farm, signs in English and Afrikaans warned: 'Keep clear of the big chickens' legs. They kick worser than a donkie.' In a special corral, brave Celia paid a tikki and rode a saddled big chicken round and round in the sawdust.

Back at school, John Stansbury, the severe-faced headmaster who beat me from time to time for good reason, awarded me the Divinity Prize. I decided to become a priest. But in September that year all saintly notions ended when the weekend film show ran a Pathé News account of the ascent of Mount Everest. Somehow I was left for years with the muddled impression that Mr Hillary and a Chinese friend had been sent up this great mountain, higher even than Table Mountain, as a wedding present for the English Queen. I, too, would become a climber of mountains and stick the British flag into fierce features of far-flung landscapes.

My mother had been brought up in another era and in different circumstances. She had married at nineteen and left her protected family environment without knowing how to boil an egg or iron a shirt. When Granny Florrie died, my mother was on her own for the first time, with nobody to turn to for advice. She could not count on the family finances to deal with life and education. Memories of my father were too strong for her to accept the various eligible proposals that came her way, but she must have often wondered whether she could continue to cope alone with the future.

In 1954 we left Constantia to travel on the liner *Winchester*

Castle back to Southampton in England. On the last night, with the house stripped of its furniture, I looked up from my bedroom window to the high slopes north of the valley and saw red tongues of fire about Tokai – summer conflagrations that blackened the woods for thousands of acres and scattered ash on our vines.

I promised to write to Archie and the Vlei gang, but I don't think I ever did.

On the Transglobe Expedition in 1979, our ship *Benjamin Bowring* anchored in Saldanha, near Cape Town, to take on fresh water. We stayed for two weeks in Cape Town to mount an export sales-orientated exhibition of our equipment, one of eight such events to be held during the course of the voyage. On a free evening I drove to Constantia with my wife Ginny and visited our old house, built by Granny Florrie thirty-four years before.

Nothing was as I remembered it. The valley was no longer the wild and wonderful place of my dreams. Residential expansion had tamed and suburbanised the woods and vineyards. The Vlei where I had roamed with Archie and the gang was now a row of neat bungalows for foreign embassy staff. Our own house, Broughton, was a transitory post for US Marines on leave and nobody had tended to the garden in years. There was no longer a view of the valley, for Granny Florrie's shrubs had flourished unchecked and the four little palm trees named after my sisters and me were now roof-high.

We wandered in silence through the old vegetable patch. No trace remained of the summerhouse, a place of bewitching memories. My mother's rockery, tended with so much care and love, had run amok. Up the valley, beside a building lot where caterpillar trucks were at work, we called on my cousin Googi Marais, whose rifle bullets at night had once caused our English nanny to pack her bags and flee. Googi was now crippled with arthritis, but he and his wife gave us tea and filled me in on the past quarter-century of happenings in our valley.

Over the next ten days I was reunited with twenty-two other cousins, one of whom, an alderman of Cape Town, showed me a family tree which proved he and I shared a close relationship with Karl Marx. I regret not having taken away a copy to shock the family back in England.

Levison Wood
Explorer and writer

As a true pioneer of our time, Sir Ranulph Fiennes has pushed the boundaries of human exploration and endurance to unfathomable limits. His ground-breaking expeditions have redefined what is possible, but have also ignited a fire within the hearts of those seeking their own extraordinary journeys.

What sets Fiennes apart is not only his awe-inspiring physical feats, but his unwavering commitment to raising awareness about important global issues, highlighting the importance of preserving our planet for future generations and raising millions for charity in the process.

Ranulph Fiennes has left an indelible mark on the world of exploration. His expeditions have inspired a sense of wonder and wanderlust in the hearts of countless individuals, challenging them to dream bigger, explore further, and make a difference in the world.

I have been fortunate enough to meet the great man on several occasions, and his words have been a guiding light in my own exploratory endeavours. His audacious journeys have taught me the value of pushing beyond my comfort zone, embracing uncertainty, and finding solace in the unknown.

What I have always found most impressive is his aura of calm confidence, humility and sense of humour. Moreover, his unwavering commitment to the belief in the potential for exploration to encourage personal growth has instilled in me a deep sense of self-belief and positivity.

As I embark on my own adventures, I am forever grateful for the guidance and inspiration that Ranulph Fiennes has provided. He has shown me that there are no limits to what can be achieved with determination, courage, and a burning passion for exploration.

May his legacy continue to inspire generations to come, reminding us to embrace the unknown and dare to dream the impossible.

In front of the Pyramids of Giza on the Egyptian leg of his seven marathons in seven days on seven continents with Mike Stroud, 2003.

7

Seven Marathons

*Ranulph Fiennes and Mike Stroud run seven
marathons in seven days on seven continents
2003*

*I*n February 2000, Ran tried to complete the final polar grail of
reaching the North Pole solo and unsupported along the North
American route. After a few days, however, his sledge fell into the
Arctic sea, along with all his food, fuel and communications gear.
Lying on the ice, Ran removed the mitt from his left hand so that
he could untangle a rope and pull the heavy sledge out of the
water. Afterwards his fingers felt numb, but soon he had such
severe frostbite that he had to abandon the whole attempt.

Back home, the ends of his fingers became mummified, but he
was told it would be five months before surgeons could safely
amputate them. After four months, Ran could not wait any longer,
so he sawed off the dead ends from all five digits on his left hand.
The remaining bits of dead finger were amputated weeks later.
Unable to mount any new expeditions for the foreseeable future,
he turned his attention to writing books.

In 2003, he was nearing the end of his biography of Captain
Scott, when he decided he needed a complete change of activity.
He phoned his friend Dr Mike Stroud, with whom he had crossed
Antarctica ten years earlier, and Stroud suggested they should run
seven marathons on each of the world's seven continents in seven

days. They would need to start in Antarctica and it would be good if they could finish the challenge by joining an official marathon in somewhere like New York.

Ran liked the idea enormously, so the two of them set about getting the sponsorship and logistics in place, while training seriously for the running ahead of them.

The day after I finished the final corrections to the text of my Scott biography, I was due to give a talk to a convention in Dunblane, so I told Ginny I would see her the following morning and I drove to Bristol Airport, arriving at the departure desk of the no-frills airline, Go, in good time. I boarded the aircraft and settled down to read a magazine. I can remember nothing that happened from that moment for the next three days and nights.

Apparently not more than a few minutes before take-off, I collapsed noiselessly and was dragged into the aisle, where a passenger with medical training gave me instant mouth-to-mouth cardiac resuscitation. The pilot called the fire service, and the fire engine accelerated across the tarmac to drop off two firemen recently trained in the use of the mobile defibrillator, which they carried on board. They applied a powerful 200-joule DC electric shock that passed right across my chest to depolarise every cell in my heart. This caused my natural pacemaker to recover and my heart was once more a regularly beating pump.

Deeply unconscious, I was then rushed to a waiting ambulance. Twice more on the journey to Bristol's Royal Infirmary and three more times in the Accident & Emergency unit I lapsed back into fibrillation. The stabilising drugs I was given proved ineffective, but the doctors managed in due course to stabilise my condition. Fearful that I would have further attacks, however, they sent me to surgery. Within just two hours of my initial collapse, I was on cardiac bypass with a machine artificially pumping and refrigerating my blood.

A consultant cardiologist, Dr Tim Cripps, commented to me much later, 'Out of the hundred thousand people a year in the UK who have a cardiac arrest, the first and only warning they get is the attack itself and only very few are lucky enough to be near a defibrillator and someone who knows how to use it.' After treating me to some examples of others who had not been so lucky, he went on, 'When you arrived in our ICU you were measured at four points on the Glasgow Coma Scale. The lowest the scale goes is level three, which Richard Hammond of *Top Gear* achieved after his car crash at 260 mph.'

Dr Cripps called the senior Bristol cardiac surgeon, Gianni Angelini, who subsequently wrote:

I was informed at my home and when I arrived was told it was quite bad . . . The situation was so urgent that we decided to go ahead and open his chest even prior to the arrival of the perfusion team . . . Two bypass grafts were performed, one using an artery called the internal mammary artery, which is behind the breastbone, the other a long segment of vein from the leg. There was serious concern about his neurological state, since we didn't know the extent and duration of his cardiac arrest at the airport and thereafter. He was kept sedated for 24 hours . . . Then woken up . . . From then on it became rather difficult to manage him, since he virtually refused any analgesia, saying he did not have a great deal of pain. And that he wanted the tubes and lines removed as soon as possible because he had to walk up and down the corridor. He was discharged five days after surgery.

Ginny had sat by my bedside day and night and watched my tube-fed, artificially ticking body, blood-smeared in places, lying in front of her for more than three days. Every now and again a nurse would enter and thump my knee or foot for a reaction. None came. This could not have been a good time for Ginny. When I eventually came to, we kissed as best we could and she told me that I had had a heart attack. It took a while to work out what she was saying and where I was. My chest had been opened up from top to bottom and later sewn up with silver wire, the knots of which I can still feel jutting proud just beneath my skin.

Leaning on Ginny's shoulder, once the pipes and tubes had all been removed from various places, I managed to walk a few paces but felt extremely sore. Ginny drove me home the next day and put me to bed with strict instructions not to move. I asked for chocolate, but she said I was never to eat chocolate again.

Some years later Mike Stroud wrote about my attack in his book *Survival of the Fittest*:

I immediately rang the hospital intensive-care unit to send best wishes to Ran and his wife Ginny. She must have been incredibly distressed, and she now faced a future without the man who had matured from childhood sweetheart into a husband and long-standing expedition partner. But although concern for them both was uppermost in my mind, I have to admit that, for me, Ran's condition also raised practical issues, because with Ran in a coma in intensive care, all thought and planning that had gone into our seven marathons project seemed to have come to nought.

This did not, however, reckon with Ran's resilience. On the fourth day after his surgery, he rang me.

'Mike?'

I immediately recognised his voice.

'Ran, how are you? How's Ginny? How's—?' My flurry of surprise was swiftly interrupted.

'Mike, I can't chat for long but I'm fine. Don't cancel anything for now.'

I guessed immediately what he was referring to, but I needed to be absolutely certain.

'You mean the marathons?'

'Yes,' he replied. 'I've been told there was a little damage so I don't see—'

'What? You mean your doctors say it's okay?' I interrupted. 'No, no,' he responded, whispering. 'I haven't asked them yet.'

Our conversation ran on for a couple more minutes, but at the end I was clear. Ran was in cloud-cuckoo-land and his specialist would soon bring him down to earth.

Then five days later he rang again.

'How's it going? When will you be home?' I started.

'Oh, very soon,' he came back, a slight laugh in his voice. 'I'm just walking off the moor.'

When it came to confessing my future marathon intentions, I had hopes that my surgeon Professor Angelini would be sympathetic. After all, he still held the Italian 800 metres record. However, I decided to approach the topic cautiously. Here is his account of his response:

I saw RF in my office for the usual post-operative check-up and he told me it was his intention to run a marathon. He asked my opinion and I said, as much as I liked running myself, I have never had a patient who had asked me a question like can I run a marathon after a heart operation. I told him he probably could, given the fact that his coronaries were now pretty well sorted out. However, I would advise him not to run in a competitive fashion. What he failed to tell me was that his intention was to run seven marathons in seven days on seven continents. Something which I would strongly advise not to do!

Meanwhile, the cardiologist, Dr Tim Cripps, decided that his colleague, Dr David Smith in Exeter, would be best qualified to decide whether or not I should be allowed to try to run a marathon, since he knew a lot more about sports cardiology. David, who was a frequent running partner and good friend to both Mike Stroud and myself and had been my team leader on the 1998 Moroccan Eco-Challenge, checked my post-operative angiograms with care and said it would be okay to run non-competitively provided I kept my heart rate low.

For my own part, I decided to see if the sponsors of our marathon project, Land Rover, would be prepared to postpone everything for a year. They were then owned by Ford, who decided that postponement was not on the cards. I must teach myself to run again in three and a half months. The bottom line, I decided, was to give it a go and if I couldn't do it, Mike would have to go solo.

So I started to walk, very slowly, on mostly flat ground, and whenever I became breathless or felt giddy, I lay down on the ground until I felt better. Sometimes, if I tripped on uneven ground, my chest hurt where the rib-cage had been slit open and it felt as though the wire ties had torn.

I took a mobile phone on each outing and kept calling or being called by Ginny. After a while she agreed that I was approaching things in a slower, more controlled manner than she had thought possible and did not seem worried by the marathon plan which, unlike most previous projects with Mike, would only last a week. Our charity, which we chose ourselves this time, was the British Heart Foundation, who support the placement of out-of-hospital defibrillators, like the one that saved me. Mike also decided, with Ginny's enthusiastic approval, to take one with us on each run.

My recovery programme, also carefully planned with Ginny's approval, stated:

3 weeks after op: walk for 5 minutes with stops, lie down when giddy
8 weeks after op: walk for 30 minutes, no stops
12 weeks after op: jog for 60 minutes, no stops
13 weeks after op: jog for 120 minutes, no stops
15 weeks after op: jog gentle (7 hour) marathon
16 weeks after op: start the 7x7x7

A total of 294 kilometres in seven days. The seven marathons would not be at fast race pace, but they would not be gentle runs either. We would need to complete each within six hours, including airport customs and security (in and out). Since none of the scheduled jumbo flights could be expected to delay take off by even one minute if we were late, I tried to foresee potential airport security problems by writing to airlines in advance, warning them of Mike's metal detector-alarming medical hand baggage and the defibrillator. Only eight weeks before departure, Mike called me. Bad news.

He had been going for a run near his home in Hampshire when his left hip began to complain. He was forced to call his wife Thea to collect him by car to take him home. In a few hours a grape-fruit-sized swelling appeared, which became a massive, blue-black bruise tracking down his thigh. He had an ultrasound check, which showed that a small muscle running from the hip to beyond the knee had torn through. The ripped ends were swimming in a pool of blood. Mike's orthopaedic and sports medicine colleagues' advice was gloomy: he would not be running anywhere for several months, let alone doing a marathon.

Mike said he was not sure he agreed with their negative prognosis and would hope to get training again after a short rest. In fact, he took only twelve days' rest, lots of aspirins, some physio and then a test half-hour outing. His hip was sore, he self-diagnosed, but workable.

Our sponsor Land Rover decided not to announce the event at all unless we could prove we were fit to run at least two full marathons before departure. Mike chose the Cardiff event a fortnight before our start date and a small marathon near Winchester a week later. Land Rover stressed that we must tell nobody at all about the project until after both trial runs were successfully done. So I was extremely worried when the Cardiff organisers sent me my running number to stick on my vest a week before their event. The number was 777! They had obviously found out about our main plan. I called Mike, but he assured me he had not told anyone, and it transpired that the number had been chosen entirely at random. We took this as a good omen.

The Cardiff course turned out to be flat, and Mike, who set the pace, went fast by my standards, finishing in around four hours. But I felt drained at the end and Mike made a mental note to add more painkillers to the medical kit.

The next marathon, seven days later, took us from Winchester to Salisbury and Mike slowed the pace slightly. We finished in

4 hours 22 minutes. I had taken Ibuprofen tablets and aspirins and felt better than in Cardiff. The Big Seven, we agreed, was at least worth having a go at. We left Heathrow on schedule on 21 October, heading for South America. Land Rover had announced the overall plan of the Challenge the day we left Britain with a simplified summary:

> The team will run their first marathon in Antarctica and the 7-day clock will tick from the moment they start. A twin-engine plane will immediately fly them back to Santiago to run the South American marathon (Number 2). From there to Sydney, Singapore, London, Cairo and finally New York. But they will lose a whole day when they cross the international date line and will have to make this up by running two marathons within one 24-hour period, a morning run in London and another that night in Cairo. If they succeed, the two runners will complete the seven runs in less than 7 x 24 hours and will see only six whole days in terms of sunrises and sunsets.

Put like that it all sounded straightforward enough. We intended to run our first leg, the Antarctic marathon, on the sub-Antarctic King George Island, part of the South Shetlands once administered by the British Antarctic Survey, but now a Chilean airbase. On 25 October, we left Punta Arenas and flew over the glaciers and mountains of Tierra del Fuego for two hours. Then our pilot had to turn back due to bad weather.

On 26 October, the forecast being better, we again taxied hopefully along the Punta Arenas runway. Rob Hall, our BBC reporter and by now good friend, announced, 'Nothing can stop us now.' A minute later, on sod's cue, the starboard engine coughed, the pilot confirmed engine failure, and our last chance of making the South Shetlands on time was lost.

A rapid conference at the Punta Arenas Airport followed. From long experience I have always believed that if Plan A fails you get going with Plan B. Our Plan B was that we would run our South

American leg immediately and here in Punta rather than in Santiago as originally planned. And while we were doing it, our local organiser would try to find another aircraft to take us to another ex-British Antarctic Survey islands group, the Falklands, for the Antarctic leg.

That afternoon we all drove out of town to a long pebble-strewn beach beside the Magellan Strait. At 6 p.m., a whistle from a member of our Chilean support team served as our starting gun and off we loped along the coast before, ten miles later, we turned inland and crossed barren moorland, where we flushed out startled groups of rhea who galloped off very much faster than we could. I managed to stay close behind Mike's shoulder all the way and our first marathon clocked in at 3 hours 45 minutes. Back in Punta Arenas, we were greeted with the news that a twin-engine jet was on hand to take us to the Falklands.

The question has been asked whether the Falklands are genuinely part of the Antarctic continent or not. Well, they aren't part of South America and the *Antarctic Dictionary* assures me Antarctica comprises the continent and its surroundings seas and islands. Support came from quite another direction with the illustrious nineteenth-century botanist Sir Joseph Hooker writing about the flora of the Falklands and South Shetlands in his *Flora Antarctica*. It was good enough for me.

'Look left, Ran.' Mike woke me from sleep on our executive jet and pointed out of one of the portholes. An RAF Jaguar fighter plane cruised a few metres from our starboard wing: the pilot's thumbs-up was clearly visible. We landed at Mount Pleasant Military Base. A giant map of the Falklands hung in the airbase commander's office and we agreed to follow a marathon route he and other officers suggested that led from close to the base to the cathedral in the islands' capital, Port Stanley. We set out with six hours to go before our jet would have to leave in order to connect with the next key flight. We had therefore to run this one in under five hours.

At first we were both painfully stiff. Army vehicles passed by every now and again, the drivers hooting and waving. Our progress was being reported on Falklands Radio. There were long climbs and the pebbly road was uneven. We passed by skull and crossbones signs, warning of 21-year-old minefields beside the track. In dry areas, dwarf shrubs known as diddle-dee spread like heather with red berries mixed with an overall dun-coloured grass, white plumed flowerheads and patches of low pig vine. Occasional rook-like birds plunged and soared over the moors.

After three hours we passed below Mount Tumbledown, site of fierce fighting during the 1982 conflict, where British paratroops assaulted Argentinian infantry dug into its upper slopes. The Governor had laid on tea and sandwiches for us at Government House but there was, unfortunately, no time to observe the diplomatic civilities as an army Land Rover rushed us back to Mount Pleasant and hasty goodbyes to the commandant.

We made it to Santiago Airport in the nick of time to catch the scheduled BA flight to Sydney with two marathons under our belt and not yet down and out, just tired and aching all over. Before we left Chile we had pared our luggage down to a single item of hand baggage. As the schedule became tighter, we would have no time to wait for baggage carousels at airports.

We reached Sydney on the morning of 29 October, raced through the airport formalities to face a barrage of questions from a curious but sympathetic media, Australians being keen on any form of sporting activity. Then we changed speedily into our running gear. Land Rover Australia had thoughtfully arranged for members of the Sydney Striders running club to run with us in a pack, which was a big help. They included the Australian Iron Man champion, who made sure we did not get lost.

The route began near the Opera House, transited the Botanic Gardens and climbed up and then down the impressive Harbour Bridge, a near nine-mile course that we were to repeat three times, thus ascending and descending the bridge's 104 steps six times. Marathons are meant to be flat. So far none of ours had been. I remember feeling drained.

But Mike was feeling much worse. It had started for him in the previous race, but now his legs were becoming tighter and stiffer in a way he could not at first understand, and the competitive edge that we used to spur each other on had not kicked in for him this time. The first signs that Mike's problems were not just fatigue appeared before we left Sydney. His urine was mixed with blood and he suffered persistent diarrhoea. This in turn led to the likelihood of dehydration. But when he weighed himself, anticipating severe weight loss, he was shocked to find that he weighed six kilos more than in Patagonia three days earlier.

This explained to him that the tightness in his legs was because of the build-up of fluid in his muscles, caused by damage to the muscle cell membranes due to extreme mechanical overwork. What was going on in Mike's body was the result of the abuse to which he was subjecting it, the actual breaking down of his muscles. Not a happy state of affairs given the fact that he had run only three out of the seven marathons and the worst part of the schedule lay immediately ahead. The hottest, most humid run would be in Singapore. And then two marathons within twenty-four hours and ever-increasing jet lag.

We arrived half-asleep and confused at Singapore Airport, and were whisked by our hosts, the Singapore Heart Foundation, to a hotel for one hour's sleep before the press conference they had fixed for 4 a.m. We awoke like zombies, stiff as boards all over. I really did not feel like getting up or walking to the bathroom, never mind trying to run somewhere. Failure, I now perceived, was eminently likely. However, a cold shower, a cup of black coffee and a well-attended press conference, at which we were reminded that we represented the UK, made me realise that withdrawal from the nightmare, at least at this stage, was not an option.

So, to the hooting of horns and the cheering of the sixty Singapore runners who were to accompany us, we set out at dawn to thread our tortured way for the next six hours through the parks and skyscrapers of Singapore. The sun rose all too quickly, as did the roar of the rush-hour traffic.

Singapore was a marathon too far for poor Mike. He was peeing blood and reduced to walking the last third on jellied legs. I was not much better. After four hours I felt faint, nauseous and could not run in a straight line. A Singaporean Army major from their Special Forces clung to my running vest to steer me. Another runner kept dousing me with water and shouting constant encouragement. He must have said 'Nearly there' a hundred times. But we never were.

My back ached. My neck was shot through with sharp pain from the weight of my hung head. I drank copiously from my camelback container of Science-in-Sport drink. I fought against the ever-increasing desire to stop running. I counted my steps. One to a hundred. One to a hundred. Again and again and again. I tried to think of home and Ginny, of the Dhofar war, of Charlie Burton, Ollie Shepard and Anton Bowring on the bridge of the *Benjamin Bowring* in a South Atlantic storm. Of anything that could even briefly take my mind away from the torture of Singapore that morning.

When the end finally came (on the parade ground where Lord Mountbatten had received the Japanese surrender fifty-eight years before), I simply fell over under the FINISH banner. The time was over five hours, but the time was immaterial. Paramedics supported me to an ambulance, shoved needles into me and gave me various drinks. A BBC Singapore man with a tape recorder came in and sat on the ambulance bunk.

'Are you giving up?' he asked. He looked blurred to me.

'Yes,' I whispered. 'It would be stupid for me to carry on. But Mike will keep going. I know he will. If one of us can do it, that will be enough.'

Mike said that run was the hardest thing he had ever done. 'I felt like shit from the word go. The prospect of doing this again in London tomorrow is really appalling.'

Three hours later and just before our next intercontinental British Airways flight, we were feted at a Singapore Heart Foundation dinner. A doctor gave Mike the report on our body checks, done at the end of the run. Mike believed we were suffering from something called rhabdomyolysis, which simple tests would confirm by measuring the level in our blood of creatine kinase (CK), which plays an important role in fuelling muscle function. The Singapore report showed that my CK level was fifty times above the norm. I was suffering from significant muscle damage.

My disappointment in learning this was soon overshadowed by Mike's exclamation as he studied the report. His own CK level was nigh on 500 times the norm, surpassing by far anything he had feared and indicating massive muscle loss. Mike was still up and running through sheer mental willpower alone.

We flew on to our next continent, Europe, where London, or rather Heathrow's immediate surroundings, had been the only choice for our fifth run if we were to fit Africa and North America into our remaining forty-eight hours. Even this thought was stressful, and I had been warned 'not to get stressed'.

Our main marathon organiser, Steven Seaton, also our Eco-Challenge companion in years gone by, had arranged for some fifty runners to accompany us on the European leg and our race leader was Hugh Jones, one of the best marathon runners Britain has ever produced and a previous London Marathon winner. He had researched for us the exact route of the original 1908 London Olympics marathon, which began at Windsor Castle and ended at the White City Stadium.

Things had changed since 1908 and the morning rush-hour traffic was in full tortoise-like flow when we set out from the castle gates at 7.30 a.m. My thoughts as my back, hips, neck and legs creaked into action were centred around the ghastly proposition that, if we managed to complete this run, we would need to begin our next marathon in Africa that same night.

The *Independent* newspaper was clearly wary of our challenge. They quoted a Loughborough University sports science professor: 'RF and MS are risking permanent damage and even death by trying to complete their challenge. They could suffer potentially fatal kidney failure because their bodies will have no time to recover between each of their 26-mile runs. They are really punishing their bodies, possibly even to the point of death. We could never get approval from an ethics committee to conduct an experiment on people like this.'

Bruce Tulloch, another racing legend, led the way. We passed by Eton College, where groups of boys in tailcoats cheered us on. I glanced up at the high dome of School Hall and remembered the long ago thrill of night-climbing. Mike, who should have been recovering in a hospital bed, somehow ran for two and a half hours before having to walk intermittently. Friends and relations from all over the UK greeted our arrival at White City before Land Rovers rushed us to Heathrow for our flight to Cairo. Mike had lost a torn toenail and was hobbling, but somehow he had completed the twenty-six miles ten minutes faster than I had finished in Singapore the previous day.

The wife of President Mubarak of Egypt was hosting our African run and using it to raise funds for one of her charities, Women for Peace. She had organised a press conference at Giza immediately below the floodlit Pyramids, so I answered the press queries in Omani-accented Arabic, which is perfectly understood in Egypt. We set out at midnight, passing the Sphinx and running alongside some sixty local runners through clamorous crowds of residents busy feasting after their Ramadan daytime fasting. There was an atmosphere everywhere of carnival and chaos, but we ran behind a hooting phalanx of police vans and two ambulances.

'One each,' Mike shouted at me.

The roadside crowds cheered and cat-called as we passed, and the route was flat tarmac all the way to the airport. We recorded our speediest time since our first Patagonian run, which completely mystified Mike from a medical point of view. We had just run, after all, two complete marathons in a single day. Circadian rhythm, Mike pondered, might be involved.

We had, by the time we finished in Cairo, chased the sun three-quarters of the way around the globe, creating about eighteen hours of jet lag. In general, Mike knew, the body can recover about one hour a day so, on our sixth day, we were twelve hours out of phase. He theorised that our time-confused bodies, during the London run, must have thought it was midnight when all hormone support is at a low ebb, whereas in Cairo we had woken up and our systems were firing on all cylinders.

We arrived at JFK Airport, New York, on time on 2 November and, with the help of a British Airways special assistant, passed rapidly through immigration and customs. My German friend, Mike Kobold, and Steven Seaton had organised things with great efficiency and we joined some 35,000 other runners at the Verrazano Narrows Bridge for the start of the New York Marathon, a far cry from our first run six-and-a-half long, long days ago in Tierra del Fuego. There, the only other runners in sight had been the odd group of rhea.

Knowing that we would be physical wrecks, if still going by New York, we had taken the precaution of assigning two strong helpers to each of us for this, the last of our seven runs. Mike Kobold would stay with Mike, and so would my American nephew, my late sister Celia's son, who was a doctor and extremely fit. Steven Seaton and a runner friend of his would, if necessary, physically push me for the twenty-six miles through the streets of the Bronx, the concrete canyons of Manhattan, and finally the green acres of Central Park.

The excitement of the great human pack surging forward to the boom of a cannon at the start momentarily made us both forget our delicate states of health, but not for long. My own main memories of the day are of fighting off the desire to stop running, bad but not as bad as in Singapore, and Steven was always there with his depth of endurance knowledge and calm encouragement.

I knew that Mike was suffering mental torture to keep going in his physical state, but I remembered many, many days on the ice at both ends of the world and over many years when he had been in dire straits and yet kept going. I felt certain he would make this last run within the rapidly dwindling time reservoir of our seven-day limit, and I was determined that this time we should cross the final line together. So I started running back to find him, which other runners must have thought quite mad.

We finished 28,362nd out of 35,000 runners. Mike went on to make a very important point:

> When, following our success, many experts in both the USA and Britain expressed disbelief at what we had achieved, they did not realise that they could have done it too. The difference is only one of perception. Whereas most people look at very big challenges, whatever the field or their walk of life, and start from the position 'I can't', Ran and I make a simple word substitution and say 'Why can't I?' 'I can't run seven marathons' easily transforms into the question, 'Why can't I run seven marathons?' Once it was asked, we felt obliged to find the answer.

The Times editorial the following day said: 'Both men are supposed to be too old to be running so far and so often. Both ignored medical scares and both kept going not by coddling or psychological bonding, but by the abrasive competitive spirit that has marked their friendship and rivalry. Their triumph against all odds is not only a magnificent publicity boost for the charities that they are supporting, it is also an inspiration for every runner, every ordinary person, tempted to give up in the face of the impossible.'

Stephen Venables
Mountaineer and writer

The only time I ever climbed with Ran was when the *Sunday Times* asked me to cover his Eiger North Face fundraiser. I accompanied him on a training jaunt up the West Flank of the Eiger. At one point, Jon Morgan, the guide, decided to dangle Ran over the edge.

Where we had stopped, the Eigerwand plummets sheer for about a thousand metres. To most climbers it is terrifying. But Ran is a military man, used to giving and taking orders, so he did what he was told and stepped backwards to lean right out over the hideous void, smiling cheerfully while I snapped photos for the newspaper. It was an impressive display of cool courage.

The following winter, I watched and reported on the actual climb from the valley. Apart from the odd dropped glove and camera, it all went very smoothly, but when he returned to the hotel after four days on the face, Ran muttered to me, 'I didn't like it.'

I am not sure that he particularly *liked* the other training climb where I joined him – on the Old Man of Hoy. My job was to come last, gently coaxing Ran across the second pitch, where you have to edge sideways over a humungous drop. Again, Ran – with virtually no climbing experience – simply got on with the job.

The only mild crisis came during the long abseil descent from the summit, when Ran passed within inches of a fulmar's nest. These sea birds are notorious for their foul-smelling projectile vomit, but my warning shout came too late, as the fulmar aimed straight for Ran's head and spattered the bullseye.

Unfazed, the victim smiled nonchalantly and explained, 'It's fine, I've got a helmet.'

'Yes, Ran,' I told him, 'but the helmet has holes in it.'

Standing on the summit of the Eiger with the mountaineer Kenton Cool, after they climbed the infamous North Face in the Alps, 2007.

8

Eiger North Face

*Ascending the 1,800-metre north face of the
Eiger, the most notorious wall in the Alps
2007*

*A*fter *his first attempt at climbing Mount Everest had failed in
2005, Ran decided to confront his lifelong fear of heights
with a more extreme challenge, climbing the infamous Nordwand,
also known as the 'Murder Wall', the North Face of the Eiger in
the Alps. He approached the respected mountaineer and climbing
instructor Kenton Cool, who agreed to lead the ascent with his
regular climbing partner Ian Parnell.*

*First Ran had to learn simple rock climbing on sea cliffs on the
Gower peninsula, on several quarry-type cliffs near Cardiff, and
the Avon and Cheddar Gorges. Then month after month throughout 2006 he flew out to Geneva to have five-day training sessions
in the Alps with Kenton Cool, who taught him how to climb using
ropes, ice axes and crampons on the mixed rock and ice conditions they would face on the Eiger.*

*The following year, at the age of sixty-three, Ran was adjudged
ready to climb the Eiger North Face.*

On 1 March 2007, I flew to Geneva and drove a rental car to
Grindelwald, where we stayed at a family-run hotel, the Grand
Regina, with a reputation among British tourists of being the best

in all Switzerland. The owner, Hans Krebs, had kindly given us accommodation free of charge because he approved of and wanted to help our Marie Curie aims.

The hotel manager, Ingo Schmoll, warned us of the consequences of the mountains not being as stable as they should normally be in mid-winter. The rate of retreat of glaciers throughout the Alps, together with the thawing of the permafrost layer, had created temporary barrages of fallen rock blocking high ravines and creating lakes. Increasingly torrential summer rains then burst the feeble dams of rubble, causing flash floods, mudslides and more loosened rock. The previous autumn the Eiger itself had suffered a major rockfall, a chunk bigger than two Empire State Buildings.

Kenton Cool, in Chamonix, was in touch with Ralph Rickli, the famous Swiss met forecaster in Berne, and with the top European weather bureau, the Met Office in Exeter. We needed a clear good weather window of at least five days and nights on the North Face if a non-skilled climber like me was to reach the summit. Kenton and I cleared the whole of March in our diaries and waited. The ITV crew, led by Philip Reay-Smith, installed themselves in a suite with a balcony looking directly opposite the Eiger, which was swiftly transformed into a studio resembling a CIA electronic snooper room, with the intention of transmitting the first ever live news footage from the Nordwand.

Philip warned me that, once his team was in Grindelwald, we must start the climb. ITV could make no open-ended commitment, since their team had to be on permanent call to go anywhere in the world at short notice. Indeed, Philip sent me an email warning me not to do the climb during the week starting 19 March, because that was ITV's 'Iraq Week' and there would be much less space on the News for non-Iraq-related items.

When I told Kenton this, he snorted, 'If the weather's good for the week of 19 March, and we haven't gone by then, we will set out at once, ITV crew or no ITV crew.' I relayed this back to Philip.

The March days slowly ticked by in Grindelwald and I began to find the bulk of the Eiger, looming over the hotel, a touch oppressive. I tried to keep busy. I went for a daily two-hour run out of the village, along hilly lanes and up the glacial ravines. As I ran I heard the intermittent explosions of avalanches from the heights of the Alpine giants all around. Then after six days of evil weather forecasts, our friendly met-experts in Berne and Exeter finally concurred and a five-day window was forecast for the middle of the month.

When Kenton confirmed our imminent departure, I tried to hide the fear, almost panic, that surged with the knowledge that we were about to start the climb. Until then there was always the doubt about the weather, the chance that we might not be able to try the climb at least until the following September. But now the die was cast, I did my best not to reveal my wobbly state of mind. Later that day, in the hostel at the foot of the Eiger, I needed to work hard to appear unfazed in the boisterous company of Kenton, Ian, the ITV crew and Stephen Venables, who was reporting for the *Sunday Times*.

We were to leave the hostel for the hour-long snow traverse to the base of the North Face at 4 a.m. the next morning and I found sleep elusive that night. I remembered a hundred similar sleepless nights before big moments, but polar fears were something I knew how to handle. Mountain fears were different. I feared my own inadequacies, of being revealed as a coward or, at best, as a wimp. Would the North Face trigger uncontrollable vertigo? Would I freeze to some cliff, unable to move, thereby risking Ian's and Kenton's lives, as well as my own? Never mind the ridicule. And what of a fall? I had by now read all the accounts by far better climbers than myself.

With fear, you must prevent, not cure. Fear must not be let in in the first place. Just do it! Keep your eyes closed and go. That is all very well when coping with rational fears about what *might* happen. But vertigo is not rational and the trigger likely to set it off was the all too real sight beneath my feet of a great beckoning, sickening void. Exactly what would it feel like to spend time cartwheeling, rushing downwards for several thousand feet?

Once my alarm went off and I began to check all my gear before a rushed breakfast, the dread thoughts and fears of the night did indeed disperse. We left on time in pitch darkness with Kenton leading.

Ian's backpack was heavier than mine, due to all the camera gear, as he was to document the climb and attempt the live ITV News broadcasts. Kenton's pack, also heavier than mine, was festooned with climbing paraphernalia, but I still felt dubious about climbing with a pack that restricted my movement, cramped my arms and limited my ability to look upwards. Dawn crept over the Alps and the mountain tops were tipped with an orange alpen-glow. The stars disappeared and the great wall above us came alive. I thought of its German nickname *Mordwand*, or Murder Wall.

Half an hour of trudging along a line of boot prints in deep snow took us to the spot Kenton decided to climb from. We said our goodbyes to Philip and Rob of ITV and to Stephen Venables. They should be able to watch our every move over the next few days, providing bad weather stayed away, through their powerful camera lenses. And at night they should be able to spot the pin-pricks of our head torches from wherever we slept.

We fixed on our crampons beneath a feature known as the First Pillar. Many climbers lose the route in this area, but Kenton seemed confident as he stared up at our first obstacle, some 2,000 feet of mixed snow gulleys, loose scree, shiny ledges of smooth, compact limestone and temporarily lodged boulders. Looking away to the flanks of the face, the lofty silhouettes of the peaks of the Wetterhorn and Mittelhorn seemed dwarfed by our own monster. Few of the infamous Eiger tragedies occurred on this first 2,000-foot climb, but the fallen detritus of many an Eiger incident lay all around us.

I remember, from one of the Eiger books, a photograph of climber Edi Rainer's body lying smashed in the scree of this catchment zone. And Chris Bonington, on his Eiger ascent, had among these rubble-strewn lower reaches passed by blood trails and a piece of flesh attached to some bone.

I knew that the world's top soloists, acrobats of the top league, could climb the Nordwand in hours, not days, without ropes, in their sticky-soled rock-shoes, as light as woollen socks. A single slip or false move would see them dead, crushed on the rock, but they survive on the confidence born of their expertise. The mere thought of climbing a single rock pitch unroped made me flinch.

In a few hours, with constant encouragement from Kenton and Ian, I had blundered my way up 1,000 feet or more of the initial rubble slopes. I felt much comforted by the thought that, if my nerve failed as the drop below grew far greater than any climb I had done before, there was a nearby escape hatch, the Eiger tunnel's gallery window or porthole, which allows tourists to look out and gasp at the airy void immediately below them.

We must have climbed some 2,000 feet up the mountain when we reached the next recognisable feature, the aptly named Shattered Pillar. I was feeling tired and my neck muscles were aching from the tug of my rucksack harness. But the weather was, as prophesied by the met offices of Berne and Exeter, holding good and clear. Every few hours I tore open a new hand-warmer bag with my teeth and inserted the two tiny pouches into my mitts. They worked well and whenever the sensitive stumps of my amputated fingers began to feel numb with cold, I positioned the hand-warmer pouch over their ends for a while.

I had never climbed on similar rock before, smooth like slate with almost nowhere to provide even the tiniest holding point for the tips of my ice axes and crampon spikes. At times I had to remove one or other of my mitts with my teeth and use my bare hand to clasp some rock bulge or slight surface imperfection to avoid a fall. This I hated to do, for my fingers, once cold, took forever to rewarm, even with my heat pouches.

Every now and again I glanced below me without thinking and felt that shock of terror I knew so well which presages the first wave of vertigo. I instantly forced my mind to concentrate on something of interest above me, usually Kenton's progress. On that first day this process worked well for me. I was, due to vanity, keen to prevent Ian and Kenton from glimpsing my fear. With Kenton I may have succeeded, but Ian Parnell was a sharp cookie and zealous in his film-making responsibilities. Philip had especially instructed him to record personal emotions and such points of human interest as discord within the group.

At some point on a steep icy slope, to my considerable alarm and dismay, one of my boots skidded off a nub of protruding rock and my left crampon swung away from my boot. Although still attached by a strap, the crampon was useless. Luckily the same crampon had come loose once before, on a frozen waterfall with Kenton a month ago. So I reined in my rising panic and, hanging from one axe and a tiny foothold, I managed, with much silent swearing, to reattach the crampon to the boot.

We came, over 2,000 feet up, to an eighty-foot-high rockface known as the Difficult Crack, which I found virtually impossible, far more technically demanding than any of my previous training ascents, and extremely testing on my puny biceps. To be more precise, my arms felt as though they were being torn from their sockets since, in the almost total absence of any reasonable footholds, I had literally to haul my body and rucksack upwards by arm-power alone. I wished I had spent more time obeying my climbing instructor Paul Twomey's piece of advice to train hard at obtaining some upper body strength.

By the time I heaved myself up the last steep and glass-smooth boulder of the Crack, I was on my very last ounce of willpower and wanted only to stop for the day and sleep. Not that there was anywhere remotely suitable in sight to lie down or even sit.

From the top of the Difficult Crack we could look immediately above us at an immense sheer wall, known as the Rote Fluh, smooth, red and infamous for its propensity to shower loose rockfalls on to the face below. A natural desire of all climbers at this point is to ascend as quickly as possible towards the base of this lethal feature, since proximity minimises the danger of being hit. With a bulky backpack, however, speed is not too easy. Balancing like a dainty gymnast in rock-shoes is a far cry from climbing heavily laden with the weight on your back ever threatening to pull your body away from the rock and out into space.

From the Crack we still had more than 8,000 feet of climbing, including traverses, on the North Face, much of which, I knew, would be a lot harder and more exposed than had been the eighty-foot-high Crack.

Kenton had planned for us to bivouac the first night at a ledge known as the Swallows Nest. Between the Difficult Crack and this refuge was the infamous Hinterstoisser Traverse, the key passage, unlocking access to the centre of the wall. It was a passage won at considerable cost by its pioneers, two German guides, Andreas Hinterstoisser and Toni Kurz, and two Austrian guides, Willy Angerer and Edi Rainer.

Their story forms a part of the forbidding history of this section of the face. In 1935 a couple of Germans, Sedlmayer and Mehringer, had climbed a record distance up the mountain, but at 3,300 metres they had frozen to death on a ledge. A year later Hinterstoisser and his companions hoping to set a new record, if not to reach the summit, had reached the ledge of the frozen bodies, which with climbers' macabre humour they named Death Bivouac, only to be themselves turned back by the weather and falling rocks. But fatally they had left no rope in place across their key traverse, and their desperate attempts to reverse their route over this slippery, vertical cliffside all failed.

So they tried to rope down to reach the railway's porthole in the rock, but disaster overtook them. One fell and dropped free to the valley below, one was strangled by the rope, and a third froze to death. The youngest German, Toni Kurz, dangled from the rope-end a mere 100 metres above the porthole, just out of reach of and conversing with his would-be rescuers. His was a slow, unenviable death.

When we reached their traverse, a relatively new-looking rope, clipped to the rock, disappeared round a bulge at the top of the great slab. My mouth felt dry and my hands weak. This was a moment of truth, and the only way I knew how to face it was by attacking the obstacle in a rush, desperate to keep my mind busy with no tiny chink into which sheer terror could claw, then spread incubus-like and render me a gibbering fool, an embarrassment to myself and to the others. This was my nightmare as I tried to find successive nicks in the glistening rock to place the steel points on my crampons. I gripped the black rope where I had watched Kenton hold it, and edged down around the bulge – and into space.

Suddenly, and with a visual impact that took my breath away, there was a panoramic view of the world below. For 2,500 feet under my boots, only the wind touched the plunging rock. My crampons skidded out of their tenuous holds. I gripped the black rope dangling from the rock as my feet scrabbled desperately to find a hold. Into my brain, unbidden, came the picture of my heavy body tearing Kenton off the cliff, and then the deadweight of us both pulling Ian away, and the rush of air as we cartwheeled through space. *Will I scream*, was my main worry, strangely enough.

My memory of that traverse is thankfully confused. I know that I swore to myself again and again that this was my last climb. I also recall, at some point during that fearful move, focusing on a sudden whiteness in the black rope upon which, in my mind, I was utterly dependent each time my crampons slipped away from the face. Somehow the rope had become frayed at this point to a single, fragile strand.

I clambered past Ian's body and savoured the blessed relief of a solid six-inch ledge under one crampon. I rested on it and felt a wave of exhaustion pass through me. So had I conquered my fear of heights? Had I vanquished my 63-year-old bogeyman of vertigo? I *had* crossed the Hinterstoisser Traverse on the great North Face of the Eiger, so surely I *must* have become a 'proper climber'. And proper climbers surely don't fear heights.

Yet I suspected that nothing had really changed. There had been no actual confrontation within myself. No fearful struggle I had bravely and finally won. My only victory thus far had been to prevent the creeping angst getting a grip on me. Day one on the Eiger was almost over without a disaster. Three or four more days, ever higher, lay ahead.

From the end of the traverse, we inched up a seventy-foot vertical crack to an eighteen-inch-wide ledge beneath an over-hang, the Swallows Nest. A scab of frozen snow was stuck to the ledge and we used our axes to flatten this out, giving us some four feet of width and almost standing up space. Ian clipped my waist harness to a rock bolt, and Kenton melted snow over a tiny gas stove. Our bivouac was comfortable but, for me, ruined by the knowledge that, as I lay with my nose up against the rock wall and my knees curled up for warmth in the lightweight sleeping bag, my backside protruded over the edge of our ledge and over the void below.

When Joe Simpson and Ray Delaney had bivouacked here seven years before us, two other climbers (Matthew Hayes from Hampshire and Phillip O'Sullivan from New Zealand) had fallen off, roped together, from an icy slope higher up and dropped past this ledge. Simpson had written: 'I thought of their endless, frictionless fall, numbed in their last moments of consciousness by the full enormity of what was happening . . . I stared down thinking of them lying there tangled in their ropes, side by side . . . We didn't hear them go. They didn't scream.'

That could have been their epitaph, I thought. 'They didn't scream.'

During the night a breeze blew ice-dust down the neck of my jacket, and small stones clattered by. I resisted the temptation of rolling over to sleep facing outwards. The clear night sky was crammed with stars, mirrored by the pinprick lights of Grindelwald in the dark valley below. Kenton woke us before dawn. He passed me an empty cloth bag which I filled with snow blocks that I cut, reluctantly, from the end of my sleeping platform. Ian asked me for some item and, unthinkingly, I threw it along the ledge to him, forgetting for an instant where we were.

This deserved and got a mouthful of abuse from the others. '*Never*,' they cried in unison, 'throw anything. Pass it over with care.' Ian went on to warn me about my boots and crampons. 'Put them on carefully. It's all too easy with cold hands trying to force a cold foot into a rigid boot to lose your grip and then, before you know it, a boot is gone – a long way. Then you are in *serious* trouble.'

Answering the call of nature during the first day's climb was something I had successfully postponed, but the moment of truth arrived on the narrow ledge. There was a sharp breeze and I felt cold. Squatting between the rock face and the void, I was thankful for the small mercy that I was up one end of the ledge and not, like Ian, in the middle. Luckily I had an empty polythene bag to hand as a receptacle. Nonetheless, I did begin to wonder how climbers cope on big mountain faces having to drink water from the soiled snow floors of oft-used ledges. But then I remembered that the London sewage system provides Londoners with oft-recycled drinking water without even the safeguard of its being boiled on Kenton's gas stove.

Shortly before sunrise, Kenton disappeared upwards from the Swallows Nest. Soon after I followed his lead on to the ice slope above our bivouac, there came an awkward leaning move over the face of a smooth rock. For a while I was flummoxed, but, stretching the axe in my good hand fully upwards, I felt its spike lodge in some unseen nook. Such moments require a blind hope that your sole hold on life will be a reliable one when you make the next move. If it isn't and your sudden bodyweight dislodges the axe's placement, you will plummet downwards hoping not to drag your colleagues with you.

Once over the rock I was on to a long, steep icy slope known as the First Ice Field, and here I heard the whistling thrum of solid matter falling past us, whether ice or rock, I'm not sure. The day before, a small stone had struck Kenton's helmet, and at the base of this First Ice Field, arrowing upwards at some 55°, a largish lump of ice caught Ian on the helmet.

With careful axe work, I crawled up two steep slopes of mixed rock and ice with extreme caution, for there was a deal of loose rubble just itching to respond to the call of Isaac Newton. After 200 feet negotiating this unstable zone, we scaled the first real ice field, which I found less difficult than anything to date. It ended all too quickly at the bottom end of a 300-foot-high near-vertical gulley of part-iced rock known as the Ice Hose. I definitely disliked this section.

More stones whistled by as I inched up the Hose but, although I found myself flinching and ducking, none made contact, and the next time I reached Kenton's belay position, he looked happy, clearly pleased we had reached the Second Ice Field intact. This was the great white sheet easily identifiable from Grindelwald. At some point as we axed our way up it, Kenton saw an ice axe whistle by us on its way down the face. We never did identify its owner. I shivered at the thought of trying to climb any distance at all on such a mountain with only one axe. The wind picked up on the wide open flank of the ice field.

An explosion sounding further down the face, as we learned later from Philip and his film crew, came from an avalanche of rock and ice roaring down the Ice Hose that we had earlier scaled. The ice climb seemed to go on and on and our ropes were usually slack between each other to the extent that I felt as though I was almost free climbing un-roped. On the many soft snow patches, I took special care to dig in my spikes and axes as deep as I could.

Philip had hired a helicopter to film our ascent of the ice fields, and he needed to collect all the film Ian Parnell had taken with the hand-held videocam. The helicopter dropped a steel hawser down towards us with a black bag on its hook. But the angle of our slope was too steep, so Ian cramponed down and then out towards the centre of the ice field. Perched on a rock, with no apparent regard for the huge drop below, he attached his film container to the swinging hook. Simply watching him made my blood run cold.

The helicopter disappeared way below us, and we finally reached the upper edge of the ice slope, following it to the left. At this point a difficult rock pitch leads up on to a triangular rock buttress called the Flat Iron. In 1961 two British climbers, Brian Nally and Barry Brewster, were progressing below the buttress when Brewster was hit by a rock and injured. Chris Bonington and Don Whillans abandoned their own ascent to attempt a rescue, but the already unconscious Brewster was swept to his death by rockfall before they could reach him, so they led a seriously disoriented Nally to safety.

Kenton, seeing that I was flagging badly on a difficult section to access the Flat Iron, had pointed upwards. 'Only two or three pitches to Death Bivouac,' he assured me. The name of the place was hardly reassuring. Just then, however, Kenton's promise of its proximity did make it sound a very welcome spot. Again we dug away at a snow-clogged ledge and cleared enough space for the three of us to lie head to toe. I slept well at Death Bivouac for I was tired, but some climbers have found its atmosphere oppressive.

That night my right arm rested on the very edge of a 3,500-foot drop, and Kenton's pan of breakfast muesli tasted none the worse for his half-joking warning that some previous climber had used his end of the ledge, from where he had scooped our brew-up snow, as the Gents.

As before, Kenton set out at dawn. He led some pitches and handed over to Ian for others. I remained always in the middle.

Since I was by far the most likely to fall, this system would hopefully minimise the chances of my body dragging both the others off the mountain with me. That, of course, assumed that neither of *them* were knocked off by a rock first.

That day, our third on the Eiger, began badly for my mental state because, expecting to continue heading in an upwards direction, we actually had to move diagonally downwards across an extremely steep slope, known as the Third Ice Field, to the base of a crucial feature known as the Ramp. This 700-foot-high left-slanting gash overhung by walls of limestone contains many nasty surprises, and some Eiger pundits describe it as the most technically difficult section on the wall.

Twice over the next few hours, inching up the central chimney of the Ramp, I came within an ace of falling, but on each occasion, my axes caught hold on some tiny unseen nub and halted my downwards rush. There were icy chimneys, awkward rock slabs, tricky and frightening overhangs, side-pulls, hand-palming off sloping holds, and the occasional hand-jamb, all techniques I had been taught by my instructor Paul Twomey on his church climbing walls in Bristol.

Near the upper reaches of the great gulley there were two or three stretches of rock that nearly defeated my every attempt. Looking down at any point during the Ramp climb would have been a big mistake, as the airy ice fields immediately below had a hypnotic effect. Looking up was not to be recommended either in the Ramp's narrower reaches, for then my rucksack lid's contents would jab the back of my neck.

Somewhere on the Ramp in 1961, an Austrian climber with a brilliant repertoire of ultra severe Alpine ascents, the 22-year-old Adolf Mayr, came to grief attempting the first ever solo ascent of the face. Down in Grindelwald, queues of tourists waited their turn to gawp at 'Adi' through the hotel telescopes. Somewhere in the mid-section, at a spot named the Waterfall Chimney, he needed to traverse across wet rock. Watchers below saw him hack at a foothold with his axe. Then he stepped sideways, missed his footing and fell 4,000 feet to his death.

Above the Ramp there were sections of slippery ice and treacherous patches of soft snow into which neither my axes nor my crampons could be trusted to hold firm. By always checking I had three reasonable holds before advancing a leg or arm to a fourth higher hold, none of the many slips that I made proved disastrous, merely heart-stopping at the time. Unbeknown to me, both my companions had been concerned that the Ramp might prove too technically difficult for my meagre rock-ability and that the expedition would end there.

At one belay I met up with Ian just below a single boulder the size of half a standard UK red postbox. As we conversed a rock struck the boulder and shattered into shards, one of which struck me hard on the helmet. The rest passed harmlessly over our heads. Just above the boulder, Kenton traversed to the right of the straight-to-heaven route we had been following for 700 feet up the gulley of the Ramp. Here we ran out of ice at a place of much loose slate aptly named the Brittle Ledges.

For a while I could find no way up one layer of slate, for every rock I tried to use for a hold simply broke off. My axes were no help. Eventually I had to remove my mitts and bury my bad hand deep into a vertical cleft to achieve the needed purchase. This move coincided with the failure of my last available hand-warmer pouch. Resupplies were unobtainable deep in my rucksack, and my hand soon grew numb with cold.

This was bad timing because, above the Brittle Ledges, Ian led up a vertical wall of slate about ninety feet high. Maybe I was too tired to think clearly, or perhaps my cold, numb left hand, incapable of gripping anything but my ice axe (and that thanks only to the crutch of its wrist loop), left me pretty much one-armed at the time.

Whatever the reason, I worked harder and with greater desperation on that single ninety-foot wall than on any previous part of the North Face. Despite the brittle nature of the rock, the first few metres up from a little snow-covered ledge on to the Brittle Crack are really overhanging. The upper twelve feet involved an appallingly exposed traverse around a corner, with space shouting at you from every direction. The tiny cracks and sparse piton placements available for my axes disappeared as I neared the top.

All apparent handhold bulges were smooth and sloped down-wards, and my bare fingers simply slid off them. My arms and my legs began to shake, my biceps to burn. Pure luck got me to the ice patch that capped the wall, into which I sank an axe with great relief and hauled myself up, a wreck, to the tiny snow ledge where a grinning Ian was belayed.

'This is it,' he said. 'We spend the night here. Lovely view.'

A bit of axe burrowing formed a fairly comfortable ledge for the three of us, and again the mental stress and physical toil of the day overcame my worries about that drop a few inches away from my sleeping position. I lost a mitt off the ledge during the night, but I had a spare immediately available. The stumps of my left-hand fingers ached, but far less than all ten fingers had hurt on most polar trips. I felt fine as I fell asleep, worried only by tales I had heard of two of the obstacles to be faced the next day, the hugely exposed Traverse of the Gods and the technical problems of the final Exit Cracks, rated more difficult than the Ramp. I had just spent hours ascending by far the most difficult climbing of my admittedly short climbing life, and yet, by repute, the worst lay ahead.

Ian recorded his night perched above the Brittle Crack, during which he was scheduled to conduct a live interview. This, accord-ing to our ITV friends, would – if it worked – be the first time ever that anyone had managed a live interview on the national news from somewhere as remote as the Eiger Nordwand. A digilink was used in order to achieve this, utilising microwaves to send high-quality television images through the air so that Philip and the ITV crew at the base of the mountain could see and talk to me. Ian recorded:

As I knelt on the edge of the drop, camera held out in one hand and the broadcast antennae in the other, I felt a muscle begin to spasm in cramp. 'Three minutes to go', and the cramp starts an inexorable rise up my back. 'Two minutes, could you hold the camera steady, Ian', and my neck has joined the knot. I try to meditate and breathe through pain. 'Thirty seconds, keep the light on Ran', and I'm gasping for air now. Must try to stop breathing. 'So, Ran, could you tell us how you keep your spirits up in such hostile terrain?' It's happening, we're live! 'Excellent, chaps, you can relax now. London says it's some of the best footage they've seen all week.'

On the morning of our fourth day on the face, I woke with a dry mouth and butterflies fluttering about in my stomach. Having just come away from the unreliable region of the Brittle Crack, I envisaged the scenario of a pendulum plunge with my full weight tearing out the feeble flaky placements, together with both Kenton and Ian who were attached to them.

Ian was behind me as I stepped out along this hellish cliffside. Suddenly, well ahead of me and appearing to be glued to the sheer wall merely by his fingertips and booted toes, Kenton disappeared around an abrupt corner. For no good reason this unsettled me badly.

Something snapped as soon as I rounded the sharp bend in the wall. I may have inadvertently allowed myself a glimpse downwards beyond my normal carefully regimented focus point – my crampon points and not an inch beyond them. The onrush of sheer terror that this error sparked coincided with a tightening of the rope between me and the still invisible Kenton.

'Give me slack,' I shouted.

I had the rope back to Ian jammed behind me round an ice nub. I had to retreat a metre to loosen it. I was teetering on my front points on a mere rock scratch. I was terrified. My voice rose to a bellow.

'GIVE ME SLACK!'

This brought a furious response from my unseen leader. Furious, but to me unintelligible, so I had no idea what his problem was, no idea that his position was precarious. He knew that, if I fell at that moment, he was unlikely to be able to maintain a hold on the mountain. He was desperately doing his best to screw ice-screws in to improve his belay point. The last thing he wanted to do was to give me slack.

Fortunately, my instant reaction to the angry tone of his voice was to get angry myself, and that eclipsed the power of the vertigo attack. I controlled myself, closed my eyes, thought of a huge plate of steaming porridge laced with maple syrup and clung to the miserable rock face. After an age, or so it seemed, I felt slack rope from Kenton, reached back to flick Ian's rope free, and crept onwards above that sickening drop until I could see the still muttering Kenton perched on a patch of naked ice.

I joined him and stayed silent as he berated me for my impatience, knowing that his moods of thunder never lasted long and were usually well deserved. There was nobody, not even Ian, who I trusted so completely in what, to me, was the most frightening environment on Earth. Without Kenton, I could never have even contemplated setting foot on the Eiger's North Face.

'Lighten up,' Ian advised Kenton. They knew each other well.

We moved fairly quickly up the steep hard ice of the White Spider, so called due to its shape – a blob of white ice with white gulleys stretching up and down from its centre for hundreds of feet. In bad weather, detritus from above can turn the Spider into a death zone for any climber caught on its face. Above and just to the right of the Spider was another, smaller ice field, the Fly.

I crawled up the Spider. I felt really tired; perhaps due to the stress of the Traverse of the Gods or because the previous three days of climbing had slowly taken their toll on my reserves of fitness. I was also getting clumsy in a place where this was inadvisable. The sun beat down from a clear sky and the extreme exertion of hauling myself and my rucksack ever upwards made me sweat. Kenton, at a belay, helped me take off my windproof jacket, but I fumbled and lost my grip on it. A breeze grabbed it and, in an instant, it slid away down the slope, gathering speed. A bad item to lose at that height on the Eiger.

We still had 1,000 feet to go straight up a maze of intricate gulleys, the notorious Exit Cracks, the final chimney of which included two rope-lengths up a near vertical ice staircase with the treads all sloping the wrong way. From the White Spider on there were many obstacles that would, back in the Avon Gorge or on the Welsh sea cliffs, have been too much for my inadequate technical skills and lack of upper body strength. But this was the last rock problem I would face.

The summit was tantalisingly close, so I attacked each new problem as though my life depended on it. Perhaps it did. The walls on both sides of various grooves and chimneys were smooth, featureless and often at eighty degrees. I remember a whitish wall called the Quartz Crack, which looked evil but turned out to be merely nasty.

The nightmare of the Exit Cracks ended with a great pendulum traverse, way to the left of our previous axis of ascent, a long icy shute and a treacherous bulge of mixed shale and snow, both ingredients being unpleasantly loose underfoot. The evening sun was welcoming as we emerged from the last of the gulleys. I craned my neck, arching my back, and saw a wonderful swathe of open sky where for four long days I had seen only the ever-rising, dark wall of the Eiger.

Above us now was only a steep wall of snow and ice leading up to a knife-edge, the summit ridge. This sharply angled snow wall was the reservoir, the source of the avalanches that sweep down the North Face. New, often wet, snow that settles here frequently fails to cohere firmly with the névé and ice beneath and sloughs away in lethal waves down the Exit Cracks, out over the Spider and beyond.

Ian led up this last steep climb, taking his time with care and caution. From an ice-screw belay I paid out Ian's rope. I could see the outline of his rucksack high above as he fixed another screw into the snow. He straightened up to move off and I felt the rope go taut. I obviously had him on too tight a leash. I quickly paid out more rope, looking down at the coils to check against knots forming. At the same moment, Ian, caught off balance by the taut rope, had slipped, fallen over on to his back and begun to slide head first down the Eiger.

He wrote later: 'I began to head down towards Grindelwald. Kenton luckily heard my screams, saw that Ran was paying *out* the rope and yelled at him. This seemed to reawaken Ran to the appropriate rope procedures and, thankfully, my downwards journey was brought to an abrupt halt.'

By dusk we had reached the knife-edge snow cornice of the summit ridge, but were still some thirty minutes and 300 metres below the actual summit further along the Mittellegi Ridge. So Kenton selected a nook on the far, southern side of the cornice, where we spent an hour digging out a platform for the sleeping bags.

We spent eleven hours in the snow dugout, and I remembered, nearly two years before, thinking I had a good chance of summitting Everest because Ian and I had spent that last pre-summit night at some 400 metres below Everest's summit ridge. Almost there. And I never made the summit. Now here we were again, a mere 300 metres below another summit. Ian considered the Eiger North Face a far more difficult ascent than Everest's North Ridge, but this time I had no cardiac troubles lying in wait, for we were at a mere 14,000, not 28,000 feet.

We left the bivouac at 9.30 a.m. and threaded our way along a classic knife-edge ridge. At 10 a.m. on the fifth day of our climb, we reached the summit.

Thanks entirely to the brilliance and the patience (usually!) of Kenton and Ian. Within half an hour of our arrival there, an evil-looking cloud bank raced over the mountain ranges to the south, soon to envelop the Eiger. Our weather forecasters had got it dead right. As we descended down the easy side of the ridge, I felt deliriously happy to be back on comparative *terra firma*. I made up my mind to steer clear of all mountains in the future . . . probably.

Ian Parnell
Mountaineer and photographer

The Eiger North Face or Nordwand is a legendary icon of mountaineering. Over sixty climbers have lost their lives trying to scale this mile-high, near vertical sweep of ice and rock. To even consider climbing the Nordwand as your first major Alpine route would be seen as verging on impossible.

I have often wondered how Ran did exactly that in 2007, accompanied by Kenton Cool and myself. The pair of us had almost forty years' climbing experience between us, including multiple trips to some of the Himalayas' toughest peaks. Ran had only recently learnt how to climb, taught by Kenton.

To tackle such a complex and potentially dangerous climb as the Eiger, you need to have a combination of well-practised technical skills coupled with the kind of mental strength that can handle challenge after challenge. It would not be unfair of me to say that Ran's technical climbing skills needed a bit more practice, say ten years or so. But he more than made up for that on the mental toughness side of the equation.

On the last day of our Eiger climb, the three of us were tied together on a rope, with Ran in the middle. Ahead of us lay a final knife-edge ridge of snow leading to the summit, with an 1,800m fall at either side.

The theory was that if one of us fell, i.e. Ran, then it was my job to throw myself off on the opposite side of the ridge to counter-balance any slip. The fact that Ran, then aged sixty-four and suffering from vertigo, ably negotiated the foot-wide crest without hesitation was a testament to how far he had come as a mountaineer.

It was also a great personal relief that I didn't have to put the counter-balance theory to the test!

Charles Westmorland, Mike Broome, Ran, Peter Loyd, Nick Holder and Anthony Brockhouse in the snow at Dover before leaving for the Nile, 1969.

9

The Nile

Navigating the Nile River from the sea to its source by Land Rover and hovercraft 1969

*B*efore taking up his new posting in command of the Reconnaissance Platoon of the Muscat Regiment in Oman in 1967, Ran had to attend a three-month course in Arabic at the Army School of Education in Beaconsfield, in Berkshire. While there, he began plans for an expedition to ascend the Nile River from mouth to source with two Land Rovers and, as an afterthought, two mini-hovercraft. With a touch of optimism, he worked out that the journey would take less than six weeks and so would fit neatly into his annual leave period from the Sultan's army. It soon became clear this would not be long enough.

Shortly before his leave was due to start in February 1969, however, Ran's hand was slightly crushed and one finger joint almost removed during a violent night exercise in the mountains north of Mizwa. This required him to return home earlier for proper medical treatment, meaning that he could now expect at least ten weeks free for his Nile expedition. So it was with a light heart that he left for England.

There was a great deal to prepare in the ten days before we were due to leave for Egypt. My then girlfriend Ginny correlated and waterproofed 400 maps of the Nile. I had written to European manufacturers requesting free goods, but the response had been poor. Two Hoverhawk two-seater hovercraft had been promised me, but only now did I discover that the maximum distance one had ever travelled non-stop was four miles round and round a gravel pit. My cousin Gubbie's father-in-law, director general of the Automobile Association, responded to my appeal with the loan of a pensioned-off diesel Land Rover painted bright yellow. All efforts to borrow a second vehicle failed.

My worldly wealth consisted of £8,000. I would need this one day to marry and buy a home. But the Nile arrangements could go ahead only through private investment on my part, since to obtain a Land Rover and travel reservations to Egypt, I would need £6,000.

My mother was adamant. The money would be lost and I would end up with nothing. It was not fair to Ginny whose father, once a millionaire, was now bankrupt and unable to leave her a penny. I argued that, once demobbed, my only career potential lay with expeditions. The £6,000 was therefore an investment needed to lay the ground for bigger, more ambitious journeys to come. This appalled my mother, who could see no end to my lunatic approach to life and my failure to settle down to a worthwhile profession.

Since there was no alternative, I frittered away my private fortune in purchasing a brand-new petrol Land Rover, there being no available diesel models. To tow the two half-ton hovercraft behind the Land Rovers, we obtained trailers specially made by a company with a flourishing business in babies' perambulators.

The White Nile Expedition team were chosen without any check on their characters. The first member was Nick Holder, an old Mons Cadet School colleague. His place on the team was assured because the idea of the expedition had been his. He had read a book called *The White Nile* by Alan Moorehead and persuaded me to put things together for a voyage up the river. After three years with the Parachute Regiment, Nick had become a razor salesman for Gillette. They had posted him to Bahrain, a difficult mission since 95 per cent of the male inhabitants were bearded and the females were happy with hairy legs. Unable to alter one of the fundamental facets of Islam, Nick had left Gillette and was unemployed.

Peter Loyd was selected chiefly because we needed somebody who could handle a hovercraft and, unable to find such a person, I decided the next best thing must be a helicopter pilot. Like Nick Holder, he had been a member of the Norwegian parachute expedition the previous year.

A volunteer movie camera man, Anthony Brockhouse, and Mike Broome, a photographer, also joined up. We now needed only a hovercraft mechanic. The owner of our sponsors, Hoverhawk Ltd, an elderly but spirited lady, summoned her son the sales director, Charles Westmorland, and told him that he would accompany us. Charlie, thirty years old, displayed neither dismay nor surprise at his mother's announcement. I was to learn that Charlie never showed any emotion other than pleasure. He was ideal expedition material apart from his laugh, which was hysterical and uncontrollable.

We decided to name our two hovercraft Baker and Burton respectively, after the explorers whose Nile exploits and writings had added so much colour and romance to the history of the river.

The team met up at Dover in mid-February 1969 during a blizzard and drove through France and Italy, then by car ferry to Alexandria, Egypt. A few perfunctory sandbags rested against shop windows, the only visible sign of the war then raging with Israel.

The British consul handed me a letter from the embassy in Cairo. This had been sent too late to my home in England and then forwarded by my mother to Alexandria:

The Egyptian Ministry of Tourism have turned down your proposed expedition. This must be a disappointment to you but I am sure you will realise that . . . due to the war . . . foreigners are suspect ... Under normal circumstances you would have been welcome.

We set out at once to Cairo to remonstrate. We had planned to take the tarmac road to the north, but heavy military movement was in progress and we were diverted to the south-east through endless miles of gravel and sand. Then a tyre burst on a trailer and the wheel nuts would not budge. Two hours later we discovered they were French nuts and unscrewed the wrong way. God knows how the Concorde functioned.

We came to the three pyramids at Gizeh by midnight. Thirst and dust were forgotten as the dazzling illuminated cones rose quite suddenly into view. The evening's *son et lumière* had ended, but the lights were still on. The moon had come out and was visible as a darting yellow boomerang between racing nimbus clouds; wild pi-dogs howled from the sands, but the glow of Cairo's lights was already visible to the east.

Next day, the British military attaché in Cairo believed that we had arrived in good faith unaware of the official refusal. But, he told us, a state of emergency had been declared that very morning. Citizen forces were to be armed, civic buildings sandbagged and blacked-out by night. Patrol centres had been hurriedly established at each Nile bridge to watch for Israeli commandos in the guise of tourists.

The sudden sight of a hovercraft, never seen before on Egyptian soil or water, could well have provoked immediate action from the guards. They might have thought it was some new Israeli infernal machine come to destroy the United Arab Republic. Hovering on any part of the Nile within Egypt was therefore out of the question.

We spent the afternoon making arrangements to fit in with the altered programme. Since we were strictly 'The White Nile Hovercraft Expedition' and the White Nile begins (or ends, strictly speaking) at Khartoum, it made little difference how much hovering we did before reaching the city. But it meant that we would have to ship the vehicles by steamer through Lake Nasser, since the roads bordering it had been submerged.

The road from Cairo lay south into the midday sun. With three of us in the front of each Land Rover, the heat grew intolerable. Shirts stayed on, for the last thing we wanted to do was offend the locals. Five miles from the last of the Cairo suburbs, the military attaché left us and everything now depended on our reception at the first road-block and checkpoint.

El Aiyat was the first village we came to and the road vanished in a seething mass of curious Arabs, fruit vendors, over-loaded mules and camels, none of whom seemed to acknowledge our right of way. '*Tayyara abyad!*' was the cry passed on from mouth to mouth in the rising din, which soon surrounded and swamped us. 'White aeroplanes!' Quite why Baker and Burton had been dubbed as such, seeing that they obviously had no wings, was difficult to work out.

Shortly before we entered the town of El Wasta, a crude barrier pole across the road halted us. There was a small hut and from this emerged an impressive looking policeman followed by a number of swarthy henchmen in grey trousers and white shirts. The former saluted and looked us over with open curiosity.

'You are the helicopter trade party from England going through Africa, yes?' I nodded vigorously. 'You are lucky,' he said. 'All others we turn back but you have the Ministry of Tourism to thank. We give you an escort south.'

Months later we discovered that we had the hovercraft to thank. One of the Egyptian ministries, perhaps of Agriculture or Defence, was interested in their potential.

All went well until our escort cars abandoned us without explanation in El Minya, their klaxons still jangling. We were left in the walled compound of a government school with a police detachment, presumably to keep guard.

One corpulent policeman, who couldn't possibly have had a change of uniform since it had been issued to him, detached himself from his fellow gate-guards on smelling our coffee and cigarettes. He sat watching us until provided with both and then formed a protective devotion to Charlie, who had been swearing at him profusely. Much to Charlie's distress, this devotion found the fat policeman bedded down next to him, and although he placed a screen of camping equipment between them, they were soon snoring loudly together, which we recorded on tape and played back, to Charlie's embarrassment, the following morning.

From El Minya we carried on south to Luxor. The town had a distinct lack of campsites but, beside the police station, we found what Charlie called a lawn. All Luxor's dogs used this patch of waste ground, as did any local with garbage to dispose of. After dinner on the lawn, by the light of a sixty-watt street lamp, we sipped Horlicks and decided to take stock. Peter unrolled our main river map. This was an impressive sight, for it was eighteen feet long, some eighteen inches of which we had so far travelled. With a wax crayon, Peter carefully marked our journey to date with camp sites and dates.

As we squatted over the map, a police officer in smart black uniform with Teutonic knee-length boots appeared with five khaki-clad underlings sporting automatic rifles.

'You will now go to my room and take this chart with you. What do you do at this time of night in the darkness of these gardens that is so secret? You will explain your actions to my chief at once.'

I think he really felt he had made a major catch, as did the rifle-toting subordinates, who directed us to an office in the police building. We spent the next two hours trying to persuade the chief that we were engaged in a harmless journey up the Nile. He responded that the hovercraft were a very good cover for our spying activities and that our radios were very similar to those used by the Israelis. After much humming and Arab hawing, we were permitted to leave without the map and warned that we were under close observation and any irregular behaviour would see us in severe trouble.

Our schedule was now a week behind the timetable set in

London to keep us just ahead of the sandstorm season in Northern Sudan and the flood season in the Sudd swamp region.

At Shellal, just south of Aswan and the site of the Nile barrage, the southerly road ended, submerged by the new reservoir. We bought tickets for the 200-mile ferry trip down Lake Nasser bound for Wadi Haifa and the Sudan. Throughout the long hot journey, any passengers from the main deck wishing to reach the dining saloon had to climb over the bonnet of a Land Rover or crawl beneath the tow-hook of a trailer. Since the floor was coated in sheep dung, oil and orange skins, most of the passengers had no desire to make the trip, so we left our kit in the vehicles for once.

The water used for cooking, washing and drinking on board was all scooped up in buckets tied to ropes, and was, even in mid-lake, spiced with green and brown algae, which lent a sewage-like quality to its texture, and on reflection, generations of steamers with no in-built latrines had indeed been plying these waters. Our water sterilisers came into their own and the Nubian deck hands got a kick out of pumping them as vigorously as possible, so that pots of sterilised tea were soon being bought by all and sundry.

Bullfrogs and the usual Arab chanting kept us from sleeping at night. Charlie had discovered one of our whisky bottles in a Land Rover, so we drank and sang Scottish ballads on the roof to the tune of a hippy's guitar. Beneath us, in the silent dancing waters, lurked the microscopic death bug bilharzia. It is a highly unpleasant and, in its later stages, agonising sickness to contract. It lives in the blood and bladders of many African river folk and kills thousands annually. Even spray from a canoe paddle can contain the worm, which landing on human skin, will burrow into a pore to escape the hot sun.

We had been warned in London about the deadly little waterborne parasites, but seeing the inviting depths of moon-silvered waters and feeling unduly merry, we dived off the deck rails and floated in the cool lake. The skipper and his crew came running from their cabins when they heard the splashes and lined the railings in their white pyjamas. When they realised it was only the English hover people gone for a swim, they shrugged and returned to their berths. A month later, Nick developed bilharzia on returning to Britain and rather wished he had resisted the temptation to go for a swim.

Early in March we finally landed at Wadi Haifa, Arabic for grassy valley, now a sprawl of wood and tin shanties in the sand. We had entered the Sudan, Africa's largest country.

The grey-blue waters of Lake Nasser lie over an Atlantis of the Nubian Desert. The mighty Aswan Dam had already caused the river here to rise an incredible 470 feet, with a further eighty feet still to go before the villagers could build permanent homes beside the new banks.

Ibrahim, the temporary commissioner of Wadi Haifa, gave me a telegram from Khartoum where the commercial attaché at our embassy, guessing at our likely arrival date, had arranged for a public hovercraft demonstration. The president and entire supreme court of the Sudan would attend. We had just eight days to hover 1,000 miles of Nile. I told Ibrahim we would set out as soon as the hovercraft were ready.

Twenty-four hours later, we left the Land Rover team of Peter, Nick and our photograher, and with much revving of the engines, slid down the beach and away over the dawn-chilled waters of the lake with hardly a ripple to mark our passage. I drove Baker with fifteen spare gallons of fuel, while Charlie Westmorland shared his cramped cab with Anthony Brockhouse, our ciné cameraman. Burton was the newer but slower craft.

Wadi Haifa's low shacks soon disappeared. The lake was so wide and the enclosing granite hills so uniform that I could identify no break in the horizon to head for. Burton soon fell behind, a fast diminishing speck only visible when the rays of the morning sun reflected from the white fibreglass hull.

Rather than lose Charlie for the rest of the day and unable to slow down without unsettling the temperamental setting of engines and skirt, I circled slowly to the east and north until I headed back towards him. Now the gap between us closed with surprising speed for there was no sound and no sensation of movement, just the faint pull on the steering wheel as a breeze caught the fins. It was a novel feeling, quite unlike any other dimension of propulsion, and exaggerated by the vast and lonely lake.

We intended to camp at Akasha, a village above the flood level, where we would await the Land Rovers and more fuel. But one of Baker's engines began to overheat. I attracted Charlie's attention and made for the nearest beach. Repair work would take some time, so we made camp.

We made radio contact with Peter Loyd. His news was also bad. Thirty miles to the east, the Land Rovers were bogged down in a trackless desert bowl surrounded by mountains. Their guide, a pitch black Haifan, insisting he knew the way, had led them from any usable trail into soft sand where a clutch had burned out. Peter was not sure how far they were from Akasha or whether they could find a way back to Wadi Haifa through the surrounding maze of sand dunes and bands of rock. The wind had obliterated their tracks behind them.

If they could replace the clutch they would attempt to return to Wadi Haifa. We had sufficient fuel, so I told Peter we would also head back once Baker was repaired. There was always the railway, which might still get us to Khartoum in time for the exhibition.

Charlie announced that Baker had blown a piston head, which would involve at least twenty-four hours of improvisation work to replace. On the second night, Anthony was woken by a primordial roar from the lake: he froze with horror in the dark as the sound of emerging bodies left the waves and began to ascend the beach. He stumbled to higher ground and, training his eyes, made out three alligator shapes in the sand. At dawn, as the wind-whipped lake turned slowly orange, Anthony discovered that his nocturnal visitors were horned lizards some four feet long. Before the sun rose they returned to the water.

Once the repairs were completed, our journey back to Wadi Haifa was enlivened by the winds, which covered the lake in a sand cloud. Charlie used compass and drift estimation to land us quite near to our old campsite and there, a day later, we rejoined the others.

The weekly train to Khartoum left the next day and Ibrahim cabled for two open wagons to be sent. These would carry our vehicles at little extra cost.

That evening the local football team, who doubled as the town band, agreed to a song-and-dance show in our camp. Between the Land Rovers we built a log fire and, unaware of any danger, Peter lit it with a match. Downwind and on the far side of a vehicle, Mike Broome, our photographer, had decided to make fire pots to provide more light for the dancers. He filled three tins with sand which he soaked in petrol from a jerry can. There was sudden thud of exploding ignition followed by shrill screams.

Peter and I peered around the Land Rover and found Mike blindly pawing himself as a ball of flames enveloped him from knees to head. There was a nightmarish second of inactivity, so sudden and unexpected was the event. Then we jumped on Mike and rolled him in the sand, heaping handfuls of it on his face and hands which were soaked in fuel. The fire kept reigniting but at length we extinguished the last flame and Mike stopped screaming. He lay curled up like a grotesque foetus and stared moaning at the layers of blistered skin that hung in shrouds from his arms, stomach and thighs. Raw and bleeding flesh showed through where we had rubbed sand on burning skin.

I gave him a morphine jab and applied loose paraffin gauze dressings to the open wounds. Not having piped water, Wadi Haifans had to defecate on the beach and the dirt was spread about by minute sand flies, so Mike's wounds were likely to be infected. The local doctor, who arrived two hours later, administered penicillin pills and did his best to swab the gritty sand from the wounds, before coating Mike in purple gentian violet. He

Ran leading his team on the first recorded descent of
the Briksdalsbre Glacier, Norway, 1970.

Ran tries to prevent branches from puncturing his boat in a massive log jam on Williston Lake, British Columbia, Canada, 1971.

Ran and Stanley Cribbett negotiate the dangerous Bridge River Rapids in British Columbia, 1971.

The two Hoverhawk two-seater hovercraft, *Baker* and *Burton*, on the banks of the River Nile, 1969.

Ran, Charlie Burton and Oliver Shepard in the Sahara Desert on the first leg of the Transglobe Expedition, 1979.

Ollie Shepard collecting skinks in the sand dunes of the Sahara for the Natural History Museum, 1979.

North Pole, Easter Day, 1982. Ran and Charlie Burton are the first men in history to reach both Poles.

Charlie and Ran in their tent. They spent three months floating hundreds of miles south on a slowly disintegrating ice floe, 1982.

Anton Bowring pours champagne aboard the *Benjamin Bowring* to celebrate the successful crossing of the Arctic Ocean, 1982.

Mike Stroud and Ran manhauling their 485-pound sledges on the first totally unsupported crossing of the Antarctic landmass, 1992.

Ran suffering the effects of UV light rays on his face from the hole in the ozone layer, Antarctica, 1992.

Ran meets his great polar rival, Norwegian explorer Børge Ousland (left), in Antarctica, 1996.

Dr Ron Blom, Nick Clapp and Ran searching for the lost city of Ubar, deep in Arabia's Empty Quarter, 1991.

Mike Stroud and Ran in New York after completing seven marathons in seven days on seven continents, 2003.

Learning the ropes on a climb of the Old Man of Hoy in the Orkneys, in training for the North Face of the Eiger, 2007.

On the notorious 'Murder Wall', the Eiger North Face, trying hard not to look down, 2007.

Climbing the North Col on Mount Everest without oxygen on his second attempt to reach the summit, 2008.

Third time lucky. Ran stands with Sherpa Tundu on the summit of Mount Everest, 2009.

mentioned 25 per cent burns, but seemed sure that the patient would survive, which was the main thing.

Later the Nubian football team came, whilst Mike slept after more morphine, and wild Nubian songs accompanied the rhythmic tap of their goatskin drums far into the night. Their white djellabia robes flowing in the fitful gusts, they danced a strange version of the foxtrot with hands clapping in unison and grinning faces jerking puppet-like to emphasise the beat. I have never met a more genuine and attractive people than the Nubians at home in their inhospitable deserts.

We left Wadi Haifa the next day on a great steel train made years ago in Birmingham. We stripped to our shorts because it was so hot. Nick opened a window but hot choking clouds of dust and soot poured in. So we sat on the wooden seats dripping in sweat, as though the carriage was a sauna. Mike's sweat ran into his wounds and the salt added to his discomfort. I fed him bananas, aiming with care at his mouth as the train jerked spitefully.

After stopping at Berber, where we bought some fizzy apple juice and lumps of crushed dates, we passed through peaceful Atbara, with its throngs of raucous street urchins and gangling camels, their purple-dyed backs marking them as bound for the slaughter house. Here the daily slave parades were once held, gleaming bodies of every hue and both sexes receiving the intimate inspections of the dealers and buyers, while onlookers cracked crude jokes as to their origins and possible destination.

The dealers obtained ivory for their slaves, and with the ivory they made fortunes selling it to Europe, where the rich made comely fans, billiard balls and keys for the pianos in their lush drawing-rooms. A far cry from the soulful drumbeat echoing along the banks of the distant Nile.

The train journey can take anything between thirty hours and two days depending on the temperament of the steam locomotives that make the trip, but we were only some eight hours behind schedule when we pulled in thankfully to Khartoum's central station.

The British military attaché met us and took Mike Broome to hospital prior to the next flight to London. I cabled Ginny to meet him with an ambulance and to arrange things with the Burns Unit at Roehampton. He was to spend eighteen months having skin graft operations before he fully recovered. After the night of that fire, I always took my own expedition pictures.

We had twelve hours in which to prepare for the well-advertised hover demonstration and drove to Gordon's Palace, which faces the confluence of the Blue and White Niles opposite Tuti Island. On a wide grassy bank beside the river we laid out radios, water sterilisers, tropical gear, medical kits, weapons, mini-rations, both Land Rovers and Baker. Sales brochures were placed on folding tables and the attaché promised a police unit to marshal the expected crowds.

The next day, we staged our show, the largest commercial demonstration ever held in Khartoum, with Peter Loyd and Nick Holder manning the equipment and Charlie thrilling the crowds that packed the banks and beaches overlooking Tuti Island. The president and his three-minister supreme court arrived in a purple Rolls-Royce and with a chauffeur in a purple uniform. I shook the eminent hands and gave the ministers a quick tour of the equipment.

The president was small and short-sighted, so Peter radioed Charlie to bring Burton close inshore. The craft approached the palace at speed and performed a succession of 360° skids right beneath the Rolls-Royce. Then Burton swung across the broad river and headed straight for the sandy shores of Tuti Island at thirty knots.

The president and the hushed crowd seemed alarmed . . . there would be an accident. But no, bucking like a thoroughbred, the little machine, accelerating still, left the water and roared over the undulating dunes between logs and other jetsam. A sudden spray arose as Burton hit the water on the far side of the island and a rapturous cheer of wonder erupted from the spectators. For half an hour, Charlie charged around the arena in fine style and the crowd never failed to produce a deep-throated 'Ooooh-ahh' at each transference from water to land and back.

The Army commander-in-chief took the radio from Peter and, speaking direct to Charlie, ordered him around the island in a series of tight loops. Other officers and presidential staff were all eager to 'have a go' but, luckily, the president took his leave after wishing us a safe journey, so Peter retrieved the radio and Charlie made good his escape.

The British Embassy staff were delighted. A flood of enquiries for sales details followed the show and our arrangements to travel south into the Great Sudd swamp and the war zone were smoothed by the presidential pleasure. A month later, the *Daily Telegraph* reported that our 'expedition was doing much to improve the friendship and goodwill between Britain and the Sudan.'

The humidity increased as we headed south. The seven-month rainy season was due and the land simmered in sultry expectation. We felt clammy and irritable. Clouds of flying, biting ants attacked us in the grasslands south of Khartoum. Scratches and sores tended to infection despite antiseptic cream. Two months earlier, during a training exercise at night, a Baluchi soldier had stomped his rifle butt on my hand and half-severed a finger. This had become swollen and reopened where the stitches had been.

We had followed the Nile for 2,000 miles but the river ran on for the same distance again. Any day now the rains would come and waterlog all tracks within 100 miles of the river. These rains annually rendered impassable an area of Sudan larger than Great Britain, a fact which I pondered as we camped by the camel beach of Ed Dueim. All our refuelling points in southern Sudan were beside the river and well off the main north–south track, easily accessible only until the grass prairies turned to marsh.

South of Ed Dueim, we hovered without problems until we met the northern outriders of water hyacinth, a modern scourge of the Nile. This purple-flowered water-cabbage floats on a buoyant tuber and grows six inches high. Triffid-like, the bulbs multiply and cover huge areas of river, obstructing all river traffic, including hovercraft. We smashed our way through many wind-blown islands of hyacinth, some of them sixty feet wide and all but covering the river from bank to bank.

I took over from Peter as a Land Rover driver for several days and I was able to see the countryside, impossible from the hovercraft, as we headed into the fringelands of the Sudd. For 100 miles either side of El Jebelain, the track was rutted with hummocks so high they could only be crossed by unhooking the trailers and hauling them over manually. Red dust clogged our nostrils and goggles.

The Nile around Malut, where we changed over driving roles, was free from hyacinth so the hovercraft made good headway. We saw herons fishing from floating islands of weed, and otter-like animals that stood on their hindlegs to watch us pass. Hippopotami scowled at us but I saw no crocodiles. Storms broke with brief intensity and I prayed that they were not the first broadside of the rains.

After each squall the river boiled for a period – a seething cauldron of spinach soup. Swirling eddies toyed with islands of rotting papyrus and half-sunken logs lurched sideways in the grip of whirlpools, making navigation tricky. We sweltered in the cockpits, trying to ration our water, and stopped only at refuelling points.

I was glad to be hovering on the day we came to Malakal, capital of the Upper Nile Province and of all the Shilluk tribal lands. The river here was just as described in the books of General Gordon's day. Avenues of shady palms hugged the eastern bank along which the townsfolk promenaded. Arabs in white robes and yellow turbans strolled by hand in hand. Shilluks, their faces and shoulders pocked with tribal cicatrices, bore bundles of hippo hide, while gangs of naked children, wide-eyed and hands held high, stopped their play to see the hovercraft slide by.

Ancient paddle-steamers, some aground, lined the banks, their cracked lattice shutters swinging with the storm swell. From the windows and low rotting passenger decks there plunged and screamed the shiny naked bodies of happy Shilluk, young and old, enjoying their poor man's funfair. Red cloaks and spears lay discarded on the roof decks.

The Malakal police appeared within minutes of our arrival and introduced us to the local Army commander. They had been expecting us for three weeks and, with the other members of the local junta, had organised and advertised a 'hoverplane show' like the Khartoum one he had heard vividly described on his radio.

'Can you do the show tomorrow?' he asked. When we agreed, he summoned runners who went off, excited, to pass on the news.

Charlie and Peter located a suitable launch site on a muddy slope between two steamers. From there, out of curiosity, they hovered upriver for some miles towards Lake No, where the river becomes known as the Bahr el Jebel, the Mountain Sea, and the true Sudd swamps began.

Our demonstration was to start at noon, but by sun-up, the tribesmen were already arriving from the outlying villages. The commissioner, chiefs and dignitaries brought shooting sticks. Everyone else crowded around the muddy arena, kept back by police with rhino-whips.

I shouldered my way through the heaving, shouting throng, coming into frequent contact with the bouncing bare breasts of excited female spectators. The ostrich feathers of soldiers' bush hats were died according to the colours of their regiments, three of which had arrived by steamer that morning from the war zone.

All was ready at the riverside by noon. The shouts of the crowd were full of anticipation. I felt apprehensive. Our audience included Shilluk, Dinka, Nuer, even the light-skinned Azande. Many had scaled lofty trees by the riverside, others, on the steamers, clung to running-boards or to the hafts of spears which they had plunged into the woodwork. Many children, pushed forward by those on the banks, stood up to their waists in the muddy shallows.

The hovercraft slid away to a roar from the watchers and accelerated through small isles of hyacinth. Charlie then launched Burton into a series of figure-of-eights perilously close to the steamers. The thousands of bunched Malakalis loved this and screamed their approval.

Then the show turned sour.

A dozen militiamen were trying to keep our landing ramp free, lashing out with their whips. A tangle of hyacinth snared Baker's skirt and Peter switched to full throttle to charge the ramp, intending to clear away the weeds. The hovercraft surged out of the water at twenty knots to climb the bank. A sign of wonder at this amphibious magic sparked a sudden scrabble at the rear of the throng. The resulting pressure at the front, quite unstoppable by the police, pushed a mass of naked children down on the ramp just as Baker roared up it. I caught a glimpse of Peter's face, mouth frozen open, as he swung the wheel in vain to avoid the human wall.

There were screams and shrieks of pain ahead and bellows of confusion behind. I fought my way down the bank as the hovercraft slid back into the Nile, sucking an unknown number of children into the mud under its skirt. Peter cut both drive engines. The propellors feathered to a standstill. With the quick reaction of a helicopter pilot, he left the engine running. Better to risk its blades cutting into a chance limb than allow the half-ton machine to sink into the mud and crush the trapped children.

Nick and I scrabbled in the mud, stretching our arms downwards as far as we could with our nostrils still above the slime. A policeman grasped a flailing limb and we lifted the skirt until a small body, all blood and filth, came clear and was passed none too gently into the screaming crowd. Two more bodies were removed soon afterwards.

'Are they alive?' I shouted. Nobody answered.

Carefully, we edged Baker out from the mud to deeper water where Peter switched off and the hovercraft's lower hull sank slowly into the water. The accident area was now awash with policemen prodding the mud with spear-butts and shouting to each other.

Nick grasped my arm. Clenched fists and shaken spears accentuated the growing anger of the chanting crowd. It was not difficult to divine that we were the source of their displeasure and I was relieved when police reinforcements appeared alongside a battered ambulance. A uniformed inspector beckoned to us and, with the others from the hovercraft, we retired under escort to the Army compound.

That night a government official arrested Peter Loyd and took him away to police HQ. I thought of our schedule, the imminent rains and the vast swamp to our south. We could ill afford a long delay in Malakal as prison visitors.

Some hours later a thoughtful officer came to tell us how things were progressing. The Malakal magistrate, a Nubian, was well aware he must be seen to dole out stiff justice to foreigners in the south just as he would in the north. The two sectors of Sudan had long been at each other's throats, the largely Christian south resentful of the Muslim government in Khartoum. Sudanese law was tough on traffic violations and manslaughter was punishable by a long gaol sentence.

By good fortune the judge received a hospital report on the victims before he reached a decision about Peter. One child had lost an ear and two had internal injuries. Otherwise none was seriously hurt. I sent a silent thank you heavenwards on hearing this.

After hours of waiting, Peter was summoned to the old judge, who told him: 'Our law is still that of the British administration and I have found no clause which covers your offence. You were driving neither a boat nor a road vehicle and there is no legislation at all concerning vehicles which hover, an omission about which I will inform Khartoum.'

Since Peter had transgressed no written law, no charge would be pressed. He received a severe warning and was dismissed. Charlie bustled us into action. The rains were coming. We left at dawn knowing that in a short while the only southerly track through the Sudd would be submerged.

The Sudd, which means 'block' in Arabic, is a meandering labyrinth of dank waterways. Only the best river pilots, who have traversed the region many times as apprentices, can afford to be confident in the swamps because the navigable channels are always changing. A single storm can alter the geography of the terrain overnight by breaking up whole islands of stinking vegetation and piling uprooted banks of reed one upon the other, crushing and suffocating any trapped creature. Dead crocodiles and hippos float bloated in newly formed streams that were previously part of the swampy mainland.

We travelled in the Land Rovers mile after mile through drenching rain. Progress was possible only in first gear and four-wheel drive. Often we de-bussed to push and pull. Mud clogged our boots like snowshoes.

We came to Mogoch, a miserable patch of high ground with only five villagers, at midnight. These people were of the Twae or Thunderbolt sub-tribe, sister clan to the Than people who lived on remote islands in the Sudd, eating only fish and hippo flesh. The next day we skidded and pushed our way to the Duk, a north–south ridge of high ground mere yards above the high-water level and, once on it, made better progress.

Bor forest lay ahead, scene of many a fatal ambush by the secessionist Anya Nya guerrillas. Nick handed out our loaded guns.

Black clouds spat forked lightning across the southern horizon and, as we entered the confines of the forest, the heavens opened. The storm broke with deafening force. Thick branches cracked and broke above us and cascades of red slime splashed up from the track. The forest was a gloomy place straight from the pages of Tolkein or Peake, with thick foliage closing above the track where grotesquely mildewed branches entwined overhead.

We crossed many gulleys over turbulent floodwater, praying as we went that haphazardly laid bridge-planks would not give way. We strained with ropes and makeshift levers each time the mud bogged our trailer. We became more fearful of being cut off by floods than of ambush. Baker came unlashed and fell down a rocky gulley *en route*. With a struggle, the hovercraft was reloaded and we pushed on. At last we came to Bor, where the Nile was briefly narrow and high-banked. We slept at once, too tired even to erect mosquito nets.

In return for signed entry permits to the next province, an active war zone, we donated Baker, damaged beyond repair, to the district commissioner of Bor. He was a keen gardener and positioned Baker in his Nile-side marrow patch as a hippo-scare. Someday I must return to Bor, if ever the interminable civil war allows, to see if it is still in residence.

With only one machine between five of us, we agreed to let Charlie Westmorland, with a triple fuel load, hover south in Burton. We would hitch a lift with the vehicles on the weekly ferry between Bor and Juba. All roads south of Bor had long been washed away by floods or destroyed by guerrillas. They had been closed to traffic for the past four years.

Sandbagged machine-gun positions decorated the stern and roof deck of the tiny tugboat, which powered two flat-top barges lashed like saddlebags to its hull. We strapped a Land Rover to each barge and fixed our mosquito nets on poles above the cargo of flour sacks.

Charlie was quite prepared to take Burton on alone to Juba, but the very real threat of Anya Nya ambushes made this course inadvisable and he agreed to compromise. So Burton hovered in long slow circles, never quite out of sight of the ferry's machine guns, and Charlie grew hourly more frustrated. His boredom was alleviated by the occasional hippo and crocodile and sometimes he showed off his hover skills by inducing skid-turns around hyacinth islands.

The ferry pilot managed to steer upriver only by bouncing his barges off the outer bank on each bend, a slow and giddy process that recurred hundreds of times during the three-day journey to Juba. Charlie estimated that, given a free rein, he could have hovered to Juba in less than one day. Nevertheless, we arrived at the Nile-side town, nerve centre of government operations in the war zone, with a sense of relief. This was a nuisance, because Charlie was rightly adamant that we should take Burton to the source of the Nile, Lake Victoria, rather than abandon the hovercraft in Juba and continue with only the Land Rovers.

Fortune intervened in the shape of Ahmed el Sherif el Habib, commander of operations in Equatoria, who came to look at Burton. I told the general about our transport problem. That night we were invited to a dance at the Juba Officers' Mess. There were no women, so staff officers danced together or with guests such as ourselves and a Japanese salesman. Jiving was the 'in' step and the favourite tune was 'Yellow Submarine' by the Beatles. After dancing with a portly colonel and the Japanese salesman, I felt my duty was done.

So apparently did the general, who winked, as I bowed my farewell, and said simply: 'All will be well for your journey, young man. I will see to it.'

We left the very next day, Burton riding high on an army truck, by river ferry to Gondokoro on the east bank. A twelve-man platoon escorted us through the forests to the Ugandan border. We crossed many river bridges, each of which was protected by a troop of armoured vehicles. All habitation between Juba and the frontier had been destroyed by brutal scorched-earth operations some years before.

Late one night our escort unloaded Burton on to the dust at Nimule, six yards on the Sudan side of the border post. Peter Loyd and Nick Holder drove away at once in the diesel Land Rover, already three weeks late back to their respective jobs.

Ninety miles from Nimule we found a merchant with a pick-up truck who agreed to take Burton south to Kampala. Back at the border post, with the help of the customs chief and his wife, we lifted the hovercraft on to the flat-back van, the suspension springs of which turned concave.

On 3 April, three weeks behind schedule, Charlie proudly took Burton over the yacht-club lawn at Gaba on to the clear surface of Lake Victoria. The East African Press turned out in strength to witness the advent of Uganda's first hovercraft and, as in the Sudan, agents were found on behalf of Hoverair to process sales orders. Businessmen and government ministers came in droves from Kampala and nearby industrial Juba.

The British military attaché introduced me to a fat corporal in the King's African Rifles named Idi Amin. The corporal was obviously of an ambitious nature since he requested a hovering lesson. Charlie, eyeing his bulk, tactfully refused.

Substantial export orders for Hoverhawks followed the expedition and the UK Ministry of Technology, impressed by the evident toughness of Burton, arranged a sales tour of Canada and the USA. Within two years, £20m in export orders from those countries alone had been placed for the little machines which, like all small hovercraft, had previously suffered from the stigma of unreliability.

We had not been able to hover up the length of the Nile, but then neither did the early explorers manage to follow its entire course. Like them, we had glimpsed the colourful interiors of the countries through which the river flows.

There are less rewarding ways of spending an Army leave.

Børge Ousland
Norwegian polar explorer

In 1996, I was planning a crossing of Antarctica, alone from coast to coast and without resupply. Ranulph Fiennes had similar plans, and naturally we both had a burning desire to be the first. The trip was described as one of the last great remaining challenges in the polar regions, and the old rivalry between Scott and Amundsen was one the media still knew how to use.

Everyone going to the South Pole gathers in Punta Arenas in Chile before departure, and it was there I met Ran for the first time. We were not completely unknown to each other. In 1990, we had both tried to be the first to reach the North Pole on skis and without resupply. Before then, I had got hold of a copy of his book about the Transglobe Expedition and I remember being hugely inspired by him, and still am.

So I was a bit excited that autumn day in 1996. Although we were equal, in a sense, he was almost twenty years older and had done so many expeditions. Ran was a tall fellow with a sharp expression on his weather-beaten face, and with his gentlemanly appearance he had a certain upper hand when we met. But even though we assessed each other a bit to start with, it didn't take long before we shared advice and experiences from the ice.

I see competition as something positive, it makes you focus that little extra, and an old-fashioned rivalry is good for both the media attention and sponsors. No great experience in life is worth anything without overcoming your fears, I usually say when I give talks. Then I think of Ran. I have always had great respect for him. When he climbed Everest at the age of sixty-five, I sent him a postcard to congratulate him on the feat. I wanted to say how impressed I am that he just keeps going and never stops.

I could not have asked for a more worthy 'competitor'. Thank you, Ran!

Ran during the first totally unsupported crossing of the Antarctic landmass with Mike Stroud, 1993.

10

South Pole

The first totally unsupported crossing
of the Antarctic landmass
1993

During their successful Transglobe Expedition in the early
1980s, Ran, Ollie Shepard and Charlie Burton had crossed
Antarctica in sixty-seven days using skidoos and refuelling
dumps. In mid-1990, Shepard and Burton approached Ran
with another suggestion. How about us making the first totally
unassisted crossing of Antarctica, they said, manhauling our
sledges like Captain Scott and his team had tried to do. Ran
thought it was a good idea, but he already had other expedi-
tion plans at the time. Then a year later, a piece of news
changed his mind.

I had done nothing about an unsupported Antarctic crossing
journey originally mooted by Ollie and Charlie, but in London I
heard that Norwegian plans for an Antarctic record-breaking
journey were afoot by Erling Kagge, our earlier rival in the north
and an exceptionally fine cross-country skier. Without delay I
started to raise sponsorship for Antarctica. With Kagge as a rival,
speed and endurance would now be a high priority for our team
and I was concerned about our collective stamina. I had recently
noticed what looked like a paunch on Charlie.

In mid-May 1991, I went to a trade fair at Olympia where Ollie had organised a sales stand for his employers. By chance, Charlie Burton was in charge of security there, so I was able to explain my worries to them both, and suggested that I ask Mike Stroud to join our team.

'He is like a bull terrier,' I stressed, 'small in stature but incredibly powerful.'

'That's great,' Charlie remonstrated, 'but where does that leave us oldies? Surely a team moves at the pace of its slowest member?' It was agreed that some thought would be given to the idea of inviting Mike along and, not long afterwards, Ollie called me to say that he and Charlie had both decided to change their role in the project. 'We would want to enjoy the experience,' Charlie told me later, 'and I know that, once you get competitive, you take any signs of enjoyment on my part as being tantamount to mutiny and a clear sign that we should be travelling faster.'

So he and Ollie took on the role of organisers from London, and I approached Mike Stroud by telephone.

I knew very little in depth about Mike. This may seem strange as he had, by 1990, already come on four of my Arctic expeditions and we had been through a great deal together. To take *friends* on stressful expeditions has always seemed to me to be foolish, since I can think of no easier way of marring a friendship forever. An expedition's aim is best achieved by individuals who can look after themselves, need little or no directing or nursing and are tough in body and mind. I look for professional or dogged people and treat any friendship resulting from an expedition as an unexpected bonus.

Polar expeditions are well known for causing stress and enmity between participants and quite why Ollie, Charlie, Mike and I had never come to blows, literally or even verbally, during our Arctic journeys remains a mystery to me.

'I know you. You like to lead from the front,' Mike observed. I conceded we would take hourly turns in navigation before he finally agreed to join. He also wrung out of me the agreement that he could conduct an extensive physiological research programme throughout the journey. This was bad news since I hate the sight of blood, especially my own, but it seemed a reasonable penalty in order to secure Mike's participation.

Prince Charles was once more our patron and he asked us to use the expedition to raise funds for multiple sclerosis research. We partly based this on members of the public pledging a penny a mile covered. Since Antarctica is over fifty times the size of Great Britain, a lot of pennies were involved.

Timing, as ever, is crucial when contemplating the Antarctic. Because the Antarctic plateau is so high and so cold, the period when humans can travel over it is severely limited. So is the availability of transport to and from Antarctica. We would be flown in on the Atlantic side and taken off by cruise ship on the Pacific side, which meant walking 1,700 miles between 1 November 1992, the very earliest flight date, and 16 February, the cruise ship's departure date. We would be pulling sledges at least sixteen miles a day for 108 days with loads likely to exceed 350 pounds, well in excess of any manhauling achievements to date.

In 1903, Scott, Shackleton and Wilson hauled loads of 175 pounds. Eight years later, on 'the worst journey in the world', Wilson, Bowers and Cherry-Garrard started out with 253 pounds. Especially unnerving for us were the much more recent observations of Reinhold Messner, the world's greatest mountaineer, and Arved Fuchs, Germany's top polar explorer, during their own crossing attempt. I had serious doubts that Mike and I could outperform such a team. Of his Antarctic journey, Messner wrote: 'With sledge-loads of 264lbs, the longest stretch would be murderously strenuous. Perhaps even impossible . . . 264lbs is a load for a horse not a human being.'

By early October the projected weight of our sledge-loads had gone up to 400 pounds. We were entering the realms of the theoretically impossible, but it was too late to back out now. To mention 400 pounds per load to anyone with the slightest knowledge of manhauling was to invite ridicule . . . so we didn't. The starting loads finally climbed to 485 pounds each. And that despite paring our gear down to minimal necessities.

On a gusty morning in late October, Ginny drove me to Heathrow. We said goodbye in the car park, for there would be many people in the terminal. I waved as she drove off and thanked God for her. I had told myself after many previous journeys that I would never again leave her at our bleak Exmoor home for the long and lonely winter. As she left I felt wretchedly guilty. It occurred to me that *I* had never spent a single night alone at our house on the moor.

As Mike Stroud and Morag Howell, in charge of our communications, chatted on the plane, I idly considered their motives in coming along. I knew Mike's. He had spent two years of his life, seven years earlier, hoping to walk to the South Pole with Robert Swan and Roger Mear but, to his dismay, the Canadian Gareth Wood was eventually selected, leaving him merely first reserve. Now, whether or not we managed to cross the whole continent, he knew that he stood a chance of at least making it to the Pole.

The KLM Boeing stopped at Sao Paulo, Montevideo, Santiago, Puerto Montt and finally Punta Arenas on the southern tip of Chile. We were met there by Annie Kershaw of Adventure Network (ANI). Annie was the widow of Giles Kershaw, our Transglobe Twin Otter pilot in Antarctica, who had later died in a gyrocopter accident. She had taken over running ANI, his polar air charter business on his death.

Her first DC6 passenger flight of the year to her tented camp and ice runway at Patriot Hills in Antarctica was scheduled to depart two days after our arrival in Punta Arenas, South America's most southerly city. Unfortunately, engine problems delayed take off for six days, the first dent in our tight schedule.

We flew south over the South Atlantic and then Antarctica for nine hours. At last, in the endless white sheet below we glimpsed a flash of tiny figures, tents and two Twin Otters. The notorious blue ice airstrip of Patriot Hills flashed beneath us. Twice our Canadian pilot rehearsed his landing to test the cross-wind. Then, with a shattering impact that could not have done any part of the DC6 much good, we struck the ice and bounced, rattling over the rippled blue surface. I do not remember any other landing even half as impressive in thirty years of arriving at remote spots in small aircraft.

Three hours later, Mike and I had transferred to one of the Twin Otters bound for Antarctica's Atlantic coastline. With us were Terry Lloyd of the new ITN film team, Rob Bowles and our radio base leader, Morag Howell. The Twin Otter ski plane roared over the ice-front of the Weddell Sea, a vertical cliff forming the seaward face of the Filchner Ice Shelf. Antarctica is composed of two vast ice-sheets divided by a mountain chain. The sheets contain ten million square kilometres of ice which, in places, is four and a half kilometres thick and moves slowly but surely seawards.

This huge wilderness provides scientists with a unique play-ground of volcanoes, fast-flowing glaciers, mobile ice sheets, katabatic winds of frightening power and a perfectly pure and sterile interior where temperatures in winter can reach −100°C. After several cautious rehearsals, our pilot found a relatively smooth stretch of snow at the point where Berkner Island meets both the ice shelf and the sea. We were set down at 78°19.8' South and 43°47' West on Antarctica's Atlantic seaboard.

Morag helped us unload and wished us well. For the next few months she would attempt to keep radio contact with us from a tent at Patriot Hills and with our UK base, which was manned by her husband Laurence Howell, known as Flo, at their home in Aberdeen. We watched the little aircraft depart until the engine noise was a distant drone and the great silence of Antarctica closed about us.

Months of unspoken apprehension were coming to a head. The key question was whether or not full loads of 485 pounds each, including the hundred days' fuel taken on at Patriot Hills, could be moved by the two of us. The main bulk was rations. These were equally important both to our chances of success and to

Mike's physiological research. Each bag was packed to provide two men with twenty-four hours of food at a daily intake of 5,200 calories. This packing system had evolved over a period of sixteen years of polar journeys, beginning with my first North Pole attempt in 1976.

The average daily intake of both Scott's and Amundsen's teams was 4,500 calories per man. This proved enough for the Norwegians, who skied unencumbered and with husky power. But to support the hard labour of the British manhaulers, the amount was insufficient and they slowly starved. The first man to weaken and die was Taff Evans, the biggest and heaviest on Scott's team, the man they 'least expected to fail'.

I considered our team's vital statistics. I was eleven years older than Mike and approaching my fiftieth birthday. I was taller by five inches and heavier by three stone. But in terms of sheer strength, especially of the vital lower limb powerbase, Mike was clinically tested as considerably stronger.

At home on our Exmoor farm, Ginny would give me twice her own food portions, although she worked harder than I did. Over the months ahead I would be consuming exactly the same calorific intake as Mike. I feared that, like the heavily built Evans on Scott's team, my performance would deteriorate first and more markedly than Mike's. I determined from the outset, therefore, to avoid my normal course of forging ahead at maximum output.

As each piece of equipment was loaded we ticked it off in our notebooks, alongside its weight, down to the nearest ounce. The total was, as we had feared, 485 pounds each, constituting far heavier loads than those of any previous polar manhaul journey on record.

We finished loading the sledges and looked at their bulk. Then at each other, and shrugged. The moment of truth had arrived. We adjusted the manhaul harnesses about our stomachs and shoulders. I leaned against the traces with my full bodyweight. The near half-ton sledge paid no attention. I looked back and spotted an eight-inch rut across the front of the runners. I tugged again with my left shoulder only, and the sledge, avoiding the rut, moved forward. I will never forget that instant. I *could* pull a 485-pound sledge. Mike was also on the move. The expedition was under way.

After a hundred yards I stopped, out of breath. I was pleased to see, looking back, that Mike was also labouring hard. The thought of pulling my sledge for an entire mile, never mind to the South Pole and beyond, was appalling. The map, or strictly speaking chart (since the sea was beneath us), showed a rash of blue lines, the crevasse symbol, running south along the foot of Berkner Island for some eighty miles.

Should we fix a safety line between us before reaching the first crevasse? I knew this was our agreed drill, but the sheer weight of the sledge had already biased me against any action beyond the sheer task of progress. Even though we were descending a gentle incline, the sledge was totally inert. The very instant I stopped pulling, it stopped moving. There was not the least glissade. I conjured up a parallel. If I were to lash together three average-sized adults, each weighing 160 pounds, dump them in a fibreglass bathtub with no legs and then drag them through sand dunes for 1,700 miles, the difficulties involved would be similar.

After two hours I felt certain we had reached the ice shelf. About a mile behind us and to our immediate north was the ice-front, a chaotic jumble of giant ice fragments where shelf met true sea ice. In every other direction there was nothing but mirage shimmer and the great white glare of Antarctica.

After five and a half hours it was time to halt, for we had been awake for twenty-four hours since leaving Punta Arenas. For navigation purposes, we must keep to a carefully timed daily schedule. I intended to use my watch and body shadow to establish direction all the way to the Pole and that meant keeping the sun due north at local midday. There were, I reasoned, only another 1,696 miles to cover and, since we had rations for a hundred days, there was yet time to find a way of increasing the daily average to sixteen miles. There must be absolutely no rest days or we would fail.

Remembering the promise I had made to Mike, I alternated the navigation with him at hourly intervals. I found this increasingly annoying, since I had spent well over twenty years leading expeditions from the front and mistrusted anyone else's navigating abilities. Another thing that annoyed me, I reflected as my legs dangled inside my first mini-crevasse of the trip, was the ignorant complacency of journalists who said that of course it was 'different nowadays' with all our technological gadgetry. Crevasses are today, just as in the time of Scott and Mawson, the chief threat to Antarctic travellers and the danger has not lessened one iota over the intervening years.

Up to my armpits in deep soft snow, with my lower torso treading air over nothingness, I only wished the gadgetry fallacy had some basis in reality. Too much movement on trying to extricate my body could collapse the whole snow-bridge in an instant. My attempts to look back at my sledge failed, for the hood of my parka and my cotton balaclava prevented sufficient lateral movement of my neck. Furthermore I had breathed into the balaclava as I fell, which had the immediate effect of misting up my goggles and the mist had frozen across the insides of the lens. To all intents and purposes I was blind, since I had no hand free to tear off the goggles.

The alloy poles leading back from my body harness to the sledge had snapped close behind me, which actually helped me by allowing sufficient movement for me to wriggle up, inch by inch, until my hips were out of the hole. The rest was easy. I replaced the broken poles with rope traces.

Many of the crevasses we were to negotiate were over a hundred feet wide with sagging bridges. The weakest point was not, as might be expected, in the centre but along the fault-line, where the bridge was joined to the crevasse wall's lip. In the most dangerous cases the whole bridge had already descended a few feet down into the maw before catching on some unseen temporary stopper. New snow had then partially filled the resulting trough.

Hauling the sledges down on to such teetering bridges presented no great physical task since gravity was on our side. If the bridge held under our initial weight, we pulled onwards over the centre span. At this point the going became singularly off-putting because, in order to manhaul our monster loads up the far side of the disintegrating bridge, maximum downward pressure with skis and sticks must be applied to its weakest point.

There were moments of sickening apprehension as our straining ski sticks plunged through the crust, or part of a sledge lurched backwards, its prow or stern having broken through. I never grew inured to the crevasse hazard and continued to sweat and silently curse as each new death trap passed beneath us.

Fifteen miles above us was a feature first discovered by the British Antarctic Survey nine years before, the hole in the ozone layer, which is also the nest where man-made pollutants called chlorofluorocarbons come to roost. Stratospheric winds carry these compounds, long used in aerosols and coolants, south, where they mix with high-altitude clouds in the cold and dark of the Antarctic winter. As the sun returns in spring, these frozen chemical clouds react with its rays, releasing chlorine molecules that temporarily dissolve the thin layer of ozone that protects earthbound life from harmful solar radiation.

Since we were travelling directly below this hazard, it made sense to cover our skin. But, hauling huge loads in our tight dog harnesses, we needed to breathe deeply, gasping for air without fogging our goggles, so the sun shone day after day on our uncovered lips and noses. Mine deteriorated rapidly. The lip scabs always stuck together overnight and, when I woke, the act of tearing my lips apart in order to speak and drink invariably opened up all the raw places. Breakfast from a communal bowl consisted of porridge oats in a gravy of blood.

Soon our minds churned over the fact that we were not averaging ten miles a day. We had to cut the loads.

'Mike, I'm chucking my duvet jacket. I have hardly worn it all week. We work so hard we will keep warm even when winter comes.'

He nodded. We both knew it was a big decision. The weather was now warm, in polar terms. Maybe we would have second thoughts later. But there would be no later if we could not get a move on now. Next morning we buried the two down-filled jackets along with the empty ration packs. I was later bitterly to regret the decision, but it is easy to be wise with hindsight.

At the end of the first week we entered a zone of great instability. Thunderous roars warned us that the whole ice shelf had entered a hyperactive phase, causing hitherto safe snow-bridges to collapse all around us into their crevasses. No amount of ice lore could keep us out of trouble here. A gaping hole opened up with an explosion of snow spray as we watched. Some ten paces ahead of Mike, and 45 feet wide by 120 feet in length, it lay directly across his intended path. Had it occurred but a few seconds later, he and his sledge would have disappeared, along with several tons of plunging snow-bridge.

All around us renewed implosions announced further cratering. The sensation was memorably frightening. We must escape at once to a safer area. But where was safer? Only the looming bulk of Berkner Island offered certain stability. We roped up with nervous fingers, fearing that at any moment the snow beneath us would open up and dump us hundreds of feet. The surface of the ice shelf all about us rumbled and reverberated again and again. Geysers of snow dust rose into the air. The feeling was similar to closing on enemy troops when under mortar fire. As each new crump exploded at random, the fear increased that the next catastrophe would have our name on it.

The nylon rope between us was sixty feet in length. We moved as fast as the sledges and the wings of fear allowed. Time stood still. I came to an abrupt halt as a wave of cold air rushed past, accompanied by the loudest and closest of the explosions. I ducked, for the all-engulfing sound seemed to pass both overhead and underfoot.

Immediately between Mike and me an immense crater appeared. One moment the ice shelf ahead was solid and white. The next a maw like the mouth of the Underworld, steaming with snow vapour, lay across our intended route, wide enough to swallow a double-decker bus. The roaring echoes of imploding snow cascading into the bowels of the ice shelf returned in successive waves, like shore ripples from an undersea volcano. Although a cold wind scoured the ice sheet, I sweated with fear. The next hour was a nightmare of apprehension; nowhere was safe. Only pure luck enabled us to escape from this volatile zone.

On the ninth day, the ice shelf showed signs of climbing towards the interior. There were no spot heights on my local chart and my small-scale map of Antarctica showed only that we were about to enter the largest crevasse field on the Filchner Ice Shelf.

Fortunately the deep drifts of the ice shelf did not extend to these wind-scoured flanks, so the going was easier than at any time since the firm coastal strip. Temperatures of around −15°C were not low enough to coarsen the surface and Mike, when navigating, set a pace that seemed to me as the day went by increasingly and unnecessarily fast.

I resolved to make no comment and at first found no difficulty in keeping hard on his heels. My shoulder blades and lower back screamed at me, but the old competitive urge came back. Why let this guy steam ahead? For almost twenty years now I had pulled sledges, in all conditions, faster than any colleague of any age, and on the northern expeditions over the past six years I had outpulled Mike, day after day, in even the worst of Arctic conditions. So, at that stage, his eleven-year advantage made no difference. Something must have happened since.

Like Shackleton, the first man to plan a crossing of Antarctica, I found myself preoccupied with the ageing process. Each new ache of muscle or tendon soon achieved obsession rating and blisters and chafing sores screamed their presence through every long and toilsome day. I swore silently when Mike was leading and moving faster than suited my pace, for then I was forced by pride to abandon the rhythm of my polar plod. Self-pity is not an attractive trait and I do not remember indulging in it on previous occasions.

As the days struggled by and the stress mounted, we faced increasing tensions between us. We could not ease the pain, the fear, above all the sheer burden of the sledge-loads by kicking our sledges, so we took it out on each other, at first silently, as had been our wont in the Arctic, but then with controlled outbursts.

After only five miles on the seventeenth day, Mike's foot blisters became painful and he told me he thought it would be sensible to stop. I said nothing in the interests of diplomacy and we camped four hours early, to my mind a dangerous precedent.

We reached the Antarctic coastline sometime during the twentieth morning. We could not actually see where the floating ice shelf stopped and the continental ice began since the joining point was covered in seamless snow, but once we crossed over we began the true continental crossing journey. At first any uphill gradient was imperceptible, but by the afternoon each and every heave on the traces required concentrated mental and physical effort. And then we reached the start of the first sastrugi field, a great rash of iron-hard furrows lying directly across our route.

I know no other way to advance when the ice gets nasty than to attack it head-on with every ounce of gristle at your disposal. Tightening my harness and stick-straps, I focused on each successive wall of ice and threw energy conservation to the winds. Towards the end of the day, after eleven hours of uphill hauling, we came to an especially rugged zone of serrated ice and Mike lagged well behind, despite my pauses for him to catch up. At the end of the final hour I had the tent up in time for his arrival and knew at once that he was livid.

Mike let rip. I had surged irresponsibly ahead despite the evil terrain and, worse, I had gone straight at the sastrugi instead of taking a sensible indirect route through the worst of it. Fortunately, the hostility we nurtured towards each other on the route almost invariably evaporated once we were in the tent, which saved the journey for both of us from becoming a non-stop nightmare.

That is not to say that our irritations with each other eased. He would surge far ahead and complain at my steady plod, when not attacking sastrugi. I was infuriated when his watch stopped because he had not put in a new battery before leaving England, despite several reminders. This meant I had to let him have mine and shout when it was my turn in front. His blister and diarrhoea stops also outraged me. I was all set to have the whole thing out with him, when he announced that the abscess on his heel was so swollen that he had decided to operate.

I watched with intense admiration as he gave himself two deep injections of anaesthetic and then plunged a scalpel deep into the swelling with diagonal incisions. Pus poured out and the swelling visibly decreased. Mike then bandaged up his heel and packed away his medical kit. I am not sure whether or not he felt faint, but I certainly did. I said nothing more about the early halts or the stricken Rolex.

Over the next three days we climbed to 5,000 feet above sea level with constant Force Eight winds in our faces. Arriving some distance ahead of Mike one evening, I began to erect the tent by fixing a safety line to my sledge before trying to slot the ten-foot alloy poles into the sleeving. The fourth and last pole was almost positioned when an especially violent blast tore the tent from my mitts and buckled one of the poles. Since I only carried a single eighteen-inch spare pole section for the entire journey, I left the bent pole in place and prayed we would be spared a big katabatic event in the days ahead.

I thought of Ginny back on Exmoor. She had lit an outsize church candle in our kitchen and intended to keep it burning day and night until I returned. It was four feet long, but so many hundreds of miles stretched ahead of us, I could not help thinking the candle would run out long before I came home.

One morning I noticed a black item behind Mike's sledge. It turned out to be a spare battery. Mike looked grim, as well he might, for he had packed the battery deep inside his load and there was no way it could have escaped but through a hole in the hull. We rolled the sledge on to one side and then the other, revealing a ragged split across its entire width. This had been caused by Mike falling twenty feet into a crevasse days earlier. We had done our best to repair it at the time, but not well enough, it now seemed. We erected the tent as a new gale blew up, unloaded, repaired and reloaded his sledge, then set off again to make mileage over the last four hours of the day.

The following day brought our first true white-out as well as sastrugi. When we camped, after a memorably nasty ten hours lurching over unseen obstacles and crashing into invisible trenches, I found both my cheeks burning and inflamed by UV rays. I had exposed my cheeks to help demist my goggles, but it had been a mistake. Mike's eyes, even though he wore goggles for all but two hours, were also affected. Soon after we camped he developed snow blindness symptoms. Only the mildest of attacks, but enough to have him lying back in considerable pain.

Since our overall speed and rate of progress for the first forty days were slightly better than for any previous Antarctic manhauling journey on record, our pace should not theoretically have caused dissension. But we were both under increasing strain and our bodies, under the stress of slow starvation combined with enormous energy expenditure, were altering chemically. Subsequent analysis of our blood samples was to show that our whole enzyme systems, everything that controlled our absorption of fat, were changing and we were recording levels of gut hormones twice as high as were previously known to science. We were adapting to our high-fat rations in a way hitherto unrecognised. Furthermore, with zero remaining body fat, we were losing muscle and weight from our hearts as well as our body mass.

By the fifth week, Mike's intermittent surges of speedy sledging were telling on him. He confided to his diary that he was feeling hypoglycaemic. He told me that he could 'feel the weight falling off'. On Christmas Eve, we were able to take full advantage for the first time of a wind driving us south and use the sails we had optimistically brought along to attach to our sledges. But on Christmas Day, the wind veered again.

I was now suffering from haemorrhoids, which at least allowed me to forget the pain in my feet due to the new aggravation. One day Mike produced from his science pack two small bottles of very expensive water for us to drink in the interest of his urine sample analysis. He told me not to spill any because each bottleful cost hundreds of pounds, and it was like atomic heavy water, but non-radioactive.

I never ceased to admire Mike's dedication to his research work. One of his science projects measured our calorific experience. The results were startling: 'When we made the ascent to the plateau, the isotopes gave daily energy expenditure of 10,670 calories in Ran and 11,650 in me. They confirmed the highest maintained energy expenditures ever documented – values that must lie close to the physiological limit.'

On our sixtieth day, Mike had a very bad time and told me he must be wrong about the effects of altitude. He was worried within himself about his ability to continue fending off negative thoughts. That night I gave Mike two chocolate squares and he seemed to appreciate the gesture. I am not good at being sympathetic. I knew that Mike was agnostic and did not expect him to gain any mental help in that direction. I had hoped, however, that he might be able to invoke his family and the knowledge that they were all gunning for him, but he seemed to scoff at this as too contrived a mental aid.

My practice was to hype up my mind during the first hour of every day, when the pain from my feet was at its worst, by simply remembering that I was not alone in facing the dreaded hours ahead. I pictured my grandfather, who had trapped in northern Canada and fought for his country all over the world. I thought of my father and uncle who were killed in the two world wars. I pictured my wife, my mother and my sisters, and I knew that all of them were right behind me, helping to suppress the ever-lurking urge to put a stop to the pain and the cold by giving up.

The last 200 miles before the Pole involved us in climbing above 10,000 feet. The altitude effects added to our debilitation and the loads were beginning to change us in many subtle ways. Mike reached the end of his tether, grinding to a halt in his tracks, head lolling, as if he were about to succumb to hypothermia. I set up the tent, got the cooker going and he accepted a mug of tepid soup in a trance. My mind was in a turmoil. I had little doubt but that he was pushing himself far too hard. I was doing likewise. We had no alternative. We had to earn our daily ration with the mileage put behind us.

On our sixty-eighth day the wind dropped and the mists cleared. Towards evening there was a *thing* ahead. For the first time in over 700 miles a man-made object was visible in the snow. Could it be the Pole? The item turned out to be a half-buried meteorological balloon. After seven hours' hauling on 16 January, on the eighty-first anniversary of Scott's sad arrival at the same point, we topped the final rise and came to the South Pole. The journey was far from over, but we had dragged to the Pole just enough stores to allow us to cross the continent and survive. If our luck held. It was a moment of sheer elation. Especially so for Mike, who had not been selected back in 1985 when Roger Mear was finalising his Pole team.

All the isolation of the past months fell away. The polar site had vastly altered, even in the twelve short years since my last visit. Strangely shaped installations on jacked-up steel legs reared monstrously in every direction from the main black-roofed dome in which over-wintering scientists lived and worked. A small huddle of nine figures had come out to greet us, but we put aside thoughts of the food available in the dome canteen as we forced ourselves to continue north. In all, we paused at the Pole for only eighty minutes.

Only then, beyond the Pole, did we discover the true meaning of *cold*. Our condition in terms of body deterioration, slow starvation, inadequate clothing, wind chill temperature, altitude, and even the day of the year, exactly matched those of Scott and his four companions as they came away from the Pole in 1912.

We learned from Morag that Erling Kagge had reached the Pole before us and had been airlifted out the previous week. The Norwegian press talked of his winning the race, but our sledges were twice as heavy and our journey twice as long, so our morale was not too badly dented by this misleading piece of media spin.

I could sense that Mike was in a bad way, despite his continued power surges. I knew that even now he would never recognise that his pace was his own worst enemy. I would never be able to 'bully' him into copying my polar plod. I could only try to compromise with him over matters of pace wherever necessary. I had my own mounting problems with harness sores, diarrhoea and haemorrhoids, and the most agonising throbbing pain in my feet. Mike diagnosed possible bone infection and put me on antibiotics.

I realised how lucky I had been for fifty years in experiencing little pain. Broken bones and teeth, torn-off digits, frostbite and chronic kidney stones had seemed unpleasant at the time. But now I knew real pain and I feared lest it overwhelm me.

On 30 January, we recorded our first barometric descent of a few hundred feet, but this welcome news was balanced by a potentially disastrous discovery. Mike had lost both his ski sticks off his sledge. Trying to share mine and progress with one each was unbalancing, and when Mike again fell behind, I gave him both, but he was once more on the edge of hypothermia and we had to camp early.

Our bodily condition was becoming highly suspect. I was not in the business of leading suicide expeditions. We were approaching the edge of our ability to cope safely with very extreme conditions and this was, we both knew, because we were starving, losing ten ounces every day through a deficiency of 3,000 calories each and every day for three months.

The next day Mike began to work out a satisfactory way of forcing his sledge to move with just one stick and I constantly checked the compass, for I knew we would need great accuracy to enter the Mill Glacier, the start of the long descent from the plateau to the Pacific coast. Mike and I needed to make no mistakes from now on. We were committed to the 9,000-foot descent as if in a rubber boat at the moment of yielding to the first pull of a great rapid.

The horizons which now opened to us were awesome, a sprawling mass of rock and ice in motion. These were the headwaters of a slow-moving ice-river. Huge open chasms leered ahead and standing ice-waves reared up at the base of black truncated cliffs.

I scanned the skies north and saw no clouds. So long as the good visibility conditions remained, I could find the best route. I felt a God-given confidence and, for the first time on this journey, the warm pleasure of challenge. I knew the rules. Never waste a minute. Pause for nothing. Here there could be no place for my polar plod. So long as the weather held, we must go like the wind.

We came at last to where the Mill joins the Beardmore Glacier and another breathtaking vista opened up. Messner and Fuchs, the only others to have attempted our route, had lost their way at this point. We had to cope with more crevasses, interrupted for a while by a field of sharp sastrugi. Unable to cross these with my skis on, I made the fatal error of unclipping and strapping them to my sledge.

The very first crevasse bridge I attempted to cross without skis was a minor affair, no more than four feet wide and similar to hundreds we had safely traversed. Because my harness waistband was unfastened, the sledge ropes did not restrain me as they should have done and my abrupt plunge into the dark shaft was halted only by the thin webbing strap of my ski stick looped over my right wrist. I dangled for a moment more surprised than frightened. The fear came as soon as I realised that only my ski stick, wedged above me and still fastened to my wrist, was postponing my imminent demise. Any movement that dislodged the stick was liable to send me downwards.

Throwing caution to the winds, I lunged upwards with my free hand, my feet scrabbling against each smooth ice-wall. With my arm strength sapping, I lifted my body high enough to reach the crevasse lip with my mitted hand and then to heave my chest over to safety. For a minute I lay shaking with relief until, with dismay, I realised that my stick and the other mitt in its wrist loop were loose down the hole. I inched to one side until I could squint down, my breath rushing out in a sigh of relief as I spotted the ski stick now loosely lodged some four feet down. Using my boots as grabs, I managed to retrieve both stick and vital mitt.

A few days later we strayed into a treacherous crevasse field, as lethal as any Marxist minefield, but our guardian angels saw us through successive obstacles of a hairy nature. At last we reached a steep slope some 500 feet above the edge of the Ross Ice Shelf and pitched our ninetieth camp. We were within half a mile of having walked over the highest, coldest, most inhospitable continent on Earth from Atlantic to Pacific. How much longer did we stand a chance of surviving? Since all our main aims were now achieved, the only practical rationale for continuing must be to reach the ship before its departure in eight days' time.

On our ninety-second travel day, clear of crevasses at last, we hauled for ten and a half hours over the floating Ross Ice Shelf. On 12 February, our ninety-fifth day of travel, the last US aeroplane left Antarctica. In five days our ship would steam out of the Ross Sea. We were still 289 nautical miles from Ross Island. The time for procrastination was over. I radioed the Twin Otter, which picked us up from the ice forty miles 'out to sea' on the Pacific Ocean.

We will never know how much farther we could have continued over the ice shelf because there are too many ifs and buts. As it was, our achievement took us into the *Guinness Book of Records* and Mike and I were awarded OBEs. If, like Scott, we had had no option but to battle on, it is my opinion that we would have died short of Ross Island.

All attempts for a century, whether by Norwegians, Russians or Americans, to cross the continent unaided and using snow-machines or dog teams had failed miserably. In hauling our own loads across this area, greater in mass by far than the United States, we have shown that manpower can indeed be superior to dog-power and, in doing so, have partly exonerated Scott's much-abused theories on the matter.

Our record in the *Guinness Book* simply states: 'The longest totally self-supporting polar sledge journey ever made and the first totally unsupported crossing of the Antarctic landmass was achieved by R. Fiennes and M. Stroud. They covered a distance of 2,170 km (1,350 miles).'

Dr Mike Stroud
World authority on human endurance

Ran and I tried four times to reach the North Pole unsupported and on our last attempt in 1990, we came incredibly close to reaching our goal. We would have tried again, had not two Norwegians claimed the prize in the same year. So we turned our attention to the south, planning another expedition as well-established friends.

Although the South Pole had already been reached by an unsupported, manhauling expedition, nobody had even considered an entire unsupported Antarctic crossing. So in 1993, we embarked on what would be a 95-day epic. Ran once more proved to be a fantastic colleague and partner in hardship. I am not saying that we did not fall out once or twice, but who would not under such incredibly difficult pressures?

In the end, we became the first men to make an unsupported crossing of the Antarctic landmass, even though our ambition had also been to cross the vast floating ice shelves on either side. However, with the availability of air drop-offs and pick-ups at the Antarctic coasts, nearly all modern journeys no longer include the ice shelves.

Since those polar expedition days, we have shared further good times, tough times and awesome times together, including the British Columbia Eco Challenge, seven marathons in seven days on seven continents, and climbing on Denali in Alaska and the Carstensz Pyramid in New Guinea.

These were also undertaken with humour and commitment and hence I have no hesitation concluding as I did in the final lines of my book about our Antarctic Crossing:

If an opportunity were to come again to step out of life . . . there is no question as to whom I would wish for a companion. I would go with Ran.

*Searching for the fabled lost city of Ubar, the Atlantis of the Sands,
in the deserts of Oman, 1990–1992.*

11

Oman

*The search for the lost city of Ubar,
the Atlantis of the Sands
1990–1992*

After making the longest and fastest unsupported journey towards the North Pole in 1990 (a record beaten four years later by the Norwegian Børge Ousland), Ran decided he had enough of being in frozen climes for a while: he vowed that future efforts would be confined to hot deserts or tropical rain forests. He remembered the legend of Ubar, the Atlantis of the Sands, which he had first heard about when he served in the Sultan's Army in Oman over twenty years before.

Back in 1968, when I was serving in Dhofar, Nashran bin Sultan, one of the Sultanate guides, told me about a lost city. 'Some say the finest city in all Arabia was Ubar, built like Paradise with pillars fashioned from gold. Allah destroyed the place and no man has been there for a thousand years. Ubar is over there' – he pointed his stick north towards the distant Qara mountains and west towards Yemen – 'in the Sands beyond the Wadi Mitan.'

Since the dawn of civilisation, trade between the West and the mysterious East had been monopolised by seafarers, Phoenicians and Muscat Arabs, and the keystone of their commerce was incense, primarily *olibanum*, or frankincense. Historic research showed that while frankincense trees were abundant elsewhere, the one and only source of superior quality frankincense was Dhofar. The guardians of the frankincense orchards possessed a monopoly on a commodity more valuable even than gold, which for 4,000 years provoked an insatiable worldwide demand.

My own early, superficial studies led me to a ready conclusion that some fabulously wealthy city was likely to have existed, because of the inescapable need for a watering place for the thousands of men and beasts involved in transporting frankincense from Dhofar to the northern markets.

Historians stress that the incense travelled from Dhofar by sea and by land. The ocean routes were at risk from storms and pirates, while the desert trails involved passage through different tribal lands, with middlemen levying taxes all the way. The routes that were chronicled in the greatest detail all led west from Dhofar's northern borders into Yemen, and this made me conclude that Nashran's missing city, Ubar, must lie on or close to that border. Somewhere there was, or once had been, a great deal more water than might be drawn from a single desert well.

The first geographers to map the Arabian Peninsula were based in Alexandria, and using information received from merchants and seafarers, they produced treatises giving the positions of the main Arab cities and trade centres. By AD 200, Alexandrian professors had recorded the existence of a major market town well into the region now known as the Empty Quarter, the greatest sand desert in the world, and gave it the name *Omanum Emporium*, meaning 'coastal market centre of Oman'. This was the first time the word Oman had appeared in writing: until then most references to the country used the Persian name Mazun.

The Qur'an was written some four centuries later and mentioned neither Ubar nor Omanum Emporium. The word of God, as passed on by the Prophet Muhammad in the Qur'an, told of desert cities whose inhabitants had behaved badly and as a result incurred the wrath of God. One of these doomed cities was described as: 'Irem of the columns, the like of which has not been created in the land.'

In the early twentieth century, Lawrence of Arabia was intensely interested in the legend of the lost city reputed to exist in the middle of the Rub al Khali. He told a colleague, 'I am convinced that the remains of an ancient civilisation are to be found in that desert. I have been told by the Arabs that ruined castles . . . have been seen by wandering Arabs in the region of Wabar. There is always some substance in these Arab tales.'

Lawrence's desert deeds inspired many of his countrymen of later generations, some not much younger than himself, such as Bertram Thomas, an administrator of Palestine and financial advisor to the Sultan of Muscat, and Harry St John Philby, the father of one of Britain's better-known spies, who would bring Ubar to the attention of the public in the West for the first time.

The two explorers exchanged terse letters on various differences of opinion. What seemed especially to niggle both men was the name for the lost city. Philby was an adviser to King Abdul Aziz of the Saudis and favoured Wabar, claiming it to be within the Saudi Arabian borders and to have actually been there. Thomas, who described Ubar as the 'Atlantis of the Sands', pointed out that Ubar was in South Arabia, where every tribal member he had ever met used the term Ubar and had never heard of Wabar. Thomas said he had unearthed evidence indicating that the lost Quranic city was well into the southern reaches of the Empty Quarter. The mystery of Ubar remained unsolved.

Our own interest evolved into a joint venture with an old friend, Nick Clapp from Los Angeles, who had edited Dr Armand Hammer's film of the Transglobe Expedition. I would liaise with Sultan Qaboos of Oman, organise sponsors and lead the expedition in the field, Nick would do the archaeological research and the filming. His researches led him to NASA in quest of space photographs, hoping these would give us a head start, but all the eventual NASA shuttle photos produced was an L-shaped site way out in the dunes. All the same, the connection between buried biblical cities and space-age technology remained a good talking point for raising sponsorship.

We began with a short reconnaissance trip in July 1990, taking along with us an eminent archaeologist from Missouri called Juris Zarins, who had a vaguely reassuring resemblance to Indiana Jones, complete with battered brown trilby. Juris did not think we had a cat in hell's chance of finding Ubar, if indeed it existed, but he was keen to have a chance to conduct archaeological work in southern Oman and if searching for Ubar provided a pretext, fair enough.

Our timing coincided with Saddam Hussein's invasion of Kuwait, but as nobody was expecting the trouble to spread to Dhofar, our visas were duly stamped. Our main guide on the ground would be Major Trevor Henry, my instructor on an SAS jungle course back in the 1970s. He told me bluntly that if there had been any surface ruins in Dhofar, they would have been spotted by oil prospectors, talkative *bedu* or land and air patrols from the Sultan's Armed Forces.

'If the city is out there at all,' he murmured, 'then, in my opinion, it will be sub-surface.'

First of all we flew by helicopter to inspect the mysterious NASA-provided *L-site*. On the ground it was as clear as in the picture taken from 160 miles in space. Different surface patterns and the movement of the sand had shaped a letter L between two separate dune formations. Juris quickly announced that it was merely an ancient lake bed, and our only excitement was his chance discovery of artefacts at a nearby pre-Islamic site. Although later, he did find some ruins with stone patterns of ancient dwellings and hearths nearby. We then flew to other possible locations that might have a bearing on the frankincense trade.

Centipedes, scorpions and spiders added interest to our trek up a side valley to a wonderful cave from where, in the past, I had once spent many days and nights ambushing Marxist soldiers. We slithered on the orange mud and avoided the dripping lianas with their colonies of stinging ants. The cave was wide and as high as a church, with a floor deep in the animal dung of centuries. Bats chirped from the dark recesses of the rock roof and Trevor led us to the mouth of an interior passage.

'Leopards live in here,' he told us, indicating the outline of feline spoor.

We searched many caves and jungle-clad ravines. In one sunny nook, Trevor pointed out aloe trees – 'very good for curing wounds' – and castor-oil trees – 'you know what that's good for' – and three deadly poisonous but pretty plants: euphorbia, the Sodom apple and datura. He led us to Jebel Kasbah, a lofty crag above a spring. Hidden by thorn and mimosa, a tangle of ruined, half-buried walls puzzled Juris. A large rectangular room, well plastered and hardly damaged over the centuries, had perhaps served as a reservoir for monsoon water. It was reasonable to deduce this was a mountain garrison from which the incense trade was once policed, an interesting fragment in our jigsaw puzzle, but not a clue to Ubar's whereabouts.

After a whirlwind tour of the plain, the mountains and the Nejd, we drove from Thamrait to my earlier Ubar hunting grounds of Shis'r and Fasad on the edge of the Sands. Both places had undergone considerable change. Where in 1968 there was only barren desert at Shis'r and a crumbling *Beau Geste* mud fort, there now flourished cultivated plots of palm, fruit and vegetables. At Shis'r there was also a modern Arab-style housing development not far from the rock cleft waterhole.

Shis'r's very location, so close to the Sands and astride the best aquifer in the region, indicated that ancient camel trains may have watered here en route for Yemen and previous visitors had recorded tracks running west from here to the Sands, which our satellite photographs had confirmed. We spent three hours wandering about a heap of rubble and Juris was delighted to find fragments of pottery and various ambiguous mounds, evidence of former springs. He was sure people had lived here longer ago than the 300 years theorised by the only previous archaeologist to have visited Shis'r.

There was plenty for Juris to explore, but as to locating Ubar, we were really no further forward. The interim report I eventually submitted to the Sultan and our sponsors made the best of a bad job.

We postponed our main expedition until the autumn of 1991, because of ongoing troubles caused by Saddam Hussein. On the day we set out, I discovered that in my rush I had collected the wrong travel bag from our London gear store. Instead of tropical shirts, sun cream and malaria tablets, I had a duffle bag with snow goggles, balaclava and mitts. I decided not to mention this to the larger party we had now assembled in case it alarmed them. They had never been to Dhofar and the entire responsibility for our wellbeing out there was in my hands. They might lose confidence in my preparations if they knew the contents of my travel bag.

Trevor Henry, so indispensable the previous year, warned me that he was due to leave Dhofar in the near future. He had earlier referred me to another Scotsman, Andy Dunsire, who had lived in Dhofar for some eighteen years and knew the country almost as well as Trevor. 'Andy works for Airwork, the aircraft engineers in Thamrait. He will give you any help you need,' he assured me.

One problem I foresaw was a lack of labour to excavate any ruins that we might locate. Juris Zarins was expecting two staff and four students from his university, but we might need six times that number of diggers. Andy saw no problems, especially when I mentioned that the American archaeology students were mostly young blondes.

Our first task involved a thorough search of the Plain and the mountains. For this work we would be comfortably based in Salalah. To the north of the mountains, the best location from which to operate in the Sands and the Central Steppes was Shis'r, for there was fresh water in this *bedu* village.

All the camping and excavation material arrived on time, so we moved to the first work site on the Plain. This was a long-abandoned well some seventy feet deep, which Ptolemy had described as the Oracle of Diana. Juris wanted to excavate the shaft itself and the ruined village around the well's mouth, so I borrowed a mobile crane from BP of Oman in Salalah.

Nick and I were lowered into the shaft inside the crane's bucket. The smell of rotting flesh was overpowering and emanated from the bloated bodies of dead foxes. I manoeuvred the corpses into polythene bags and swatted at the fat flies that settled on my arms. I tried to keep my thoughts off the glistening carpet of insect life that crawled, leapt and slithered in that foul-smelling hole.

Even inside the bucket we were attended by a host of flying, biting insects, but the stench lessened once the foxes' bodies were gone. Subsequent lowerings took us back with shovels and we began the task of hoisting debris into the buckets. Each time we raised a new item, be it a tattered tent canvas or stinking mattress, hundreds of disturbed spiders, cockroaches, scorpions and unidentifiable creatures of all imaginable shapes and sizes scuttled away.

The well shaft was some sixty feet in diameter and Juris assumed that Ptolemy and others had noted the site as an oracle because, in ancient times, some local priest had hidden down the shaft and shouted up oracular responses to questions from paying visitors. This being so, we should find traces of a cave or crevice halfway down the shaft.

Andy Dunshire, an experienced caver, fixed two harnesses to one of the Land Rovers parked above and we descended twenty feet to attack a suspect protuberance with pickaxes and brushes. In a while, four well-cut plastered stone slabs were clearly delineated but further work began to dislodge them, so we never discovered if they led to a horizontal passageway, long since choked with dirt, which might have hidden some trickster and acted as an echo chamber to his prophetic platitudes.

The deep stratum of modern garbage and animal bones that formed the floor of the shaft defeated our attempts to reach detritus from earlier times, so we left the Naheez valley and headed north, via Fasad, with eight days' supply of food, fuel and water.

In Fasad, I asked the Imam, a gentle Rashidi named Mohamed Mabhowt, if he would take us to two nameless spots out in the Sands, the *L-site* and the ancient camel track that we had visited on the 1990 reconnaissances by helicopter. Ron Blom, our team geologist and interpreter of satellite images, produced one of his NASA pictures, taken from 160 miles above Earth, and clearly delineating every sand dune. Mohamed made various grunting sounds that indicated comprehension if not recognition and agreed to accompany us.

The next day we set off into the desert using the satellite pictures as though they were maps. This was a slow process involving many interesting debates between the film director, the explorer, the space scientist and the Imam of Fasad, through whose familiar home terrain we were hesitantly creeping. If only we could have given him a familiar name as our desired goal and he would quickly have taken us there by the best available route.

We camped for the night between the dunes and under the stars, and at the break of day, the clear and mellow voice of the Imam sounded the morning incantation to God. The soul of Arabia, the thunder of the Saracens and the spirit of the desert came together in the passion of the mullah's voice. No God could ignore such a sound. '*Allahu Akbar, Allahu Akbar . . .*'

Soon after dawn, and carrying all the filming gear, we plodded to the ridge of the highest dune, filling our shoes with sand and exposing the unfit to the less unfit. The view made the effort worthwhile: mile upon mile of crests and peaks, battlements and moving shadows. To capture the colouring, wonderfully soft and diffuse, would have taxed the most subtle of artists.

The ancient camel tracks at this point were clearly shown by satellite image to disappear underneath the sand dune to our immediate east. We searched with binoculars, but not until late afternoon, when the harshness began to fade from the desert light, could we distinguish the tracks. There were two main trails that, as they became easier to see with the naked eye, did indeed appear to vanish beneath a three-hundred foot mountain of sand. This certainly seemed to provide an argument that the track had been in use many centuries ago. Exactly how old? That is difficult to say, but camels were not used as load-carrying beasts before 2500 BC, and so, if the track *is* older, then only humans, mules and horses can have used it.

This is where Nick Clapp and I have a divergence of opinion. He believes that the NASA-produced images showing a network of tracks converging on the region of Shis'r led us to the assumption that Ubar must be somewhere along an arc of tracks that included those at Shis'r and stretched all the way to the Sands and beyond.

Juris, on the other hand, agrees that our only reason for basing ourselves at Shis'r was its excellent position as a base from which to work the region to the north of the mountains. This had always been the plan and no NASA data amended it. Shis'r was only one of a dozen places of potential interest both for clue-searching and for film-making. Later, in 1992, Juris told me, 'I didn't think Shis'r was Ubar even when we started digging there.'

I knew well from my Arab Army days that there were three main aquifers running north into Dhofar's southern fringe of the Empty Quarter. The water at Fasad is very sulphurous, and at Mugshin highly salty, but Shis'r's water, that of the Wadi Ghadun aquifer, is famous for its sweetness. Since water availability is an obvious key to the siting of cities, one did not need to be an archaeologist or a student of satellite maps to deduce that Shis'r could itself be a candidate for Ubar.

Nevertheless we had all, including Juris, no idea that we might find the city at Shis'r any more than a number of other sites that our original space images showed as interesting blips, such as the *L-site* (the most promising), or Heilat Araka, or merely places reported by Trevor and *bedu* informants. We intended to dig and film at them all.

The only reason Shis'r stood out was its suitability as a base camp. Militating against Shis'r was the fact that the explorers Thomas, Thesiger and Phillips, later archaeologists and every Omani we spoke to, all wrote off the Shis'r ruins as a mere 300 years old or less.

When first I planned which areas were most suitable for Juris to visit, the key person who judged the value of each site (whether a suspect NASA blip in the Sands, an old village in the steppes or a nest of ruins on the Plain) was Trevor Henry. But in the mountains, where our clues would consist mainly of cave drawings, and in the maze of *nej'd* wadis running north (where the pecked rock, graves and triliths mostly lay), our chief guide and adviser would be a remarkable Dhofari of the Shahra tribe named Ali Ahmed Ali Mahash.

Ali had decided, without official prompting or support, to make a systematic survey of all the caves in Dhofar. Since there are many thousands of caves, often deep and inaccessible, in the *nej'd*, the mountains and along the coast, his intentions were enormously ambitious. He had no formal training and could only use his spare time for the project.

Over the months, Ali drew up individual groupings of different symbols that formed the cave writing at various sites. He intended to decipher the unknown early alphabet of his ancestors. To find out how the pictures were painted, he mixed dyes from over 130 different sources, vegetable and mineral, in a backroom in his Salalah home.

Ali was enthusiastic about our work and agreed to take us to his discoveries. Whether or not the paintings or graffiti would provide us with clues, we would only know when Juris could see the sites for himself. Over a three-week period, Ali took us by vehicle and on foot to remote and wonderful places all over Dhofar.

Ginny came out to establish a proper HF communications network with radio sets based at Shis'r, Thamrait and in each of our vehicles. When the archaeologists arrived and we separated into groups, good long-distance communication would speed up the search and help in an emergency. Meanwhile Ali took the two of us to the homesteads of his people, the Shahra, high on the grassland downs of Kizit, where they are cattle herders, and deep in the Wadi Darbat, where they keep thousands of camel.

The caves near each settlement reflected in their paintings the business of the region. Camel drawings were omnipresent, depicting them walking, trotting or being milked by herders. However, pictures of camels being ridden immediately told those of us who had previously listened to Juris that the paintings must be later than 2500 BC, when camels were first domesticated. We were fast becoming amateur archaeologists.

With only a few of the more inaccessible caves to explore, we thanked Ali and made our way over the mountains back to Shis'r with two lorryloads of food and equipment.

Juris's archaeological team arrived not long before Christmas, all in their twenties and none with previous experience of Arabia. The five girls were blessed with long hair, pretty faces and good figures. I thanked God (and Juris) for an excellent selection process and felt confident there would be no problem in Andy Dunsire finding a great number of volunteer diggers from among his Airwork colleagues at Thamrait. If the attraction of the actual digging was not enough, this bunch of American belles would surely do the trick.

I handed out *shemagh* headcloths, sand goggles, camp-beds and water bottles to everyone. Together with the anticipated influx of Thamrait expatriates, we should total up to forty diggers on a good day.

Once we were established at Shis'r, two partly different programmes had to be followed. Juris and his diggers were to excavate all hopeful sites in the immediate area for a month and then move south to work for a further two months in the mountain and on the Plain, based in Salalah. Nick Clapp, his wife Kay and the camera team, with both Andy and Ali Ahmed kindly ready to take them more or less anywhere they wished, would complete the documentary.

The month of December rushed by with preparations and a good deal of filming work. Three days before Christmas, I overheard two Omani students, who worked with us on loan from the Ministry of National Heritage and Culture, commenting on the fact that we had been in Shis'r for ten days, the dig teams were ready and yet all we seemed to do was film each other. This seemed a fair summary, but it would not sound good at all in the wrong quarters.

On Christmas Eve, I had a quiet but urgent word with Juris and suggested he start digging *anywhere*, so that the Ministry students could see the action. So he took his dig team some 200 yards from our camp to the rubble around the old Shis'r well. Desultory work began.

Two days later Juris looked smug. I asked him why, but he was guarded.

'The dig,' he muttered. 'It's good . . . interesting.'

'Is it four hundred years old,' I pressed him, 'like they say?'

'No,' he replied, winked and returned to the room where retrieved artefacts were beginning to be spread all over the improvised shelves. The team were buried in site maps, lists and hushed discussions. There was an unmistakable air of excitement.

At first Juris concentrated his small force on or close to the original rubble pile. Within a week, the outline of the rock heap had taken on the clear-cut silhouette of a ruined tower connected by low battlements to a second round tower and a beautifully built horseshoe tower to its east. Pottery and flints were hourly unearthed including, to Juris's great pleasure, both Roman and Greek-style urns from the period that would have been Ubar's heyday.

'You ask me when I began to think Shis'r was Ubar,' Juris was later to stress, 'but there was *no* one single day that I said, "Oh God, this is Ubar or this is Omanum Emporium." Until we find an inscription, we can *never* one hundred per cent say that.'

Early in January 1992, Juris found a piece of red pottery identical to the style of the Jemdet Nassir period in Uruq, Mesopotamia. If carbon dating proved this to be so, it would predate previous thinking as to the start of trade between Mesopotamia and south Arabia from 4000 to 5000 BC. He was not yet ready to go out on a limb and say we had discovered Ubar, but he was clear that our Shis'r dig was already proving to be a very important Roman-period site and probably went back at least 4,000 years.

'Why did the middle of the walled citadel collapse?' I asked him. It was as though a bomb had blown out a crater, leaving only the outer walls and towers with a few rooms and hearths on the inside of the walls. How many other internal structures there might have been before the collapse may never be known.

'As with many well-built walled caravanserai,' Juris said, 'this was built around a strategically sited waterhole – and what could be more of a controlling site than this?' He paused, looking down into the sandy pit. 'I suspect that as they used up more and more water during a dry period, the water table lowered and the immediate surrounds fell in to form a typical dolina or karst collapse. An earthquake may have even assisted by undermining the solutional cavity.'

When free time was available, I took a shovel and pickaxe to the site and attacked any area that did not require more delicate attention using trowel and handbrush. But the archaeologists in our team, who were allergic to shovels, would shout and chase me away, so Ginny and I spent more time plodding about in the desert six or seven miles east of the site, searching for subsidiary camps, rich in axe heads and Fasad points, arrowheads from between the sixth and fourth millennia BC. Once these were located, I would fetch Juris with his position-locating gear to plot each new satellite site.

In the days when the area was verdant, travellers would have camped within sight of the many-towered citadel, but far enough away to settle their camels and sort out their loads. Altogether we found thirty-five such campsites to the north, west and east of the citadel and up to eight miles away from it.

The central site would have appeared majestic and without equal in the land to the *bedu* cameleers. For 560 miles of desert in any direction, there was no edifice even a quarter of the size of Shis'r, or Ubar as I now described it. The walls and towers would have stood out to the weary and thirsty traveller from up to twenty miles away – to them indeed a city of the desert.

Of our site, Juris told me: 'So far we have walls and towers that are square and round and horseshoe-shaped. There was clearly a central tower, an inner sanctum and an outer wall which had a minimum height of between ten and fifteen feet and a consistent thickness of eighty centimetres. Some of the original rooms, complete with hearths, did not collapse into the sink-hole and these have already yielded rich finds for the key periods between the second millennium BC and around AD 300, when trading activities seem to have dropped off.'

As we dug down, we found the original building work of our city was excellent, consisting of semi-dressed stones cemented with a white plaster similar to that used in the north of the peninsula by contemporary peoples such as the Nabataeans of Petra.

Our archaeologists came across the only ancient chess set ever to be found in South Arabia, six soapstone pieces, each two or three inches high and well-polished by the fingers of the players, had lain buried for over a thousand years. After a month the diggers were three feet down in places and pottery from Rome, Greece and Syria joined Celadon and Ming pieces from China, glass bracelets of bright clear colours from Aden and Neolithic flint weapons from 5000 BC.

Words of our discovery soon reached the Omani and Gulf press and tourists in Land Rovers began to arrive from Salalah. Was this

Ubar? Was it Irem? If so, where were the golden pillars and the whole fabulous city? The fantasies of the *Arabian Nights* had a lot to answer for.

By the end of January we had found no major inscription, but nine towers were unearthed, some 60 per cent of the main outer wall and over 6,000 individual artefacts.

Andy Dunsire had told me of a cave system 600 feet down at the base of a giant sinkhole called Tawi Ateer, the Well of Birds. He had promised to show me a great cavern, which I hoped might contain wall writings or at least paintings, for it was known, certainly until the advent of recent rockfalls, that Dhofaris used to descend into the hole by way of vertiginous pathways.

Andy drove me with a Range Rover full of his friends to the village of Tawi Ateer on the high plateau of the *jebel* and a mile to the north, and we trekked into the dry bush with rucksacks and ropes. His three friends were to camp at the end of the 600-foot deep crater to ensure that our descent ropes were not removed during the night.

Because I was inept with the special rope techniques Andy used, he took an hour to make everything ready. I felt a touch giddy, for the cry of pigeons and the starling-like Tristram's grackle echoing around the vast natural chamber kept reminding me of the long drop down to the cave system.

By the time we were ready, dusk had filled the huge, perfectly rounded cauldron and as Andy encouraged me to let go of the safety rope by the crater lip, stars were already appearing in a sky of midnight blue. I could not see below me and my helmet torch, striking a rock, went dead. This had the advantage of making it impossible to see the hundreds of yards of thin rope dangling down into the void between my swinging feet.

After many minutes of painfully slow descent, the two-inch-long alloy crocodile clasp, which slid down the rope at great speed, suddenly came sharp up against a knot of rope coils. I winced as the rope elasticated. I imagined the feel of it breaking and the sudden rush of air.

Panic was not far off. Sweat stung my eyes. Because all my body weight rested on the point where the metal teeth were jammed against the knot and since there could be no upward impetus from my dangling legs, it took me many long minutes to free the impediment without disentangling my lifeline by mistake. For a while I despaired, then a lucky tug freed the coil, and ten minutes later I arrived shaky kneed at the floor of the great shaft.

The stench of civet dung hung about in the warm air and I heard the scrabble of the striped cats in the darkness. Andy arrived after twenty minutes and I followed him via boulders and sloping ledges, past stalactites and a descending series of passages, to the edge of a scum-laden lake. The beam of his head torch disturbed a cloud of flying creepy-crawlies.

On a previous visit, Andy had secreted two Land Rover inner tubes close by, and stripping down to our pants and desert boots, we slipped into the evil-smelling waters. Andy beckoned me away from one side wall, where a swarm of giant mosquito-like insects rose in anger from their nests.

'There are blind fish in the caves.' Andy pointed downwards and added, 'Keep close.' I nodded, needing no second warning.

For fifty minutes I swam on my black tube and soon gave up any attempt to memorise our tortuous route. Sometimes the ceiling of the tunnel approached within inches of the water and, copying Andy, I turned over and swam on my back. There was just enough room to breathe and then, when the gap improved slightly, to haul on a long cord attached to my tube to pull it under the obstacle.

I kept a nagging claustrophobic fear at bay through total trust in Andy's cavemanship, if that is the right term. But it came to me how easily he might suffer a heart attack, for he was well into his fifties. How then would I find my way out of these evil waterways? Certainly not by memory.

My faith in Andy collapsed and my inner fears surged when his white beard lifted from the oily surface and he spluttered, 'Which way did we enter this chamber?'

I told him and he disagreed. We bobbed under an even lower ledge with no more than three inches' clearance and I smelled putrefied flesh close at hand. An animal skull with wet, green flesh attached in floating ribbons nodded against my shoulder – some civet or goat lured to its death by thirst.

After half an hour, Andy shook his head, dislodging all manner of flying insects. 'I can't understand it,' he grunted. 'The main passageway must be underwater. I just can't locate it.' So we gave up and, to my considerable relief, he found no difficulty in retracing his route to the entry point.

We slept on a ledge free of civet dung until dawn when, back at the base of the crater and the single length of rope, Andy attached two special grips to my foot and shoulder.

'You go first. If you get into trouble, shout, but do not look down.'

After about two hundred feet, the tautly stretched rope felt as thin as string. The swish and shriek of disturbed grackles and my empty stomach combined to make the climb unenjoyable, but I managed to force from my mind the tiniest thought about the ever-increasing drop below.

When Andy joined me at the upper rim of the crater, he looked disappointed. 'Never mind,' he said, 'we'll come back when the water level drops.'

My enthusiasm to find the cave graffiti had lessened, but I took care not to show it.

Some five weeks after the first key finds at Shis'r, a police van with four armed officers arrived around midnight with a summons for me to go at once to the Palace in Muscat. The police drove me to Salalah and, by Royal Oman Police flight, I reached Muscat the next morning. A royal limousine took me to Seeb Palace, where various new ambassadors were being accredited.

After an hour's wait in what must rank among the most splendid palaces in the world, I was shown in to His Majesty Sultan Qaboo's *majlis*. He was delighted with the success of the expedition and keen to ensure continued excavation at Shis'r until the ruins were finally revealed. He asked me to give him a list of actions I thought might best be taken to follow up the discovery.

'Is it Ubar?' he asked me.

'I believe so, Your Majesty. It is difficult to know what else it could be.'

The warmth of his smile and the strength of his handshake reminded me of meeting his father twenty-four years earlier. I felt that the long years of hoping, the setbacks and the false trails all been worthwhile.

I asked in my report to Sultan Qaboos that Ali Ahmed be appointed Field Director for Archaeology in Dhofar, that Juris be contracted to continue excavations and that the Shis'r site be protected against damage by visitors.

Back in Salalah I handed over all the equipment and organisational details to Juris. I was also able to hand Ali Ahmed more than 13,000 artefacts fully computerised with individual reference numbers. The search for Ubar was over. Apart from the archaeologists, all the team left Oman early in February.

Each new artefact had helped to fill in the puzzle that Juris needed to reconstruct about Shis'r's unknown past.

Between 8000 and 6000 BC the region was too arid for humans. In 5000 BC, with wetter weather, Neolithic folk from Syria and further east had arrived and built hearths. Even then, Juris believed, they traded in incense and travelled the then less arid interior, now the Sands, on foot and, after 4000 BC, by donkey. By the seventh century AD, when the Qur'an and later Islamic writers described the fabled city, the site itself was gone, a place only of fanciful legend.

The decline would partly have been due to the natural catastrophe that caused the town's collapse between AD 100 and 300, but Roman power faded in AD 300, Christianity spread and the demand for incense dwindled. Without the Dhofar frankincense trade, the key to Shis'r's former glories, the inhabitants of the half-ruined site returned to a *bedu* existence and for 700 years only squatters and nomads needing water came to Shis'r.

After AD 1000, the time of the Ming china and the chess set, the horse trade brought back a second lesser glow to the wounded city and then, in 1970, Sultan Qaboos built homes, a mosque and a school there. Now the Bait Masan tribe, descendants in all likelihood of those early arrowhead makers and incense traders, have made it their permanent home. They too will leave their traces in the ground at Shis'r or Ubar, the Atlantis of the Sands.

The carbon dating tests eventually confirmed Juris's hunch and the worldwide attention aroused by the expedition brought tourists and television teams aplenty to Shis'r. Sultan Qaboos recognised that oil revenues would diminish in time and tourism could offer a lucrative alternative source of income. I like to think that the eventual success of my long search for Ubar has in a small way repaid the people of Oman, the country that has given me some of the best times of my life.

Kenton Cool
Mountaineer

Sitting on top of the Eiger in Switzerland in 2007, after our successful ascent of the notorious North Face, I felt a mixture of relief and pride in what we had just achieved.

Years later, I realise that it wasn't so much the climb that was important (raising money for charity to one side), more the journey to get there. Weeks, possibly even months spent with Ran in the Alps helping him to hone the skill set needed for one of the biggest Alpine Faces, taught me a lot.

Each time we met he'd leave me a little bit richer in knowledge, a little wiser about the world, even though I was meant to be the teacher.

I look back on our time together with a warm fondness, like a son feels for his father, in spite of the numerous times Ran attempted to sabotage our climbs by dropping head torches down icy cliffs or failing to bring crucial pieces of equipment with him.

All these 'failures' can be forgiven, because Ran is Ran and this brings with it a certain stoicism, which can get you out of any scrape.

The time he allowed his boots to fill with snow at an open bivouac, when the morning finally came, he simply pushed his feet into the cold, damp boots and proclaimed himself ready for the day ahead.

That sunny March day on top of the Eiger represented the beginning of the end of our days climbing together. Looking at Ran's grizzly, bearded face, I was yet to realise what he had planted within me, but I knew it was there.

As the mist rolled in, for a while it looked like we might be stuck, but I didn't mind at all.

I simply had to channel my inner Ran.

At the North Col camp on his first attempt at summitting Mount Everest in 2005. Ran succeeded four years later, at the age of sixty-five.

12

Mount Everest

*Ran's three attempts to become the oldest
British person to climb Everest
2005–2009*

*S*hortly after Ran returned from his seventh marathon in seven
days on seven continents in New York in 2003, his wife Ginny was
diagnosed with stomach cancer. She died a few months later in
February 2004, at the age of fifty-six. The couple had been married
for thirty-four years and Ginny had helped to organise all his expeditions from the River Nile and the Transglobe Expedition to the Lost
City of Ubar. She was the first woman to be awarded the Polar Medal
by the Queen and to be voted as a member of the Antarctic Club.

Three months after her death, Ran felt he needed to do something
to break himself out of his misery. At the suggestion of his friend
Sibusiso Vilane, he joined a UK mountain tour company called
Jagged Globe, with the intention of climbing Mount Everest. Its
boss, Simon Lowe, explained they could not take anybody who was
'sixty, cardiac-challenged and missing some digits', so Ran joined
two of their mountaineering courses, starting in the Alps and
progressing to volcanoes in Ecuador, involving climbs up to 20,000
feet, which would introduce him to the effects of high altitude.

Following his Ecuadorian guide's good report, Ran was
accepted for Jagged Globe's projected 2005 attempt on Everest via
the Tibetan north side.

The British Heart Foundation took on my Everest project as a charity-raising tool. The aim was to raise £2 million specifically for a new scanner unit for children with heart trouble at the Great Ormond Street Children's Hospital.

I gave a talk after a fundraising dinner for twelve well-heeled businessmen in a North Yorkshire castle, and the host, Paul Sykes, a fiery Yorkshireman, asked if I was planning any more expeditions. I told him about Everest and he agreed to sponsor the project financially, as he approved of the plan and the charity aim.

At a lecture I had given to the Chester branch of the Royal Geographical Society the previous summer, I had met one of their members, Louise Millington, and had since taken her out when she wasn't busy with the horse transporting company she had built up based from her Cheshire home. She was thirty-six, full of life, mercurial and she jolted me out of my miserable state. We agreed to marry in March 2005 and honeymoon at the Everest Base Camp in Tibet.

Abbie, Ginny's sister and closest relative, said to the press:

Ran and Ginny were in love with each other for all their adult lives. Ran was devastated by Ginny's illness and death, and he has had a desperately long, lonely year without her. To see him happy again with Louise is wonderful. He still grieves for Ginny, but she wouldn't want him to be sad or lonely. In her last days she had urged him to marry again, and everyone in the family is one hundred per cent supportive of his decision. We all wish Ran and Louise every happiness.

During the run-up weeks to Everest, I had a severe bout of bronchitis. Louise was worried and booked me to see various lung, chest amd heart specialists. The results were disappointing. They showed a limitation in my airways, probably due to my previous smoking. Additionally, my ability to saturate oxygen, a key function when exerting yourself at high altitude, was badly impaired.

Coupled with my cardiac status, which dictated never getting seriously out of breath, I was not an ideal candidate for an Everest attempt.

March the 7th was my sixty-first birthday. Five days later Louise and I were married, and a fortnight after that we left Heathrow bound for Kathmandu in Nepal. At the airport a reporter from *The Times* interviewed Louise and asked her all the usual questions. She admitted she was worried about the altitude and the strain on my heart. This reminded me of Sherpa Tenzing's account of his wife's reaction, when told he was joining John Hunt's 1953 attempt on Everest.

'You are too weak,' she said. 'You will get ill again, or you will slip on the ice and fall and kill yourself.'

'No, I will look out for myself,' he told her. 'Just like I always have.' Adventuring husbands have always been having these prior-to-departure conversations.

Those members of our team we did not meet at Heathrow we caught up with in Kathmandu, where we were introduced to our group leader. He was a tall Scotsman named David Hamilton. His number two, Neal Short from Liverpool, was small and mild-mannered. The rest of the group included my South African friend, Sibusiso, at whose suggestion I had become involved in the first place, and the professional freelance climbing photographer Ian Parnell, who was covering my climb for *The Times* and, with minimal equipment training, was organising live TV coverage for *BBC Breakfast*.

Two other South Africans in our group, Alex Harris and Mark Campbell, were both experienced climbers and good friends of Sibusio. Tore Rasmussen was a Norwegian businessman and hobby climber; Jens Bojen, born in Denmark, was now a Grimsby businessman, with a lifelong experience of North Sea fishing; and Fred Ziel, from California, was our doctor. Rosalind Buckton had once very nearly been the first British woman to climb Everest and, although now in her late fifties, was keen to succeed on this her second attempt.

The general opinion of the more experienced climbers in our group was that our Tibetan northern route was a bigger challenge than the Nepalese southern route pioneered by John Hunt's British expedition in 1953, which made the first ascent. This was because our route involved more time spent higher than 8,400 metres, in the notorious 'Death Zone'. The twin words 'altitude' and 'acclimatisation' were on our group's lips much of the time. Sensible application of the latter, the old hands constantly assured us, would be our main way of defeating the potentially lethal effects of the former.

We travelled north-east towards the Nepalese/Tibetan border in jeeps, our gear on high-back lorries. The border town of Zhangmu buzzed with groups similar to ours, and all with the same thing on their minds . . . the summit. As we joined various queues in the complex process of passing through Chinese customs, security and immigration, I met nine climbers of different nationalities.

From Zhangmu the road, evilly potholed and often edged with sheer drops to our immediate left and cliff walls to the right, fought its tortuous way up the sheer and rugged gorge of the Bhote Kosi. A thousand feet below roiled and roared the fearsome rapids of the Bhote Kosi heading back south to Nepal.

An hour or so north of Nyalam, our convoy eased into the main Himalayan range between India and Asia, the mightiest geographical feature on the Earth's surface. It boasts more than a hundred peaks in excess of 24,000 feet (7,315 metres) above sea level, and includes all the famed fourteen 8,000ers, the trophy peaks whose summits are 'collected' by many dedicated high alitiude climbers.

For many hours we travelled on up over the high dusty Tibetan Plateau until our road began to turn east, and we came to the village of Tingri, from where our group headed on a switchback drive over the Pang La pass. We stopped at the highest point from where Everest was now clearly visible, crested by a plume of ice crystal 'smoke', indicating violent winds on the summit ridge. The highest mountain on Earth was certainly no visual let-down.

Some four hours after the Pang La, we came to the Rongbuk Monastery, close to the original Base Camp used by the pioneering British expeditions of the 1920s. It was from here that George Mallory and Andrew Irvine set out in 1924, never to return.

Then we climbed sharply up a narrow valley, the Rongbuk Gorge, which widened quite suddenly to become a bleak, flat plain some 500 metres wide between high hills, with Everest dead ahead. This plain, home to the modern Everest Base Camp, was dotted with the colourful tents of at least a dozen expedition groups, and was swept by a bitter cold wind from the glaciers above.

Louise and I shared a two-man tent, which was hardly a honeymoon suite, and there was a fairly cramped communal tent for meals and various stores tents. We spent two weeks in Base Camp, sometimes trudging a few miles upwards on the Everest trail or back downhill to the Rongbuk Monastery. Acclimatisation was the main aim of our existence. Louise suffered severe headaches, but stayed with me for a fortnight before returning to England, just before David Hamilton decided we were ready to try our first trek up to the Advance Base Camp. Our gear was taken by sixty-five yaks, with drivers who whistled and yelled at their animals when the trail was especially narrow or slippery.

I knew that all 2005 summit bids had to be completed by the first week of June, because that was the annual date for the arrival of the monsoon winds, which would make Everest lethal. I still had about fifty days in which to reach the top.

I slept well that night at the first interim camp at 5,500 metres, and next morning our group moved on up the glacial valley, with sharkfin pinnacles of ice towering above each side of the trail, known as the Magic Highway. I kept up with the others without trouble, and after five hours came to the tents of the second interim camp at 6,088 metres, approximately 20,000 feet.

We were all dog-tired and most of us had headaches since, despite our cautious acclimatisation, we were for the first time above 17,000 feet, where the human body starts to deteriorate, indeed to rot. It literally starts to consume itself for energy. Sleeping becomes a problem, muscle wasting and weight loss take place, and this process of deterioration continues more quickly the higher the altitude.

That night, with no warning at all and a nasty shock, I jerked up gasping for air with a terrible sensation of suffocation. My heart beat wildly. The phenomenon passed as quickly as it came and I felt drowsy again, but within minutes it happened again. There was no way I could get any sleep. Next day, I learned that my problem was an ailment known as Cheyne-Stokes 'periodic breathing'.

A standard cure is for the victim to take Diamox tablets just before going to bed. However, with my lung problem, I was already taking the maximum advised dose of two tablets daily. The only answer was to use oxygen whenever I needed to sleep at or above the height of that camp at 20,000 feet.

Early next day our group pushed on upwards until, rounding a sharpish bend, all of a sudden, the stupendous mass of Everest's North-East Ridge was revealed, ever ascending to the wind-driven streamer that raged along the impossibly high summit ridge at a height of 29,029 feet, where jumbo jets fly.

After an hour I clambered up scree and loose boulders, over small melt pools and past the first outlying tents of the waiting congregation of aspirant summiteers. This was Advance Base Camp – ABC.

David's plan, now that all the Jagged Globe group, apart from a badly coughing Rosalind, had reached ABC in good condition, was to have us sleep only one night there, then descend all the way back to Base Camp. This was part of the generally accepted acclimatisation policy of 'climb high, sleep low'. We would recuperate for a while at Base Camp, then come back up (in a single day next time) to ABC *and* climb the formidable ice slopes that give access to the North Col. Then back down. And so on until we and the weather were ready for a final four- or five-day push from ABC to the summit. It was the yo-yo principle of bouncing up and down. This is how the body and the brain learn to cope with inadequate oxygen.

My second return journey to ABC took a full day. After resting for forty-eight hours, I joined David and the others for my first trip from ABC to the North Col. We were starting out from a point already 1,600 feet higher than Mont Blanc (where twenty years before I had been violently sick from altitude) and, within ten minutes of climbing into what Tibetans call 'the poison gas' – the thin air of high altitude – I was already feeling geriatric. It seemed as though, at 21,000 feet, my personal tree-line was broached.

I lagged behind everyone, constantly needing to rest my lungs and my legs. It was a novel experience, for I normally prized my ability not to need a rest for many hours of adventure racing and ultra marathons in wild country. I felt wretched and, when David dropped back to check on me, I apologised and felt ashamed. He was kind and stayed close as I trudged on for an hour over rocks, ice and snow to the base of the North Col ascent.

Fixed ropes were in place all the way from this point to the summit of Everest, put there and maintained by Sherpas from all the groups. Using a simple hand device called an ascendeur (to grip the rope when tugged downwards, but to slide along the rope when pulled upwards), I followed David up a succession of very steep snow slopes. In my free hand I grasped my ice axe. Everybody climbed in this manner, pretty much all the way up the mountain. You do not need to be a 'proper' technical climber for Everest. But you do need to be altitude fit, which I clearly wasn't. All the others in the group (except poor Rosalind, who had to return home due to her lung trouble) made it to the North Col that day and spent the night there.

David saw me back down to ABC and gave me a gentle but not too subtle warning that my current form would not see me much higher than the North Col. My speed must improve.

Various other sorties followed, then it was back once more to Base Camp. A few days later, on 27 April, I did manage the North

Col, extremely slowly, but in time to make it in daylight and to spend the night there at 7,066 metres and using oxygen before heading back down to ABC.

After one more spell in Base Camp, we made our last ascent to ABC by the third week of May and stayed there, with small local excursions from time to time, eagerly awaiting our chance for the final push. David allocated a Sherpa to each climber. I was matched with Nima Dorje Sherpa (or Boca Lama), the smallest and most humorous ever-grinning dwarf of a Nepali.

At last, on 31 May, half of our group left ABC for their summit attempt. David had sensibly divided us into a fast-moving greyhound group of Sibu, Tore, Alex and Fred, led by him, while group two, led by Neal, would be Mark, Jens, Ian and me.

On the other side of Everest, only a single day of less strong winds is needed to climb from the South Col to the summit and back. Jagged Globe's group on that side, led by Kenton Cool, summitted on 31 May. That same day I made it up to the North Col camp with the rest of group two. Group one were, by then, two camps ahead of us and experiencing high winds.

The North Col camp, in the lee of a great snow wall, was the last haven of shelter all the way to the summit. I tottered into one of the four tents our Sherpas had erected for us, fairly near to the snow wall and surrounded by some ninety or more other tents. The toilet arrangements were simple. You squatted as near as was safely possible to the edge of the ice precipice on the far side of the encampment. Slipping on the ice there would be a bad idea, for the resulting fall would be over 1,000 feet.

Sleeping with oxygen, our group stayed there awaiting orders from David to come on up once his group had vacated our tents. This leapfrog shuffle would involve the three camps between the North Col and the summit.

Eventually our number two group set out from Col Camp. The sky was clear and the winds manageable, so we all made good time up the long steep snow ramps to where shattered shale underfoot gradually replaced the snow, and the fixed ropes edged to the right, at first gently then, for the last hour, at quite a steep gradient.

This 7,500-metre camp was much smaller than the Col Camp and the few dozen tents there were tattered. Our own two tents had survived well and we all slept on oxygen. Each time I woke to knock frozen dribble from my mask, I intoned, 'Only two days to the top and two million quid in the kitty.'

Let me explain to anyone who is not a climber how Everest hopefuls who are upwards-trudgers like me haul themselves up the many thousands of feet from the base of the North Col, where the fixed rope starts, to the summit where it stops.

You have a climbing harness around your waist and crutch and to a strong point on the belt's front just above your tummy button there is attached a steel karabiner (or krab). A loop or sling is attached to this krab. Another detachable device, also on your sling, is clipped on to the fixed ropes that lead you up the mountain. This is called a jumar (or ascendeur), and has metal teeth. Slide the jumar up the rope and it runs along smoothly, but any downwards pull and the jumar's teeth will clench the rope and stop you falling.

Because there are hundreds of knots and fixed points along the rope line, you always use two of these slings and never unclip one until the other is attached to the rope beyond the obstacle. Many of the bodies lying along the rope line and below it are there because they slipped and fell when briefly unattached to the mountain or a rope. You can't add to the number of corpses who died from that particular fate so long as you always use the two-sling system – *and* so long as the fixed rope does not break or come loose. It pays to keep checking every rope that you intend to rely on.

The 7,500-metre 'camp' was in reality a raggedy series of ledges, anywhere big enough for a tiny tent to be pitched with guy ropes tied mostly around rocks in lieu of tent pegs. The recent big winds that had held up David's group had rendered many of the tents I passed mere skeletal tent-pole hoops attached to wildly fluttering bits of material. Cylinders and food packs and bric-a-brac lay all around. Every so often a couple of climbers would slowly descend, and I would unclip myself to let them pass down the rope. They often moved like zombies and were unrecognisable in their hooded, goggled sameness. One of them was our doctor, Fred Ziel, who had sensibly turned round too sick to continue.

I kept checking that my oxygen system's pipes were not snagged, nor the mask workings frozen, but I never managed to discover why, every so often in strong winds, the oxygen stopped coming and I had to tear my mouth from the mask and try to gulp in air. I had set out from 7,500 metres an hour earlier than Ian, Jens, Mark and Neal in order to reach the next camp at the same time as them. Halfway through the morning, Mark caught up with me. We lifted tired arms in greeting. There was no point in trying to communicate verbally as the wind tore away the words.

At 7,900 metres the camp was perched on tiny tilted ledges and felt, I thought, unpleasantly exposed. But I also enjoyed a new feeling of anticipation because the summit ridge, which for the past seventy days had seemed so high as to be unobtainable, now for the first time looked within reasonable grasp. How many other hopeful folk had reached this point and likewise felt they could make it, only to die within forty-eight hours? A good many. At least one out of every ten. The most famous were, of course, Mallory and Irvine.

To this day it is unclear if they reached the summit in 1924, but it is certain that nobody else did until, twenty-nine years later, a British Commonwealth expedition under John Hunt, an Army colonel, finally placed two of its climbers, Edmund Hillary from New Zealand and Sherpa Tenzing Norgay from Nepal, on the summit of Everest from the southern side on 29 May 1953. News of their success was flashed to London just before the coronation of Queen Elizabeth II.

By the end of 2006, records showed that, in the seventy-six years since George Mallory's death not far from my 7,900 metres tent, 2,062 climbers had reached the summit and 203 of them died on the mountain. Since there were ten climbers in our two groups, I wondered if any would succumb to this Everest law of decimation. Five climbers had died on the mountain already during the past month, I knew, and maybe more, since there were a number of lone climbers as yet unaccounted for at ABC.

The good weather spell was still with us at dawn on 3 June. Today we would move into the so-called Death Zone, above which the majority of North Ridge climber fatalities take place. Our next camp lay, at 8,400 metres, higher than all but five of the world's mountain summits.

Two hours later, above 8,000 metres (26,246 feet), I was preoccupied with not slipping off the shale and ice, aware of, but studiously avoiding, any glimpse of the sharp drop to my right and focusing on slow but continuous movement to keep ahead of the others in my group. I had, as usual, set out an hour ahead of them and was determined to keep that lead. Luckily I felt stronger than before, probably because the oxygen system was working better as there was less wind.

There were some very steep sections where I had a problem passing other climbers descending in a dazed, clumsy state. I tried speaking to one, who knocked his pack hard against me as he slipped down past me, but there was no reply. He looked exhausted. I passed by a climber curled up on a tiny ledge. As I cautiously unclipped to get by him, I asked if he was okay. There was no reply, but his hooded, masked head nodded slowly.

It struck me that, if he was dying, I might well be accused of being one of those callous climbers who pass by the near dead without offering aid. But I had passed several such inert individuals and I myself had been passed as I rested, completely winded, on some tiny perch, too tired even to acknowledge a passing greeting.

When a climber near the summit of Mount Everest reaches a stage of exhaustion and oxygen starvation so severe that he can no longer move on his own initiative, he is typically left to die. It is simply impossible for one climber to descend such treacherous terrain carrying or dragging the inert body of another. The mountain is littered with the bodies of climbers who have simply sat down and died of exposure. Sibusiso nearly joined their ranks.

I came at last to the exposed series of ledges at 8,400 metres on which perched a few battered tents. I saw Sibu sitting outside one. I waved to him and he waved back slowly. He looked tired. I assumed he was on his way down from the summit with David and the others. The last fifty metres up to one of the two colour-coded Jagged Globe tents took me twenty minutes, for my oxygen pipe kept snagging on my rucksack but, for the first time, I arrived within a few minutes of Ian, Jens, Neal and Mark.

We crawled into our tents tired but exhilarated. After seventy days we were nearly there. The tent was pitched on a slope. The Sherpas had done their best to find a flat spot, but there were none. Ian, my own Sherpa, Boca Lama, and I tried to get ready for our night in the Death Camp, unpacking our rucksacks and checking our oxygen systems without upsetting each other's space, all in a tiny two-man tent pitched on rocks and ice. Any item that escaped through the entry door was liable to slide, then fall for many thousands of feet to the snow terraces and glaciers below. Various dead bodies had been found in the tents here, including an Indian climber the previous week.

Sibu nearly died that day when his oxygen ran out, although we did not know this until the following morning when one of our Sherpas found him slouched beside the ropes an hour or two below the tents.

So why on earth do people want to risk their lives on Everest year after year? George Mallory, in fact, had a very reasonable motive for his Everest trials. Curiosity. Nobody had yet reached the summit. Nobody knew if the human body could survive at that altitude. On a more cynical level another British climber, Stephen Venables, observed, 'Everest is prime *Guinness Book of Records* territory.'

From the Death Camp, the final climb ascends and traverses a steep stretch of striated limestone, known as the Yellow Band, mostly by way of a part-snow-filled gulley where many old ropes can cause confusion, especially since this section must be done at night. However, the great motivating thought is that from the tents to the summit ridge is a mere 300 metres in height.

I struggled into my boots, pack and oxygen system, said good-bye to Ian and the other three and, with Boca Lama a few yards behind, grinning as usual, began the fairly steep climb up the fixed ropes with new batteries in my head torch. The others would start out in an hour at 11 p.m. In seven or eight hours, on a fixed rope the whole way, I hoped to be on the summit of Everest. We moved off into the night, pitch black beyond the cone of our torch lights. There were slippery rocks, snow patches and a bewildering choice of upwards-leading ropes, some frayed almost through, others brand new. In the torch light it paid to take time.

I found myself panting far more than on the previous climb, despite taking it slowly, perhaps because of the gradient. I felt cold despite the exertion, and I felt dizzy, too. Something was wrong but nothing I could identify, so I kept going in a stop-start way, gasping for breath every few metres. Then, some forty minutes after setting out, my world caved in.

Somebody, it seemed, had clamped powerful arms around my chest and was squeezing the life out of me. And the surgical wire that held my ribs together felt as though it was tearing through my chest. My thoughts were simple: I am having another heart attack. I will be dead in minutes. No defibrillator on hand this time. Then I remembered that Louise had pestered me to carry special pills with me – Glycerine Tri-Nitrate (GTN). You put one under your tongue where it fizzes and causes your system to dilate in all the right places. I tore at my jacket pocket and, removing my mitts, crammed at least six tablets under my tongue before swallowing.

I clung to the rope, hanging out over the great drop and waiting to die. My one glimpse of Boca Lama, who said nothing, was of his usual big grin as my torch light lit up his features. Five minutes later I was still alive. The tablets, if you were lucky, I knew could stave off a heart attack and give you time to get to a cardiac unit. They are *not* a means of avoiding an attack in order to allow you to continue climbing. This might not be my own end, but it *was* definitely the signal to descend to lower altitudes at once.

Some twenty minutes later we were back down in the Death Camp. There was no tent to enter as our group were in the act of booting and kitting up, using all available tent space. So I waited outside with Boca Lama until Ian and the others had disappeared up into the night.

'I must go down quickly,' I told Boca Lama. He shook his head and the grin disappeared. It would, he explained, be too dangerous to descend until we could 'see our feet'. That meant dawn in five hours' time.

I knew my best hope of survival was to lose height rapidly. The tightness had gone from my chest, but the sharp discomfort around the stitch-wires was still there. I contemplated going on down without Boca Lama, but decided against it. Going up an icy, slippery, steep slope in the darkness is a lot safer than descending one.

Statistically, the vast majority of accidents happen on the descent. The concentration of going up seems to disappear to be replaced by a weary nonchalance. Nothing matters apart from a longing for warmth and comfort. Lost in these thoughts, you become careless. The focus gone and the mind weary, it is all too easy to lose your footing or clip carelessly into a rope. Three thousand metres of void waited directly below our tent.

Nine times Everest climber, Ed Viesturs, has two favourite sayings: 'Just because you love the mountains doesn't mean the mountains love you' and 'Getting to the top is optional. Getting down is mandatory.'

Dawn came eventually and we descended without a break to the North Col, where we rested for two hours, then on down to ABC for the night. My Everest was over. If I had feared a scathing reaction from the press, I was pleasantly surprised. *The Times* correspondent wrote:

Aborting his climb will be seen by the mountain community as a wise and courageous decision. Duncan Chessell, who has led thirty-five Himalayan expeditions, said, 'For a 60-year-old man to make it even this far is extraordinary. You would expect only fifty per cent of climbers to reach anywhere near this high, especially during this season.'

I congratulated my fellow Jagged Globe climbers, especially Sibu, who was the first black person to climb Everest from both sides, and Jens, who was a year older than me. Fred, who had recovered from his illness but still looked weak, assured me that he would be having another go, his third, in a year or so. I thanked David, Neal and our wonderful team of Sherpas, especially Boca Lama, for what had truly been a great experience. Would I try again? Not for a while. Maybe never, but I hate saying 'Never again'.

Within a day, I was back down in Base Camp, and forty-eight hours after that I was checked out in Harley Street for new cardiac damage. None was evident, so it is likely that on Everest I had mere angina warnings. What would have happened if I had not heeded them or had not had the GTN tablets, it is impossible to know. I learnt later that, on the other side of the mountain a Scottish climber, 49-year-old Robert Milne, died of a heart attack on the same night and at the same height as I had my attack. I assume he had no GTN pills with him.

The tangible declared aim of my Everest attempt, all costs of which were sponsored by the generosity of Paul Sykes, had been to raise £2 million for an MRI Scanner Unit and Catheter Laboratory in the Great Ormond Street Hospital for Children in London. The British Heart Foundation eventually raised the £2 million through the Ran Fiennes Healthy Hearts Appeal, despite my failure on the mountain, and I cut the ribbon to officially open the gleaming new clinic. Its purpose is purely for heart research, and it will enable BHF medical professionals to explore the heart disease that affects children, helping them to develop new interventional techniques with the aim of saving young lives.

Since our 'honeymoon' at the Everest Base Camp had been a non-event, Louise and I took up the kind offer of John Costello, who had checked out my lungs prior to Everest, to stay for a week in his family villa in southern Spain. A couple of months later, Louise told me that she was pregnant and, on Easter Day 2006, our daughter Elizabeth gave her first yell. A month later I was sixty-two years old and changed my first nappy.

Although I had resolved not to climb any more mountains, my failure on Everest when so close to the summit continued to rankle, and I could not forget the letter I had subsequently received from my guide on the climb, Neil Short of Jagged Globe. He had written, 'As you were so close, I often wonder whether you are tempted to give it another go.'

I reflected that Marie Curie headquarters were, as always, desperate for funds to use to train more nurses, and Neil would hardly have bothered to suggest having another go at the Big One if he didn't think me still capable of making it to the top. Also, in the back of my mind, I knew that my great rival Børge Ousland must surely be planning to try again, in order to achieve the internationally sought adventurers' crown of being the first person to cross both ice caps and summit the so-called 'Third Pole', which was Everest. Why not at least try to beat the great Norwegian?

What finally decided me was when I switched on Radio Four in a traffic jam and heard the gravelly tones of the world's greatest mountaineer, the Italian Reinhold Messner, declaring that the tourist route on the Nepal side of Everest was definitely easier in many ways than the Tibet climb. So I phoned Kenton Cool, with whom I had climbed the North Face of the Eiger and was at that time taking folk up Everest annually, as one of the guides hired by Himalayan Guides Nepal.

That April 2008 saw me yet again chorusing 'Yes, Kenton' and 'No, Kenton,' as he put me through my acclimatisation training from the Nepali Base Camp. He chose, as my personal Sherpa, a patient and friendly man in his early twenties from Kathmandu who was named Tundu Sherpa, and by mid-May I became confident that, by following his every suggestion and by using oxygen from about 19,000 feet, I could make it this time.

But, to my shame and annoyance, I failed once more, and precisely four years after my Tibetan debacle, I had again let down my sponsor, Paul Sykes, and the charity Marie Curie. This time, my heart and my spine behaved themselves immaculately but, at a rock known as the Buttress, which is about a five-hour plod from the summit, I found myself fearing that, if I carried on, I would surely die.

This uninvited fixation was not helped by two death sites that we passed, one of which was where my Sherpa Tundu's father died, and the other where the Scots climber, Robert Milne, had died four years earlier, on the same night that I had my angina seizure on the Tibetan side.

We passed where both of the two bodies had become partially exposed due to the weather conditions over the past year. Then, close by the Buttress, we came across the body of a famous Swiss climber who had, earlier that day, reached the summit without using oxygen support, but died of hypoxia on his descent. Sherpas were covering his body with snow.

Back down in Base Camp, I apologised to Tundu and Kenton for wasting their time, and, unable to sleep in my tent, I analysed the reasons for my failure as best I could. My conclusion was that over the past four years, my body's performance at some point around the so-called Death Zone of 27,000 feet had deteriorated, but that all the way from Base Camp my innate competitive nature had kept me, although exhausted, plugging on in my ongoing attempt to keep up with Kenton (or in Tibet, with Neil and Ian). I had, therefore, pushed myself too hard and this had proved my undoing. That, plus on this occasion a probable feeling of apprehension brought on by passing the three bodies.

To my surprise, back in London I found that Marie Curie had netted a further £1 million from my Nepal-side near miss and were keen that I have yet another go. They had achieved their fundraising success by hiring a remarkably fit, professional camer-aman, Dave Carter, who had successfully filmed my ascent up to Camp Two, above the notorious Khumbu Icefall, and transmitted his footage back to *BBC Breakfast*.

Once I had worked out, or at least surmised, that my past fail-ures were due to trying too hard all the way up the long lower slopes, which left me exhausted on reaching the Death Zone, I persuaded myself that if only I could accept a nice and easy (geri-atric) pace, then all would be well.

Paul Sykes agreed to sponsor me, providing it really was the final attempt and that Marie Curie remained our charity of choice.

So I went back to Marie Curie's Thames-side HQ (beside that of MI5) and made a deal. I would try Everest one last time, on condi-tion that they agreed not to allow their highly efficient media department to publicise the attempt until, and if, I was definitely on the summit, and *not* just *nearly* there.

They found it difficult to accept this condition, since the longer the PR lead time they had, the more donations they would garner from the public. However, they persuaded BBC Television News to film the attempt for the national news, which would greatly increase the fundraising potential of the project, and the BBC also agreed that they would keep all their footage off air, *until* I had summited.

Back at the Nepalese Everest Base Camp, the famous Scottish boss of Himalayan Guides Nepal, Henry Todd, agreed that I could again have the ever-patient Tundu as my Sherpa, and this time I would go without a European guide, even Kenton, who would be leading another party.

The idea was that, since Tundu climbed with the speed of a mountain goat, there would be no point at all in my making any effort to move faster than a rate with which my body felt happy.

So in late April of 2009, I found myself back in the Nepalese base camp, where I trained hard with Tundu on and above the ledge later ravaged by the 2015 Nepali earthquake, which killed some of Henry's guides and injured him.

In a separate tent, the BBC News team of producer Mark Giorgio and reporter Andy North filmed our preparations and local excitements such as nearby avalanches. Their cameraman had had to be evacuated by emergency helicopter after falling ill with potentially fatal altitude sickness on the journey up to Base Camp, so Mark and Andy had to teach themselves how to use all the camera and satellite transmission gear brought up on four yaks.

They trained Tundu to use a specific camera for the ascent of and above the notorious Khumbu Icefall. Kenton set out from the South Col camp on the same night in late May, but a couple of hours after Tundu and I had headed upwards. We passed by the burial sites that this time were covered in snow, and the moonlit slopes were swept only by a soft breeze. Ideal conditions for the steep upper ridges and the Hillary Step.

Keeping to a very slow pace all the way and cosseted by the patient Tundu, I reached the summit, at some 29,029 feet (8,848 metres) above sea level, about an hour or two before dawn.

Tundu shook my hand and, aware that it is stupid to linger in such a place with a limited amount of oxygen and the ever-uncertain weather prospects that had recently killed many climbers, he said, 'Now we go down, Ran, very slowly.'

I reminded him that we *must* first film our reaching of the summit. The team of Mark and Andy had spent over a month producing a great documentary for BBC TV, which simply had to have the 'headline shot' of us on the summit.

Tundu shrugged and unpacked the camera gear. 'Not enough light yet,' he noted.

'We must wait then,' I said. 'Dawn will be soon.'

'Maybe an hour. Very cold. Not too much oxygen. Better we go down. We can film "like" the summit later.'

Knowing how indignant, if not irate, Mark and Andy were likely to be if they were told that we had reached the top but failed to produce any evidence on camera of doing so, I shook my head. I was more fearful of them than any bad consequences of waiting for the light, such as getting cold and running out of oxygen. I thought of our sponsors and of Marie Curie and knew that we could not go down without film, or at least a photo of being on the summit, unless it was a matter of life and death. Tundu shrugged again and, looking resigned, joined me to sit in a huddle on the open space of the summit.

About an hour later and to my intense relief, a well-known Mexican climber arrived and, after greetings, kindly agreed to photograph us. The BBC used that picture in their news headlines and it appeared in newspapers all over the world. Before he left, Kenton's group arrived and he fixed my mobile so that I could call Louise whilst still on the summit.

Then, with obvious relief, Tundu led the way down to the Hillary Step. Tundu was a really great person and I was privileged to have been led by him. Sadly he died in an avalanche in 2017.

Marie Curie's PR made the most of my 'third time lucky' climb and Everest helped to raise the charity total of all my fundraising activities over the years to more than £18 million. Although, based on the fact that I was the first ever Old Age Pensioner to have summited, the *Daily Mail* merely commented:

'It was, of course, easy for him as he had a bus pass.'

Bear Grylls
Adventurer and television presenter

I have always considered it an unspoken privilege to share three unusual things in common with the great legend and explorer, Sir Ranulph Fiennes. Firstly, he and I both survived Eton; secondly, both of us are amongst a small number of boys ever to climb the highest school building by night. And thirdly, we both served as soldiers with 21 SAS Regiment.

Where I had the record as the youngest Brit to climb Everest, Ran became the oldest British climber to do so. A much harder accolade to achieve indeed. And that is typical Ran for you. Always that little bit further and always the best. It is why, even to this day, I remain in awe at all he has accomplished. Some of his record-breaking feats have been with long-time friends, but many have been done alone. Again, much tougher and less forgiving when things go wrong.

Ran's success is based on a rare combination of qualities developed to the highest level. He is obviously immensely strong physically, but it's his mental strength I admire most. To be able to carry on under the most brutal conditions, for such long periods, is a testament to his incredible mental fortitude and willpower.

On top of all this, let's not forget he has pretty much always been the leader of his expeditions, so bearing the added burden of responsibility and stress. He once said that he looks for people who are solid and not given to extremes of behaviour. Time and experience have taught him the value of strong, humble, stable character in the face of adversity.

'No dramas' is an old-school quality, but it is key to great expeditions. Prepare well and stay drama-free. Just head down and do the job.

He is a father, a husband, a friend to many and an inspiration to millions. Myself included. And Ran, we love you for it.

Acknowledgements

Ranulph Fiennes:
I would like to give thanks to my long-suffering family and to Charlie Burton, Oliver Shepard, Mike Stroud, Simon Gault, Geoff Newman, Mary Gibbs, Simon Grimes, Ben Howkins, Nick Holder, Peter Loyd, Monty Don, Tim Peake, Ben Fogle, Bear Grylls, Simon Reeves, Steve Holland, James Dyson and Paul Sykes.

Thanks also to the patron of the Transglobe Expedition, King Charles (then the Prince of Wales), to the crews and oceanographers of the *Benjamin Bowring,* and the great skills of Giles Kershaw, Gerry Nicholson and Karl Z'berg; to all the sponsors of our projects; and all the members of our endeavours since those in a little canoe with my sister Gill in our teens.

Also a huge thank you and apologies to all those my memory has failed to acknowledge here.

Barry Johnston:
I would like to express my grateful thanks to Sir Ranulph Fiennes for his help and advice in the compilation of *Around the World in 80 Years.*

Special thanks to Ran's friends and fellow explorers who contributed their tributes to him for the book: Anton Bowring, Kenton Cool, Monty Don, Bear Grylls, Erling Kagge, Børge

Ousland, Ian Parnell, Oliver Shepard, Dr Mike Stroud, Stephen Venables and Levison Wood.

Finally, many thanks to the excellent team at Hodder & Stoughton: Christian Duck, Rupert Lancaster, Ciara Mongey, Matt Everett and Juliet Brightmore.

Picture Acknowledgements

Colour inset pages 1–8
Author's collection: pages 1, 3, 4 centre right, 5 above.
© Bryn Campbell: pages 2, 4 below left.
Contreras/BBC: page 8 below.
© Mike Hoover: page 4 above left.
Howell, Fiennes, Stroud: page 5 centre right.
© George Ollen: page 6 above.
Courtesy of Børge Ousland: page 5 below.
© Ian Parnell: pages 7 below, 8 above.
REUTERS/Chip East/Bridgeman Images: page 6 below.
© Stephen Venables: page 7 above.

Chapter openers
Chapters 1 and 5: Mirrorpix/Alamy.
Chapters 2, 3, 4, 6, 11: Author's collection.
Chapter 7: Salah Ibrahim/EPA/Shutterstock.
Chapter 8: © Kenton Cool Archive.
Chapter 9: Daily Express/Getty Images.
Chapter 10: Howell, Fiennes, Stroud.
Chapter 12: © Ian Parnell.

Hardback edition endpapers: Charlie Burton and Ranulph Fiennes in their two-man Boston Whaler entering the 2,000-mile section of the ice floes of the North West Passage en route to their crossing of the Arctic Ocean, 1981.

Index